Women in England 1870–1950

Women in England 1870–1950:

Sexual Divisions and Social Change

JANE LEWIS

Lecturer in Social Administration
London School of Economics

WHEATSHEAF BOOKS • SUSSEX

INDIANA UNIVERSITY PRESS • BLOOMINGTON

First published in Great Britain in 1984 by
WHEATSHEAF BOOKS LTD
A MEMBER OF THE HARVESTER PRESS GROUP
Publisher: John Spiers
Director of Publications: Edward Elgar
16 Ship Street, Brighton, Sussex
and in the USA by
INDIANA UNIVERSITY PRESS
Tenth and Morton Streets, Bloomington, Indiana

British Library Cataloguing in Publication Data
Lewis, Jane
Women in England 1870–1950.
1. Women—England—Social condition
I. Title
305.4′2′0942 HQ1593

ISBN 0–7108–0186–6
ISBN 0–7108–0191–2 Pbk

Library of Congress Cataloging in Publication Data

Lewis, Jane (Jane E.)
Women in England, 1870–1950

Includes bibliographical references.
1. Working class women—England—History. 2. Middle class women—England—History. 3. Mothers—England—History. 4. Family—England—History. 5. Sexual division of labor—England—History. I. Title
HQ1599.E5L49 1985 305.4′0942 84–48437
ISBN 0-253-36608-9 (Indiana University Press)
ISBN 0-253-28926-2 (Indiana University Press : pbk.)

1 2 3 4 5 88 87 86 85 84

Photoset in 10/11pt Bembo by Witwell Limited, Liverpool
Printed in Great Britain by Whitstable Litho Ltd, Whitstable, Kent

Contents

List of Tables

Preface

As a relatively new field of study, women's history has engendered huge enthusiasm and the volume of work that has been done in the relatively short period of ten years since Sheila Rowbotham showed the range of issues that might be addressed in *Hidden from History* is enormous. However, much of this either remains unpublished or is tucked away in relatively inaccessible journals; and hence this attempt to proved a brief review of some of the issues and themes that have emerged.

I owe a great debt to the large number of people who have permitted me access to their hitherto unpublished work. I would also like to thank the following scholars and friends who have read all or part of the book for me: Brian Abel Smith, Leonore Davidoff, Celia Davies, Olwen Hufton, Angela John, Judy Lown, Mark Shrimpton, Deborah Thom, and Jeff Weeks. Mark Shrimpton's help was also invaluable in compiling the statistical material and Barbara Meredith provided a constant source of encouragement while giving expert help in the preparation of the manuscript.

Introduction

It is very difficult to reach a balanced assessment of the changes in the position of women during the late nineteenth century and the first half of the twentieth century. During this period women were gradually spared the ordeal of frequent pregnancies and painful childbirth, with a commensurate improvement in their health, while their access to better education and employment opportunities and to public office increased dramatically. Such gains were reflected in women's greater visibility in society.[1] Male pen-names amongst women writers became rarer as women writers became more numerous and more accepted. Women working alongside men in offices were a common enough sight in the 1930s, whereas such a practice was virtually unheard of a generation earlier. And women increasingly worked together, whether as feminists, as middle class women determined 'to do good', or as working class women engaged in mutual support and self-help. Such women also expressed themselves more publicly, leaving more records of their feelings and experiences than are available for earlier periods, although the vast majority of wives, mothers and working women and girls remained inarticulate.

However, there are few historians and fewer feminists who would now accept Ivy Pinchbeck's optimistic view that industrialisation proved an unmixed blessing for women. Writing in 1930, Pinchbeck believed that by creating the possibility for men to earn a wage sufficient to keep a wife and children, the industrial revolution had freed women from the double burden of work inside and outside the home, enabling them to pursue the childrearing and household tasks they were particularly fitted for.[2] But in a male-dominated society women's *choice* of activities was severely circumscribed: the role of men never became a soul-searching matter in the same way as did that of women. 'The Woman Question' was hotly debated in late nineteenth-century periodical literature and has never entirely disappeared since. Whether the source be popular magazines or the Census, women's activities have always been described in relation to those of men and never on their own terms. As the American feminist C.P. Gilman observed during the late nineteenth century, the world was 'man-made' and women were defined in relation to it.[3] Traditional and scientific belief, customary practice and the law combined to prescribe the bounds of women's sphere. Neither men nor women were able easily to transgress the boundaries marking the sexual divisions in society, the only difference being that while women wanted access to the male sphere, men showed relatively little interest in that assigned to women. Nor is there much evidence to support the view of some writers that the recent past has seen an increasing symmetry in the roles of men and women.[4]

The nature of sexual divisions has varied considerably over time and for women of different social classes. Leonore Davidoff and Catherine Hall have described how between 1780 and 1850 separate spheres for men and women emerged amongst the middle class.[5] As the workplace became separated from the home, so a private, domestic sphere was created for women, divorced from the public world of work, office and citizenship. Moreover, during the early period of industrialisation this separation of spheres between the public and the private was given legal sanction: married women were not permitted to own property or make contracts in their own names. They were thus shut out from the world of business. Furthermore, the 1832 Reform Bill made their exclusion from political citizenship explicit for the first time. Increasingly, family and home were seen as a refuge from the harsh world outside. Mid-nineteenth-century evangelical writers such as Sarah Ellis and Hannah More urged women to pay the utmost attention to their home duties:

> Not only must the house be neat and clean but it must be so ordered as to suit the tastes of all, as far as may be without annoyance or offence to any. Not only must a constant system of activity be established, but peace must be preserved or happiness will be destroyed... Not only must an appearance of outward order and comfort be kept up, but around every domestic scene there must be a strong wall of confidence which no internal suspicion can undermine, no external enemy break through.[6]

The boundary between the public (male) and the private (female) spheres was more closely defined in respect to political citizenship and office and work within the home than it was in respect to paid employment. While increasing numbers of single middle class women went out to work during the late nineteenth and early twentieth centuries, it was only during the two World Wars that married middle class women were expected to take up paid work; working class women often having no option but to work in order to make ends meet. At the workplace, sexual divisions between men's and women's work ensured that the majority of women found themselves in low paid, low status jobs. Such circumstances denied middle class women the opportunity of achieving self-fulfilment and personal autonomy through a career, and condemned working class women to 'double-toil' inside and outside their homes. Such an unrelievedly bleak picture was of course never true for all, and yet is still the case for some.

The boundary between public and private shifted considerably during the period, chiefly as a result of women entering the public sphere. Increasing numbers of single women took up paid employment, and married middle class women began to undertake voluntary philanthropic work and play a significant role in local government. The achievement of the vote by women over thirty in 1918 and by women over 21 in 1929 also meant that more women were invited to serve on government committees and appointed bodies. Nevertheless a division of labour between women and men in the public sphere was preserved. Jobs were sexually segregated and women undertaking committee work were generally confined to bodies concerned with 'women's issues'.

Women also made substantial gains within the boundaries of their sphere, for example in respect to their legal rights as wives and mothers in matters of divorce, property and guardianship over children. The move towards recognising the mother's claim to the children of a marriage as not merely equal but superior to the father's was particularly marked, and served also to reinforce the idea of the primacy of women's role as wife and mother. The sexual division of labour within the home changed but little. George Orwell's experience in 1937 of a Manchester working class housewife's unease at his offer to help with the washing up (virtually the limit of Orwell's contribution to the housework in his own family) and her comment that 'Lads up here expect to be waited on'[7] was probably representative, although in the few areas where there was a tradition of married women working—as in the Lancashire cotton mills—things were ordered somewhat differently.

However, there was no simple progressive erosion of the boundaries between male and female worlds. Socio-economic changes which might logically have been expected to result in the blurring of sexual divisions were often balanced by attitudes and beliefs which served to reinforce those divisions. For example, between 1870 and 1950 the birth rate fell amongst women of all classes, theoretically giving women considerably more time and energy to devote to activities outside the home, while at the same time the ideology of domesticity was reformulated. Whereas in its mid-nineteenth century form it had stressed the importance of female gentility and 'accomplishments', by the turn of the century higher standards of mothercraft were demanded, and by the inter-war years a more personal involvement in housekeeping was required. Similarly, while the shift in the balance of economic activity from manufacturing to service industry during the period favoured the employment of women, beliefs as to what work women were suitable for and capable of, combined with the restrictions imposed on women by the changed sexual division of labour within the home, ensured that women tended to remain at the lower end of any particular job hierarchy. Within male-dominated society the boundaries of change were in large measure set by men: male doctors defined female sexuality, male scientists defined women's intellectual ability, male legislators their legal capacity, male employers and trade unionists their position at work and husbands their degree of personal, emotional and financial security.

Yet this is to deny that women had any voice in determining their position in society. Indeed, the portrayal of women as victims was common in early work on the history of women. The relationship between the nineteenth-century doctor and his female patient, for example, was characterised as one of simple sexual hostility and exploitation.[8] Attention focused on the sexual violence implicit in such practices as ovariotomy and the invasion of the uterus commonly performed by doctors who were convinced that the creation of women had involved taking a uterus and building a woman round it. This view of women as victims provoked two types of response. The first emphasised the process of modernisation by which late nineteenth-century women began to adopt individualistic values and assert control over their lives.[9] In this interpretation women's increased resort to the medical profession, for example, was linked to the increasing use of contraception, making the role of women in the patient/doctor relationship one of active agent rather than victim.

The second type of response argued that there was little evidence to suggest anything but that a majority of women acquiesced or colluded in their oppression.[10] This might be explained by the active opposition of many women to the suffrage movement, or the way in which many female pioneers of education favoured a curriculum for girls that emphasised domestic subjects, or how so many working class wives accepted that as breadwinners their husbands should earn a family wage and with it their own position as housewives first and wage earners second.

Yet neither of these interpretations has sufficient flexibility or depth to encompass the wide variation of women's behaviour and beliefs. The one asserts women's independence of action to the exclusion of any consideration of male power and control, and the other ignores the possibility of independent action by women. A more promising line of inquiry is to begin with the way in which women have interpreted their own situations. In the view of one American historian, women have redefined in their own terms the male dominated worlds in which they have found themselves, creating a woman's culture.[11] This means that they have often attached a different meaning to institutions and the relationships they share with men (the family being the most obvious example), and these meanings have varied over time according to factors such as class position, marital status and relationship to the labour market. Thus, while in many instances women appear to have accepted the role prescriptions set by men, they may well have had their own reasons for doing so. Women opposing the vote, for instance, did not necessarily accept the view of many male anti-suffragists that they should be denied it because they were intrinsically inferior, rather they believed for the most part that women's talents were equal but different to men's and that women's essentially domestic skills were better employed in local rather than national politics. If women's motivation is often more complex than at first appears, then so the outcome of their actions has often differed from what has been expected. For example, many working class mothers welcomed the early twentieth-century infant welfare clinics, which were intended to raise the standards of infant care and to inculcate a proper sense of maternal responsibility; but they attended the clinics to see the doctor or nurse about their child's progress, and ignored classes on mothercraft and housecraft.

Some women who developed a radically different notion of their role from the one prescribed, consciously rebelled. But women's power of collective organisation throughout the nineteenth and early twentieth centuries was weaker than men's. For the most part, meanings were negotiated by individual women either explicitly or implicitly, and resulted in either capitulation, usually on the part of the woman, or compromise (for instance in the matter of family size). The example of one woman's life is perhaps instructive. Francie Nicol's tale of her life in South Shields provides a complete picture of courtship, childbirth, marital relations and work as a lodging-house keeper and small businesswoman.[12] Her attitudes could be interpreted as fatalistic: painful childbirth and a drunken husband are to be endured and hard times expected. All her efforts are directed towards the defence and preservation of her family. It is for the sake of her children that she opens a fish and chip shop and when her husband drinks away the profits it is for them that she tries again. The limitations imposed on her by class, poverty, a poor education, ignorance of her own body and marital dependency, are all too clear to an observer, but she never complains or refers to them directly; they are the unstated boundaries within which she behaves independently and with unlimited vitality and resourcefulness. She cannot be categorised as either victim or free agent.

This book is an attempt to make a contribution towards our understanding of the changing nature of the boundaries of women's lives and how their experience within them was constructed. This requires consideration of women's experience as a whole. Juliet Mitchell early identified four structures to which women relate: production, reproduction, socialisation (by family, school, the media) and sexuality; and previous historical work has demonstrated the crucial importance of the interplay between women's position in the family and in the labour market in particular.[13] Change in one area of women's lives, for instance in terms of increasing job opportunities, did not necessarily bring about change in the others, with the result that potentially liberating developments were not realised. Working class women for example ended up performing 'double-toil' inside and outside the home.

In a short volume of this kind the structure may tend to be overly schematic. Divisions between social classes, for example, have been broadly drawn, but it should be remembered that the determination of women's social class is in itself highly problematic. It cannot always be assumed that the housewife shares her husband's socio-economic class. There will also inevitably be gaps in the account, dictated in part by space, but also by the research that remains to be done. The rich complexity of regional variations has been merely signalled rather than described or explained in detail, and while Welsh data have been used in the tables (because of the way in which British social and economic data is collected), I have not attempted to deal with the significant differences in the Welsh experience. Difficulties have also arisen from the scant attention that has been paid to the whole area of women's work—the inter-war years in particular are virtually uncharted territory—and to the position of lower middle class women in the home. Finally, it has been suggested to me that the text errs on the side of earnestness. Perhaps it has been infused along the way by the moral seriousness of so many of its nineteenth-century subjects, but when women's past has so often been either trivialised and/or reduced to a paragraph, I am not sure to what extent that is a bad thing.

NOTES

In order to keep the number of notes to a minimum, references within paragraphs have been grouped together where possible. All places of publication are London unless otherwise stated.

1. Roy Porter has reflected on the invisibility of women in the eighteenth century in his *English Society in the Eighteenth Century* (Harmondsworth: Penguin, 1982), p. 36.
2. Ivy Pinchbeck, *Women Workers and the Industrial Revolution* (Routledge & Kegan Paul, 1930).
3. C.P Gilman, *The Man Made World* (T. Fisher Unwin, 1911).
4. Michael Young and Peter Wilmott, *The Symmetrical Family* (New York: Pantheon Books, 1973) is a classic example.
5. Leonore Davidoff and Catherine Hall, 'The Architecture of Public and Private Life: English Middle Class Society in a Provincial Town, 1780–1850', in *The Pursuit of Urban History*, ed. Anthony Sutcliffe (Edward Arnold, 1983), pp. 326–46.
6. J.A. Banks and Olive Banks. *Feminism and Family Planning in Victorian England* (Liverpool: Liverpool University Press, 1964).
7. Bernard Crick, *George Orwell. A Life* (Harmondsworth Penguin, 1980), p. 280.
8. G.J Barker Benfield, *The Horrors of the Half-Known Life* (New York: Harper, 1976); and Ann Douglas Wood, 'The Fashionable Diseases: Women's Complaints and their Treatment in Nineteenth Century America', in *Clio's Consciousness Raised*, eds. Lois Banner and Mary Hartman (New York: Harper & Row, 1974), pp. 1-22.
9. Patricia Branca, *Silent Sisterhood* (Croom Helm, 1975); and Daniel Scott Smith, 'Family Limitation, Sexual Control and Domestic Feminism in Victorian America', in *Clio's Consciousness Raised*, eds. Banner and Hartman, pp. 119-136.
10. For a discussion of this point see Vicky Randall, *Women and Politics* (Macmillan, 1982), pp 24-26; Jacques Donzelot, *The Policing of Families* (Hutchinson, 1977), argues that women acquiesced in the reformulation of the ideology of domesticity in the late nineteenth century (see below pp. 86–87).
11. Gerda Lerner, 'Politics and Culture in Women's History', *Feminist Studies* **6** (Spring 1980), pp. 49-54.

12. Joe Robinson, *The Life and Times of Francie Nichol of South Shields* (Allen and Unwin, 1975).
13. Juliet Mitchell, *Women's Estate* (Harmondsworth: Penguin, 1971); and Louise Tilly and Joan Scott, *Women Work and Family* (New York: Holt Rinehart, 1978).

I FAMILY, MARRIAGE AND MOTHERHOOD

1 Patterns of Marriage and Motherhood

For all women marriage conferred a higher status than spinsterhood, which connoted failure. This was particularly the case before World War I, but marriage remained the normative expectation of women of all classes to the end of the period. Spinsterhood was often referred to as 'failure in business' in middle class households, leading Cicely Hamilton to write bitterly about 'marriage as a trade' in 1909.[1] Prior to World War I, a majority of spinsters faced an often lonely and marginal life in their parents' home or in the households of a male relative. The prospect of remaining unmarried was undoubtedly materially harsher for working class women, because the average wage they could command in the late nineteenth and early twentieth-centuries was below subsistence level.

Marriage, then, was part of the typical experience of women throughout the period. Between 1871 and 1951 the proportion of adult females who were (or had been) married never fell below 60 per cent, reaching 75 per cent in 1951 (Table 1), and when young unmarried women are excluded, the figure becomes much higher. Thus the proportion of women reaching their late forties who were (or had been) married fell from a high of 88 per cent in the

Table 1: Selected demographic characteristics, England and Wales, 1871–1951

	Percentage of women ever married		*Sex ratio (F/M x 100)*		*'Excess' women (F-M) '000s*	
Year	*Age 15+*	*Age 45–49*	*All ages*	*Age 15–44*	*All ages*	*Age 15–44*
1871	63.9	87.6	105.3	107.9	594	382
1881	63.3	87.7	105.4	106.6	694	369
1891	61.3	87.1	106.1	107.5	882	479
1901	60.5	85.7	106.8	108.2	1070	613
1911	61.0	83.5	106.8	108.0	1178	664
1921	63.2	83.2	109.6	114.2	1736	1174
1931	64.6	83.2	108.8	109.4	1686	842
1951[a]	75.2	84.8	108.2	103.2	1726	290

Sources: 1961 Census, Registrar General's Annual Reports (various), 1971 Census, *Age, Marital Condition and General Tables*, Table 6 (HMSO 1974), p. 13.

a. There is no Census data for 1941.

late nineteenth century to a low of 83 per cent in 1921 and 1931. The rest of the period saw both an increase in the popularity and duration of marriage, with life expectancies for both men and women improving and the divorce rate remaining low.

There were nevertheless many women who never married. This was partly due to the imbalance in the sex ratio, which increased steadily from 1871 to 1911, and dramatically as a result of World War I. This 'excess' of women caused considerable anguish, particularly in the nineteenth century, because it became inevitable that some women would not be able to fulfil their 'natural destiny' of marriage and motherhood. The problem was considered particularly vexing because, as the research of contemporaries showed, it affected middle class women most. In 1892, Clara Collet, a social investigator, reported that in the richer suburbs unmarried women aged 35-45 outnumbered unmarried men by over three to one, and only one-third of these were domestic servants.[2]

Those women who were not married by their late twenties stood a very real chance of never marrying. For most of the period about one-third of those unmarried by age 25-29 failed to marry during their reproductive years (the figure rising from 27 per cent in 1871 to 35 per cent in 1931). Despite the fact that contemporary comment was no stronger than it had been in the nineteenth century, World War I had a dramatic effect on the marriage expectations of women, and it may be hypothesised that there were concomitant changes in attitudes towards the desirability of careers for daughters of middle class parents. Of those women who were single and in their late twenties in 1921, 50 per cent remained unmarried a decade later: this figure is particularly striking when compared with that for men, of whom only 30 per cent failed to marry.

There were also changes in the numbers and age distribution of widowed and divorced women. In general, the numbers of widows in the 15-44 age group remained fairly constant at about 200,000 throughout the period, despite steady increases in the total population. The exceptions were the increase during immediate post-World War I years, and the decrease in 1951 to only 150,000. By 1951, only 6 per cent of all widows were in the 15-44 age group, compared to nearly 20 per cent in 1871 and 1881. In contrast, the proportion of all widows aged 65 or more increased from 38 per cent to nearly 60 per cent, while their numbers rose from 386,000 in 1871 to 1,529,000 in 1951, doubling between 1871 and 1921, and almost doubling again during the following thirty years, reflecting increased longevity amongst women. Generally speaking, a widower or divorced man was three times as likely to remarry as his female counterpart throughout the period. This was due to both the 'surplus' of women and conventions regarding the marriageability of older women.

Prior to 1914 divorce was largely confined to the middle and upper classes. Changes in the aid given to poor petitioners in 1914, together with the effects of World War I, produced an increase in the divorce rate after 1918, but it was not until 1946 that legal aid became freely available and therefore not until 1951 that divorce petitions began to come from a cross section of the population.[3] Prior to World War II working class couples made use of judicial separation machinery rather than divorce, but the number of informal separations was undoubtedly larger than the number that came to court.[4]

Within marriage the most important change experienced by women was the steady decline in the fertility rate until after World War II (Table 2), while in the 1870s there were over 295 legitimate live births per 1000 married women aged 15-44, this figure had dropped to 222 by the first decade of the twentieth century and to only 111 by the 1930s. The 1940s saw a very slight increase, accounted for entirely by the post-war 'baby boom'. Illegitimate fertility rates also decreased, both in absolute terms and relative to marital fertility, except for the war years. Peter Laslett has suggested that the illegitimate fertility rate may be seen as a subset of general fertility.[5] Until the 1930s, illegitimacy was primarily a rural phenomenon, although there were wide differences in the illegitimacy rate between regions and between different groups of women. For example, the ability to bear sons remained important in early twentieth-century farming communities. An elderly fenwoman remembered her husband-to-be demanding 'What you got under your apron? I got to see if you're any good. I ain't going to buy a piggy-in-a-

Table 2: Selected fertility characteristics, England and Wales, 1871–1951

	Fertility rate[a]		*Average family size*[b]	*Family size (all F married under age 45) %*[b]		
Period	*Legitimate*	*Illegitimate*		0 – 2	3 + 4	5+
1871	295.5	15.1				
1881	274.6	12.6				
1891	280.3	9.6				
1901	221.6	8.2	3.4	44.8	27.7	27.5
1911	173.5	8.1	3.04	49.5	28.2	22.3
1921	143.6	6.3	2.54	59.4	25.8	14.8
1931	111.1	5.6	2.10	67.6	22.0	10.4
1941	113.7	11.6	2.00	69.8	21.0	9.2

a. Births *per* 1000 married/unmarried women age 15 – 44. Figures relate to the decade commencing in the year indicated (i.e. 1871–1880, 1881–1890 etc).

b. Figures relate to women first married in the decade commencing in the year previously indicated (i.e. 1900–1909, 1910–1919, etc), and are for Great Britain.

Sources: *Register General's Statistical Review, 1951, Tables Pt II, Civil*, Table C, (HMSO, 1953), p. 8; and Peter R. Cox, *Demography*, 5th Ed, (Cambridge: Cambridge University Press 1976), p.89.

poke'.[6] A 1911 survey showed that 46 per cent of the illegitimate children in Britain were born to women who had worked in domestic service.[7] John Gillis has shown from a study of the London Foundling Hospital that higher servants, such as ladies' maids, seem to have been particularly vulnerable, which may be explained by the contradictions they experienced in attempting to combine customs of courtship and marriage appropriate to women of their class backgrounds with the standards of conduct expected by their employers. Intercourse did not usually take place until marriage was promised, and marriage failed to take place usually because of job difficulties on the part of the man.[8] In 1938 the Population Statistics Act required the age of the mother at the birth of the child to be recorded, and these new data revealed that one-seventh of all children born between 1938 and 1939 were premaritally conceived. The rise in the illegitimacy rate during World War II resulted from many marriages not taking place (owing to conscription and general wartime dislocation), rather than from a rise in premarital conceptions.[9]

The decline in the general fertility rate was matched by a reduction in family size. In the first decade of this century 55 per cent of women had three or more children and 25 per cent more than five, but by the 1940s these figures were 30 per cent and 9 per cent respectively. However, there were also marked class differences. In general the wives of men in working class occupations had larger families, marrying earlier and giving birth earlier in marriage, with more conceptions and live births. The period saw a similar decline in the number of live births for both manual and non-manual families, but the differential between these groups remained great, and indeed widened, until the inter-war years. Between 1870 and 1879, the number of births to the families of male manual workers was 25 per cent higher than those to non-manual families, but this widened to 42 per cent for the period 1910–1924. The fact that manual workers married on average, and throughout the period, about a year earlier helped contribute to this, as did the fact that there was about fifty per cent more childlessness among non-manual families.

The variations among specific occupational groups were often even more extreme. Labourers' wives who married at age 20 to 24 during the first decade of this century had on average 4.8 live births, or over 80 per cent more than the wives of professionals. (And, of course professionals tended on average to marry later and hence have even fewer live births, so the difference between the reproductive experience of the two groups was in fact even greater.) The marital fertility of agricultural labourers actually rose during the late nineteenth century relative to other social groups,[10] and this, together with their low levels of infant mortality, resulted in a large average family size.

Thus, while marriage was an experience common to women of all classes, there were substantial differences between middle and working class women in terms of first, their realistic expectations of marriage given the greater surplus of women amongst the middle class (at least prior to World War I), second, their experiences of marriage breakdown, and third, their patterns of childbearing within marriage. As the following chapters will show, the separation between the public and private spheres was much more rigidly maintained for middle class than for working class women. While working class women increasingly went out to work, usually out of economic necessity, philanthropists and policy makers increasingly urged them to pay more attention to their duties as wives and mothers, which only tended to exacerbate the difficulties they experienced. The struggle of working class women against scarce resources and ill health continued thoughout the period, while progress in terms of the reform of property laws relating to married women, of the divorce laws, and the change in attitudes towards the expression of female sexuality within marriage primarily benefited middle class women. Nevertheless, by the early 1950s the extremes of difference between working and middle class women's experiences, which had been the result chiefly of poverty on the one hand, and a cloistered existence in a home where at least the heavy chores were performed by domestic servants on the other, had disappeared.

NOTES

1. Cicely Hamilton, *Marriage as a Trade* (Chapman and Hall, 1909).
2. Clara E. Collet, *Educated Working Women* (P.S. King, 1902), p. 39.
3. G. Rowntree and N. Carrier, 'The Resort to Divorce in England and Wales', *Population Studies* **11** (March 1958), pp. 188-233.
4. O.R. McGregor, Louis Blom-Cooper and Colin Gibson, *Separate Spouses* (Duckworth, 1970), p. 32.
5. Peter Laslett, 'Introduction: Comparing Illegitimacy over Time and between Cultures', in *Bastardy and its Comparative History*, eds. Peter Laslett, Karla Oosterveen, and Richard Smith (Edward Arnold, 1980), p. 40.
6. Mary Chamberlain, *Fenwomen. A Portrait of Women in an English Village*, 1st ed., 1975 (Routledge & Kegan Paul, 1983), p. 72.
7. Nigel Middleton, *When Family Failed* (Gollancz, 1971), p. 270.
8. John Gillis, 'Servants, Sexual Relations and the Risks of Illegitimacy in London, 1801-1900', *Feminist Studies* **5** (Spring 1979), pp. 142-173.
9. Sheila Ferguson and Hilde Fitzgerald, *Studies in the Social Services* (HMSO, 1954), pp. 90-93.
10. W.A. Armstrong, 'The Influence of Demographic Factors on the Position of the Agricultural Labourer in England and Wales, 1750-1914', *The Agricultural History Review* **29** (1981), pp. 71-82. I am grateful to Janet Blackman for this reference.

2 Working Class Women

Introduction

Most commentators on late nineteenth and early twentieth-century working class life have been struck by the prosaic attitudes of working class couples towards marriage. One writer described couples entering and leaving church in the 1870s as 'cool and businesslike, as though having paid the deposit on the purchase of a donkey or a handsome barrow, they were just going in with their witnesses to settle the bargain'.[1] Little seems to have changed by the 1900s, when compared to funerals, marriages were tame events. In London, weddings usually took place on Saturday, so that a day's work was not lost, and in Middlesborough, Lady Bell, the wife of the ironmaster, recorded that marriage was 'merely an incident in the daily work'.[2] Parents often did not attend, and at most the couple might take a day off to celebrate. By the outbreak of World War II rather more was being made of the ceremony itself, but it would appear that the reasons given by working class couples heading for the altar were still somewhat pragmatic. Slater and Woodside found the the couples they interviewed in the 1940s showed 'a mutual liking canalised by prudential and social considerations'.[3]

Certainly marriage was very much a practical necessity for working class girls, and the chief hope was for a good bargain. Music hall songs showed that both men and women had a down-to-earth view of the advantages and disadvantages of marriage. Girls of all classes preferred marriage to being 'left on the shelf', but working class girls needed a husband above all for economic support. The average weekly wage of young women workers over the age of eighteen in non-textile industries was 12/11d in 1906, a sum that did not permit a fully independent existence. As one woman who lost her job in 1921 recalled:

> It didn't bother me, I knew I was engaged to be married, and in those days as soon as you were going to be married you left your job . . . that is the only thing we girls had to look forward to, getting married and going on our own, getting our bottom drawer together and things like that. . .[4]

Most girls were aware of the realities of household labour and the difficulties of household management that awaited them after marriage. Many would have helped their mothers, especially on washdays, minding the baby or turning the mangle, some, like the young Louise Jermy, at the expense of health as well as leisure.[5] Yet only a very few seem to have consciously resolved to make a different life. On the whole expectations were confined—doubtless realistically—to hoping for a 'good husband': that is one who brought home a regular wage and with whom a relationship could be built upon mutual respect. From his study of working class autobiographies, John Burnett has concluded that the virtues of a marriage partner tended to be described in terms of solid calculation, and that compatibility of temperament and affection seemed to be more important than sexual attraction.[6]

It is by no means clear that working class girls regarded the constituents of marital happiness as being substantially different from those prized by middle class girls, but the realities of economic contraints meant that their priorities were ordered rather differently. Amongst the one-third of the urban population of London and York whom Booth and Rowntree found to be in poverty at the end of the nineteenth century, the chief concern of the married women was to provide food, clothing and shelter for themselves and their children. It is therefore not surprising that, as Ellen Ross has pointed out, the marital relationship did not enjoin romantic love or verbal and sexual intimacy, but required financial obligations, services and activities that were gender specific.[7] It is important to remember that this conclusion was reached on the basis of urban evidence, for it is likely that the degree of sex segregation or jointness of marital relationships varied widely from region to region. Gill Burke has shown that in Cornish mining villages, for example, the worlds of men and women were close until the 1880s and 1890s.[8] Cornish mining families tended to live in rural villages apart from the mines, and while very few married women worked full-time, husbands and wives took part in the life of their communities, attending the annual fairs and suppers and working together at harvest time. With the rapid decline in the mining industry during the late nineteenth century, men were forced to work longer hours or to seek work abroad and this shared life largely disappeared.

For both town and country women it seems that children were the centre of their worlds. Mrs Pember Reeves commented on this in her study of Lambeth, published in 1913, as did Slater and Woodside after a survey carried out during the 1940s. One of their respondents commented: 'A child is *your* life; men can go out and find their pleasures outside'.[9] Husbands were expected above all to make regular contributions to the family exchequer. Mrs Pember Reeves noted that the Lambeth housewives she visited 'seemed to expect judgement to be passed on the absent man according to the amount he allowed them.'[10] When money ran short, whether through neglect, illness or even death of the breadwinner, women would resort first to kin and to neighbours. In large part it was neighbourliness that distinguished the behaviour of working from lower middle class women, although Lady Bell observed that even prior to World War I working class women in Middlesborough saw virtue in keeping themselves to themselves.[11] Neighbourliness among the poor suffered greatly during the inter-war years, when unemployment rather than low wages became the chief cause of poverty. Under the twin pressures of moving to seek work and household means-tested benefits, community solidarity tended to disintegrate. When family and neighbours failed, women resorted to the pawnshop and other ready means of obtaining credit or to whatever part-time work was available—hawking goods, taking in washing or going out charring. The typical pattern of female activities among the poor and the very poor included borrowing, bartering and pawning, as well as housekeeping chores and paid employment, which do not fit neatly into the realm of either production or consumption.[12] Any woman who had to go further than this and shoulder the burden of full-time work in addition to her domestic duties was often pitied by other married women.[13] (The problems these women faced as workers are considered in Part II.)

Evidence suggests that working class wives were prepared to put up with occasional drinking bouts by their husbands and the physical abuse that sometimes accompanied them rather than lose the economic support normally provided. It is also possible that late nineteenth- and early twentieth-century working class women expected a greater degree of drunkenness and violence on the part of husbands than would be tolerated today. But it is not easy to differentiate between the views of middle class commentators and those of working class women themselves on this issue. It does however, seem likely that working class wives were tolerant of occasional abuse, provided that husbands had what they considered 'just cause'.[14] In this context the 1912 Minority Report on Divorce may have been right in its opinion that 'a blow in one class of life might not be the unforgiveable injury it would be in another'.[15] Working class marriages may perhaps be best considered as economic and emotional support systems. Wives were not unaware of the pressures experienced by men at the workplace and on the whole tended to accept the burden of domestic responsibilities that fell to their lot, and which, if left undone or mismanaged, might provoke some kind of outburst from their husbands.

Above the level of the very poor, notions of respectability acted as a curb on abusive or violent behaviour within the family and increasingly dictated that married women should not work outside the home.[16] However, evidence regarding the latter, which is more plentiful than that on family violence, shows that it is hard to draw clear lines of demarcation between different sections of the working class. For example, the experience of members of the Women's Cooperative Guild, who in both their own estimation and that of observers were adjudged respectable married women, shows that family misfortune, particularly in the form of sickness and unemployment, could quickly plunge a family into poverty, whereupon the wife would probably resort to strategies similar to those of her poorer sister.[17] She would still invoke the aid of neighbours but would be more likely to take in lodgers or do homework in the form of sewing, for example, than use credit systems (especially the pawnshop) or go out to work. During the inter-war years the trend seems to have been towards increasing privatisation of the respectable working class family.[18] Men in regular employment found their real wages rising and many families moved out to the new housing estates, where evidence rapidly came to light of female depression arising primarily from physical isolation.[19]

The importance of the economic support provided by husbands is neatly illustrated by working class women's attitudes towards marriage breakdown. Miss E. Lidgett, a Poor Law Guardian,[20] provided some interesting and not untypical evidence in this regard to the Royal Commission on Divorce in 1912. She described a case where the Guardians had taken a whole family into the workhouse, the father being 'hopelessly out of work'. Eventually, in what would then have been interpreted as a generous gesture on the part of the Poor Law authorities, the wife was freed in order to give her a second chance to build up a home. She immediately began to live with another man and had more children by him, complaining to Miss Lidgett that the Guardians would not then allow her to visit her children by her first husband, who remained in the workhouse. She 'stoutly defended' her new home, saying that her first husband 'was no husband for her, and the one that worked for her she respected'. While Miss Lidgett showed some appreciation of the woman's circumstances, she was unable to condone her course of action.[21]

Irregular marriage relations was one of the main areas of working class family life giving rise to middle class anxiety during the period. The Majority Report of the Royal Commission on Divorce used the existence of large numbers of working class common-law marriages as an argument in favour of relaxing the divorce law and thus permitting remarriage.[22] Bastardy law, on the other hand, remained extremely harsh, with the result that the unmarried mother who was rejected by her family had very little recourse other than the workhouse. It is a moot point as to how far the apparent relaxation of attitudes towards unmarried mothers during World War I resulted in any real shifts in policy during the inter-war years. The tenets of late nineteenth- and early twentieth-century middle class respectability imposed rules which were much stricter than the principle of legitimacy required, but which were consistent with the concern to regulate family life and promote a particular family form. The harshness of the bastardy laws should therefore be read as an expression of the state's desire to reaffirm moral values, particularly as they governed female sexual behaviour, as well as a determination to curtail the burden of expenditure this particular group imposed on the community. A similar effort to control the boundaries within which sexuality might legally be expressed was inherent in the late Victorian attempt to regulate prostitution.[23]

A second major middle class concern was for working class parents to accept certain standards and codes of behaviour. Throughout the period policy makers and social investigators were anxious that husbands should fulfil their obligation to maintain dependent wives and children. The philanthropist Helen Bosanquet drew eagerly on the work of the French sociologist Frederick Le Play to argue that the 'stable family' with its male breadwinner was 'the only known way of ensuring with any approach to success, that one generation will exert itself in the interests and for the sake of another'.[24] This concern was balanced by a profound distrust of the male worker's desire and ability to provide. Lord Shaftesbury voiced the common belief that working class women were 'much superior to the men in tact, sound judgement, and economy, and yet melancholy to say there were instances every day of the homes of such industrious women being swept away by the rapacity of bad husbands'.[25] Politicians offered such women limited protection in the form of maintenance provisions and legal protection of their earnings.

At the same time as working class women were offered a measure of protection, more emphasis was placed on their responsibilities at home. The working class family was increasingly subjected to closer supervision, first by visitors attached to voluntary organisations like the Charity Organisation Society (COS), and later by state officials, such as school attendance officers and health visitors, who attempted to exact new standards of behaviour from the working class wife in respect to domestic duties and childrearing practices. As the ideology of motherhood strengthened during the early twentieth century in response to the high infant mortality rate and the implications it was feared to have for the health and welfare of an imperial nation, so the pressures exerted on working class mothers increased.[26] The rhetoric of maternalism was applied to women of all classes, but with differential effect. In the case of working class women, Anna Martin, a suffragist, observed that mothers were being 'ordered by the law to perform the impossible and punished if they fail'.[27] A woman who kept a child home from school to mind the baby while she worked broke the law, and if she left the baby alone and it injured itself, she was also liable to prosecution.

Throughout the period the needs of mothers were not considered in relation to providing a solution to the difficulties they faced (for example in combining paid employment and motherhood), but rather in respect to a precise concept of motherhood as a social function.[28] Working class women attempting to solve the problem of scarce resources by borrowing, pawning or taking paid employment, were condemned for either mismanaging or neglecting their home responsibilities, while under the guise of protection, efforts were made to limit their employment to 'suitable' occupations.

NOTES

1. Quoted in Gareth Stedman Jones, 'Working Class Culture and Working Class Politics in London, 1870-1900', *Journal of Social History* **7** (Summer 1974), p. 491.
2. Lady Florence Bell, *At the Works: A Study of a Manufacturing Town*, 1st edn. 1902

(Thomas Nelson, 1911), p. 256.

3. Eliot Slater and Moya Woodside, *Patterns of Marriage* (Cassell and Co., 1951) p. 119.
4. E.A. Roberts, 'The Working Class Family in Barrow and Lancaster, 1890-1930', unpublished PhD. Diss., University of Lancaster, 1978, p. 76.
5. Louise Jermy, *The Memories of a Working Woman* (Norwich: Goose and Son, 1934), pp. 28-9.
6. John Burnett, *Destiny Obscure: Autobiographies of Childhood, Education and Family from the 1820s to the 1920s* (Allen Lane, 1982), p. 258.
7. Ellen Ross, '"Fierce Questions and Taunts": Married Life in Working Class London 1870-1914', *Feminist Studies* **8** (Fall 1982), p. 578.
8. Gill Burke, The Cornish Miner and the Cornish Mining Industry, 1870-1921', unpublished PhD. Diss., University of London, 1982.
9. Slater and Woodside, *Patterns of Marriage*, p. 141.
10. Magdalen Stuart Pember Reeves, *Round about a Pound a Week* (G. Bell and Sons, 1934), p. 17.
11. Thea Thompson, *Edwardian Childhoods* (Routledge & Kegan Paul, 1981), p. 105; and Bell, *At the Works*, pp. 318–19.
12. Ross, 'Fierce Questions and Taunts'.
13. Roberts, 'The Working Class Family', p. 53.
14. Nancy Tomes, '"A Torrent of Abuse": Crimes of Violence between Working Class Men and Women in London, 1840-1875', *Journal of Social History* **11** (Spring 1978), pp. 328-345; and Iris Minor, 'Working Class Women and Matrimonial Law Reform, 1890-1914', in *Ideology and the Labour Movement*, eds. David E. Martin and David Rubinstein (Croom Helm, 1979), pp. 103-124.
15. PP., 'Report of the Royal Commission on Divorce and Matrimonial Causes', Cd. 6478, 1912-13, XVIII, 143, p. 181.
16. Peter Stearns, 'Working Class Women in Britain 1890-1914', in *Suffer and be Still*, ed. Martha Vicinus (Bloomington, Indiana: Indiana University Press, 1973), pp. 100-120.
17. Margaret Llewellyn Davies, *Maternity: Letters from Working Women* (G. Bell, 1915).
18. Diana Gittens, *Fair Sex: Family Size and Structure, 1900-1939* (Hutchinson, 1982).
19. Jane Lewis and Barbara Brookes, 'A Reassessment of the Work of the Peckham Health Centre, 1926-1951', *Millbank Memorial Quarterly: Health and Society* **61** (1983), pp. 307-48.
20. Relief was provided to the destitute (ideally in a workhouse but often in their own homes) under the Poor Law Amendment Act of 1834. The Act was administered locally by boards of guardians and was not completely dismantled until the introduction of new social security legislation during the late 1940s. See Derek Fraser, *The Evolution of the Welfare State* (Macmillan, 1973); and Pat Thane, *Foundations of the Welfare State* (Longman, 1982).
21. PP., 'Minutes of Evidence to the Royal Commission on Divorce and Matrimonial Causes', Vol. II, Cd. 6480, 1912-13, XVIII, Q. 20120.
22. Cd. 6478, pp. 37 and 96.
23. On the issue of state regulation of sexuality see Jeffrey Weeks, *Sex Politics and Society: The Regulation of Sexuality since 1800* (Longman, 1981); and Judith R. Walkowitz, *Prostitution and Victorian Society* (Cambridge: Cambridge University

Press, 1980).

24. Helen Bosanquet, *The Family* (Macmillan, 1906), p. 199 and 222.
25. House of Lords, Debates, 1870, CCII, col. 613.
26. See for example: Anna Davin, 'Imperialism and Motherhood', *History Workship Journal* No. 5 (Spring 1978), pp. 9–65; and Jane Lewis *The Politics of Motherhood* (Croom Helm, 1980).
27. Anna Martin, *The Married Woman Worker* (NUWSS, 1911), pp. 36–7.
28. Denise Riley, 'The Free Mothers: Pronatalism and Working Women in Industry at the End of the War', *History Workship Journal* No. 11 (Spring 1981), pp. 59–118.

Family Size and Fertility Control

Working class family size remained large throughout the period. In the 1950s two social investigators reported the reluctance of a working class informant to go for a walk with his family on a middle class housing estate because 'they look at you and say, Oh look at all those children!'[1] Nevertheless, by the end of the inter-war period the working class fertility rate was dropping as rapidly as that of the middle class, with the result that the two-child family was fast ceasing to be a middle class phenomenon. Indeed, by the outbreak of World War II, there is considerable evidence that working class families were not responding to the call by the Royal Commission on Population and policy makers for larger families (a result of anxiety regarding the dramatic decline in the birth rate during the 1930s). Slater and Woodside met with comments such as 'I want some fun out of life; I'm not interested in raising the birth rate'.[2] There are then two aspects of the working class fertility pattern to be explained: first the slower rate of decline during the period before World War I, and second, the rapid decrease during the inter-war years.

Late nineteenth- and early twentieth-century working class wives have often been characterised as fatalistic in their attitudes towards childbirth.[3] The very few working class women who have left a record of their conscious decision to limit their families usually mention the plight of their mothers as the decisive factor. Hannah Mitchell, for example wrote of her mother-in-law: 'Poor soul! I never knew her. Child-bearing and cooking for twenty years. . . she must have been worn out before she died a comparatively young woman. So I was definitely determined not to begin where she left off'.[4] Jessie Stephen, an active trade unionist, ended up teaching her own mother about birth control when the latter was 42 years old.[5]

However, failure to limit fertility should not necessarily be interpreted as fatalism. Jessie Stephen's mother wished she had not had so many children and did not desire to have more. Similarly, the letters published by the Women's Cooperative Guild (WCG) in 1915 regarding the maternity experiences of 160 of their members whose husbands earned between 24 and 40 shillings a week and who mostly had been married during the 1890s, showed that women with large families bitterly regretted it, chiefly because of the hard labour necessary to sustain a large family. One Guild member felt that three children had reduced her to a household drudge and in desperation resorted to propping up Lowell and Longfellow over her washtub and learning passages off by heart on washday.[6]

The Guild members were not asked about birth control in the questionnaire that elicited these letters, so it is all the more surprising that twenty women volunteered the information that they either used or approved of contraception. But what comes across from the letters is an overwhelming ignorance about female physiology and sexuality, the difficulty of gaining access to information, and a lack of privacy in their homes that would have rendered the use of female methods of birth control extremely difficult. Similar problems undoubtedly faced many working class women throughout the period. Many of Rosemary Cook's respondents in the Rhondda, who had given birth to children during the inter-war years, said that birth control had been out of the question despite the fact that the birth rate for the Rhondda fell dramatically during the inter-war period.[7] Similarly, when in the late 1930s a leading obstetrician asked women in Aberdeen how many children they would like to have, he received the response: 'Aye Doctor, I shall have me number'.[8] And in 1938, the editor of *Woman's Own* judged from her postbag that ignorance of sex was as widespread as ever,[9] a view born out in 1948 by a woman who explained that:

> having your normal period wasn't ever mentioned, I was just sent along to the lav, my sister came with me, she said 'you wear this', and that was that—My mother never even mentioned it . . . you got married and you had children, I didn't know there was such a thing that you could not have them and it just went on and on.[10]

The social taboo placed on discussion of birth control and sexuality, and the acceptance by a majority of middle class women of the idea that they lacked sexual drives—what Judith Walkowitz has called the doctrine of passionlessness[11]—meant that little information was likely to come within the purview of women generally.

It is also important to consider the views of working class husbands. Jessie Stephens' mother had initially refused to contemplate birth control because her husband did not consider it 'natural'. When she began to use contraception at the age of 42 she probably did so without her husband's knowledge, but this would have been difficult for most working class women, given the lack of privacy in their homes. As late as 1956 a team of investigators described the plight of a woman in a mining village whose husband refused to use a sheath and who, because she had no bathroom could not use a cap. The woman's sister made an appointment for both to go to a birth control clinic, but in the end neither attended.[12] The organisation required to travel to the clinic and to sustain the project through to conclusion proved too much. A similar picture of female powerlessness and male dominance in respect to fertility control is given in a 1950 portrait of families in Ship Street, Liverpool.[13]

Perhaps not surprisingly, we have copious evidence throughout the period of women who felt no sexual pleasure because of the fear of pregnancy, and there is here some indication that working class women may have internalised middle class ideas of passionlessness and its correlate: male sensuality. In 1912 Eleanor Barton, a spokeswoman for the WCG (albeit herself middle class), voiced the opinion that 'women suffer a great deal through their husbands' sensuality, and that is more evident amongst working people than other classes, simply because the conditions of life lend themselves to that sort of thing, and they have not been taught the proper uses of their bodies'.[14] More straightforward were the comments recorded by Leonora Eyles of women in the early 1920s who declared that they would not mind married life so much if it were not for bedtime,[15] or the anecdote related by a birth control pioneer to a 1930 conference on the provision of birth control information by public health authorities:

I was asking a women why she did not keep herself more tidy and make herself attractive to her husband. 'I don't want to be attractive to him', she replied, 'Every time I am attractive to him, it means another kid'.[16]

Women with uncooperative husbands were forced to resort either to wiles such as these or to abortion. In this connection, it is interesting to note that Hannah Mitchell had the agreement of her husband to use birth control: 'Fortunately my husband had the courage of his socialist convictions on this point'.[17]

Quantitatively abortion was probably the most important *female* initiative in family limitation throughout the period, particularly among the very poor. During the 1890s and early 1900s the *British Medical Journal* traced the diffusion of abortion involving the use of lead plaster as an abortifacient from Leicester to Birmingham, Nottingham, Sheffield and through some of the large Yorkshire towns.[18] This substance was scheduled as a poison at the end of World War I. By 1914, Ethel Elderton concluded that abortion was common in 26 out of 104 registration districts north of the Humber.[19] These districts were primarily urban and working class and eleven were textile areas. Abortifacient pills, usually ineffectual, were widely advertised in newspapers. A typical example read:

Ladies Only/THE LADY MONTROSE/MIRACULOUS/FEMALE TABULES/Are positively unequalled for all/FEMALE AILMENTS. The most OBSTINATE/obstructions, Irregularities, etc./of the female system are removed in a few doses.[20]

Such remedies were expensive at 2/9d or 4/6d a box; 'extra strength' pills were dearer. The mixture of ten herbs, gin and salts consumed by a York woman provided a cheaper alternative at 10d a pint. Other remedies included a liquid produced by soaking nails and pennies in water, gunpowder, gold leaf from painters' shops, and even rat poison. The professional abortionist was a last resort. The more desperate remedies undoubtedly reflected desperate motives. A women quoted in Ethel Elderton's 1914 study declared that she'd 'rather swallow the druggist's shop and the man in't than have another kid'.[21]

Among northern textile workers poverty and the need to work probably played the most important part in the decision to seek an abortion, but it is also important to remember that working class women viewed abortion as a natural and permissible strategy. As late as 1938, a government Inter-Departmental Committee on Abortion found that 'many mothers seemed not to understand that self-induced abortion was illegal. They assumed it was legal before the third month [before quickening], and only outside the law when procured by another person'.[22] Abortion decisions and practices were very much part of a female culture and to some extent must be considered apart from, rather than as an alternative to, other methods of birth control. For example, it cannot be argued that poor women resorted to abortion because doctors withheld information about other birth control methods. Such women went to doctors but rarely on their own account, largely because they could not afford to do so. However, there is evidence to suggest that some women distrusted other methods of birth control, and particularly that of male withdrawal; not all women could reckon on either being able to 'push him out of the way when I think it's near',[23] or on their husbands' constant exercise of self-control.

It is difficult to assess the incidence of abortion. The British Medical Association estimated that 20 per cent of abortions were criminal and using that figure David Glass calculated that a total of 68,000 criminal abortions took place in 1935. However, a practising midwife in a small colliery village during the 1930s believed that of 227 miscarriages amongst 122 women over a period of seven years, few were accidental. Prosecutions for abortion doubled between 1900 and 1910 and doubled again during the next twenty years, but this may merely indicate more vigilance on the part of the authorities rather than increasing incidence.[24] Since the Royal Commission on Population found that out of a sample of 7,625 pregnancies only 147 resulted in criminal abortions (equal to 2 per cent of all pregnancies and 17 per cent of all abortions),[25] it is unlikely that changes in the abortion rate played a major part in accounting for the decrease in working class fertility.

Indeed, withdrawal was undoubtedly the main method by which the decline in working class fertility was achieved, and it continued to be as common a method of birth control as the sheath in post-World War II Britain.[26] While the percentage of middle class people using mechanical methods of birth control increased from 9 per cent to 40 per cent between 1910 and 1930, the comparable figures for the working class were 1 per cent and 28 per cent.[27] One of the main reasons for the popularity of withdrawal, especially prior to World War I, was its cheapness; sheaths cost an average of 2/- to 3/- a dozen, during a period when the average weekly wage of a labourer did not rise above 20/- a week. The importance of withdrawal brings us back to the issue of women's sexual dependency and the fact that some degree of male cooperation was necessary, if only a willingness to be pushed out of the way. Thus attention must be given to male motives for using contraception.

In his latest book on fertility decline, J.A. Banks dismisses the argument that fertility control results from economically rational behaviour.[28] The introduction of compulsory elementary education after 1870 may have prompted a re-evaluation of the cost of children because it seriously diminished the contribution the child could make to the family economy. But on the whole, there is little evidence to suggest a link between male wage levels and fertility. For example, the size of agricultural labourers' families, one of the poorest paid occupational groups, remained high. Instead Banks stresses the importance of the development of a meritocratic career pattern for men and a concomitant future-time perspective on the part of all the mainly middle class occupational groups whose fertility rates fell fastest during the late nineteenth century. The fertility rate of railway workers declined rapidly following the expansion of promotion hierarchies at the end of the century. It is also interesting to note that even though the fertility rate of female textile workers was low from the beginning of the period, this was not the case in Preston, probably because the women weavers tended to be married to general labourers rather than to fellow textile workers, again suggesting that it was the occupational status and attitudes of the husband that were more important.[29] Certainly this view parallels both Sidney Webb's famous 1905 observation, that it was the thrifty of all classes who were limiting their families, and the classic complaint of social investigators that the large families of the very poor resulted from their 'intense devotion to the present moment and their blind forgetfulness of past and future'.[30] (There was of course little incentive to plan for the future when work was often obtained on a casual basis and wages were irregular.) The argument is strengthened still further by evidence from clinic data between the wars which show that the most popular method of birth control among skilled manual workers was the sheath.[31] However, in attributing prime importance to male decision-making on birth control, Banks is dismissive of the part women may have played.[32] We may accept that male cooperation was needed for fertility to fall, while at the same time arguing that the opinions of wives may also have had an important effect on husbands. Ethel Elderton found that in Chorlton working class wives talked freely about birth control and said that they 'made their husbands take precautions'.[33]

The dynamics of decision-making and the exercise of power within the family are difficult to investigate today, let alone for the past. But consideration of the process by which family size was negotiated between husband and wife is crucial, especially when evidence suggests that the couples who were most successful in controlling their fertility between the wars were those who discussed the issue and reached agreement. Diana Gittens has concluded that couples whose worlds increasingly centred on the home, rather than on the culture of the workplace or on the spouses' respective circles of friends, most frequently achieved their ideal family size.[34] Such joint relationships could occur between spouses of very different backgrounds. In the case of families where both husband and wife worked in the textile industry, joint role relationships were common and involved a large amount of sex role equality. In the absence of a family wage, husbands often shared household tasks, and major decisions, including that of family size, would be discussed jointly. Gittens has also suggested that female textile workers' apparently greater knowledge of birth control methods emanated from their female friends and acquaintances at work (although Elizabeth Roberts' findings have not borne this out).[35] In contrast, female domestic servants led isolated work lives prior to marriage and their marriages usually involved a traditional sexual division of labour; but they also tended to enjoy a joint role relationship with their husbands in the sense that the husband spent his non-working hours with his wife and children, and they too tended to be successful in limiting the size of their families. However, all the evidence concerning mining villages, where fertility rates continued to be high until the 1930s and where the average age at marriage was also significantly lower than the national average, suggests that role relationships within marriage were segregated.

During the inter-war period birth control was discussed more openly than ever before. For example, women in the Labour Party made sure that resolutions asking for the provision of birth control information via local authority clinics came before the Party's Annual Conference in 1925, 1926 and 1927. The 1927 Conference heard a moving appeal on the issue from a miner's wife who referred to the women's support for male trade unionists during the 1926 General Strike: 'Surely you will not turn the women down on this question because it was the women who stood four-square with you in your dispute?'[36] In this context, it is likely that changes in the nature of marital relations resulting from the increasingly private nature of family life, together with an increasing tendency by working people to plan for the future, were the most important variables explaining the decrease in working class fertility during the inter-war years, at a time when the employed working man enjoyed a more regular and higher real wage than ever before. It also seems that unemployment, the chief cause of poverty during the inter-war period, resulted in a different outlook from that induced by pre-World War I poverty, which was caused primarily by low wages. The Commission for the Special Areas unsuccessfully recommended the setting up of birth control clinics in areas of high unemployment, believing the birth rate to be undesirably high.[37] But in the Rhondda fertility declined dramatically between 1911 and 1931, especially amongst younger couples. In Lancashire the effect of unemployment was less dramatic, possibly because wife or child could continue to earn.

The birth control methods most commonly used by working class families were as readily available in 1870 as they were in 1950. To explain why they were not employed as frequently as they were amongst the middle class until the inter-war period involves consideration of the complicated relationship between the occupational characteristics of *both* husband and wife with their respective values and expectations and how they related to each other.

NOTES

1. Quoted in Brian Harrison, 'Underneath the Victorians', *Victorian Studies* X (March 1967), p. 258.
2. Eliot Slater and Moya Woodside, *Patterns of Marriage* (Cassell, 1951), p. 189.
3. Peter Stearns, 'Working Class Women in Britain 1890-1914', in *Suffer and be Still*, ed. Martha Vicinus (Bloomington: Indiana University Press, 1973), pp. 100-120.
4. Hannah Mitchell, *The Hard Way Up*, 1st ed. 1968 (Virago, 1977) p. 96.
5. Sheila Rowbotham, *A New World for Women. Stella Browne: Socialist Feminist* (Pluto, 1977), p. 40.
6. Margaret Llewellyn Davies, *Maternity: Letters of Working Women* (G. Bell, 1915), p. 47; see also Pat Knight, 'Women and Abortion in Victorian and Edwardian England', *History Workshop Journal* No. 4 (Autumn 1977), pp. 57-68.
7. Rosemary Cook, '"Tidy Women": Women in the Rhondda between the Wars', *Oral History* **10** (Autumn 1982), pp. 40-46.
8. Quoted in Derek Gill, *Illegitimacy, Sexuality and the Status of Women* (Oxford: Blackwell, 1972), p. 175.
9. Cynthia L. White, *Women's Magazines 1693-1968* (Michael Joseph, 1970), p. 108.
10. Joan Busfield and Michael Paddon, *Thinking about Children* (Cambridge: Cambridge University Press, 1977), p. 237.
11. Judith R. Walkowitz, 'Male Vice and Feminist Virtue: Feminism and the Politics of Prostitution in Nineteenth Century Britain' *History Workshop Journal* No. 13 (Spring 1982), pp. 79-83.
12. N. Dennis, I. Henriques and C. Slaughter, *Coal is Our Life: An Analysis of a Yorkshire Mining Community* (Tavistock, 1956), p. 208.
13. Madeleine Kerr, *The People of Ship Street* (Routledge & Kegan Paul, 1958).
14. PP., 'Minutes of Evidence to the Royal Commission on Divorce and Matrimonial Law Reform', Cd. 6481, 1912-13, XVIII, Q. 37147.
15. Leonora Eyles, *The Woman in the Little House* (Grant Richards, 1922) p. 129.
16. Linda Ward, 'The Right to Choose: A Study of Women's Fight for Birth Control Provisions', unpublished PhD. Diss., Bristol University, 1981, p. 49.
17. Mitchell, *Hard Way Up*, p. 102.
18. Frank M. Pope, 'Two Cases of Poisoning by the Self-Administration of "Diachylon"—Lead Plaster for the purpose of Procuring Abortion', *British Medical Journal*, 1 July 1893, pp. 9-10; and Arthur Hill and W. B. Ransom, 'Plumbism from the Ingestion of Dachylon as an Abortifacient', *British Medical Journal*, 24 February 1906, pp. 428-30.
19. Ethel Elderton, *Report on the English Birthrate* (Dulau, 1916).
20. Angus McLaren, *Birth Control in Nineteenth Century England* (Croom Helm, 1978), pp. 232-3.
21. Elderton, *Report on the English Birthrate*, p. 176; and see also Barbara Brookes, 'Abortion in England 1919-39. Legal Theory and Social Practice', unpublished PhD. Diss., Bryn Mawr University, 1982, p. 176.
22. Quoted in Angus McLaren, 'Women's Work and the Regulation of Family Size', *History Workshop Journal* No. 4 (Autumn 1977), p. 75.
23. Slater and Woodside, *Patterns of Marriage*, p. 198.
24. Brookes, 'Abortion in England 1919-39', pp. 37 and 167.

25. E. Lewis Faning, 'Report on an Enquiry into Family Limitation and its Influence on Human Fertility during the past Fifty Years', *Papers of the Royal Commission on Population*, Vol. I (HMSO, 1949), pp. 171 and 173.
26. Griselda Rowntree and Rachel M. Pierce, 'Birth Control in Britain', *Population Studies* **15** (July, 1961), pp. 3-31.
27. Diana Gittens, *Fair Sex. Family Size and Structure 1900-1939* (Hutchinson, 1982), p. 162.
28. J. A. Banks, *Victorian Values. Secularism and the Size of Families* (Routledge & Kegan Paul, 1981).
29. E. A. Roberts, 'Working Wives and their Families', in *Population and Society in Britain, 1850-1980*, eds. T. Barker and M. Drake (Batsford Academic Press, 1982), p. 154.
30. *The Times*, 5 September 1905, p. 10; and Helen Bosanquet, *Rich and Poor* (Macmillan, 1896), p. 40.
31. Gittens, *Fair Sex*, p. 170.
32. Banks, *Victorian Values*, p. 39.
33. Elderton, *The English Birth Rate*, p. 61.
34. Busfield and Paddon, *Thinking about Children*, also develop the idea of negotiation between spouses on the issue of fertility control.
35. Roberts, 'Working Wives and their Families'. p. 154.
36. Ward, 'The Right to Choose', p. 145.
37. Jane Lewis, *The Politics of Motherhood* (Croom Helm, 1980), p. 207.

Health and Welfare

The relationship between the improvement in women's health and their emancipation has been widely noted. Early in the 1950s, Richard Titmuss pointed out that the average working class woman marrying in her teens or early twenties during the 1890s experienced ten pregnancies and spent fifteen years in pregnancy and nursing compared with an average of four years so spent by her counterpart in the years following World War II. Titmuss felt that changes in patterns of pregnancy and childbirth had been a much more important factor in explaining changes in women's position in society than the acquisition of legal rights.[1] More recently, Edward Shorter has made a similar case for improvements in women's health status generally as a pre-requisite to an active feminist movement.[2] Certainly women's mortality rates have improved significantly faster than those for men (Table 3), but it is difficult to come to any general conclusions about health status for the period 1870–1950, particularly in respect to working class women. Nor is the connection between improvements in health and feminism clear in the lives of individuals; large numbers of active middle class feminists were also chronic invalids.

What is striking from the admittedly patchy evidence regarding the health status of working class women is the apparent lack of any real improvement during the period. It is interesting that wives aged under 45 suffered a higher mortality rate than unmarried women prior to World War I, and that the difference is not explicable solely in terms of maternal mortality. In 1913, Mrs. Pember Reeves commented that it came as a shock to realise that working class wives in Lambeth who looked as it they were 'in the dull middle of middle age' were in fact young.[3] Commenting on the ageing process

Table 3: Comparative Mortality Indices (1938 = 100) England and Wales, 1871 to 1950

Period	*Males*	*Females*	*Adjusted ratio (M/F)*
1871–80	2.09	2.27	1.15
1881–90	1.93	2.09	1.16
1891–00	1.87	2.01	1.17
1901–10	1.59	1.69	1.19
1911–20	1.45	1.49	1.25
1921–30	1.16	1.22	1.25
1931–40	1.07	1.10	1.31
1941–50	0.92	0.89	1.38

Source: Registrar General, *Statistical Review of England and Wales, 1951*, Pt 1, Table 3 (HMSO, 1953), p. 4.

in the 1950s, Viola Klein remarked that women generally looked old at 40, which may indicate some improvement.[4] However, a 1939 survey of the health of 1,250 working class wives found only 31.3 per cent to be in good health, 22.3 per cent were categorised as 'indifferent', 15.2 per cent as 'bad' and 31.2 per cent as 'very grave'.[5] Similarly in a 1947 survey of 2,807 women (conducted as part of the Ministry of Labour's campaign to stimulate the recruitment of women to industry), older married women in particular often gave health problems as a reason for not working outside the home; 37 per cent of those aged between 45 and 60 mentioned ill-health to the interviewer.[6] The women in the 1939 survey reported a large amount of debilitating illness, especially anaemia, headaches, constipation with or without haemorrhoids, rheumatism, gynaecological disorders, toothache and varicose veins. These findings are reminiscent of the self-reported morbid conditions of the Women's Cooperative Guild members published in 1915.[7] National health insurance statistics, which recorded the health experience of the small proportion of married women who worked in insurable occupations, also indicated that the health of married working class women left much to be desired. By 1931-32 married women were experiencing 140 per cent more sickness than the insurance commissioners had anticipated, compared with the 25 per cent more sickness experienced by unmarried women and the less-than-expected sickness rates of men.[8] Mary MacArthur, a leading woman trade unionist, believed that these figures could be attributed to the 'treble strain of child-bearing, wage-earning and household drudgery'.[9] Moreover, women had singularly low expectations of health. A Cardiff woman, aged 35 in 1939, suffered from decayed teeth, bronchitis every winter and a prolapsed uterus dating from her second pregnancy, yet she did not consider herself ill.[10] Moreover, as the 1939 survey showed, few women sought medical attention for their ailments. The National Health Insurance Act of 1911 provided access to a general practitioner for all insured workers, male and female, but not for their dependants, who were mainly women and children. Women, whose responsibility it was to look after the family budget, were notoriously reluctant to incur the additional expense of a doctor's bill on their own account. It was for this reason that one woman diarist writing during World War II was convinced that the introduction of a national health service would mean more to women than to men.[11]

CONDITIONS OF MOTHERHOOD

The causes of the low health status of working class wives were related to frequent pregnancies, poor nutrition, hard household labour in often depressing conditions, and lack of leisure. Most working class women's autobiographies tell of hard work and financial anxiety prior to childbirth, poor quality attendance and great pain during labour, with a swift return to domestic and/or paid employment after the birth. Hannah Mitchell's matter-of-fact account is typical:

> one Friday, having done my weekend cleaning and baked a batch of bread during the day, I hoped for a good night's rest, but I scarcely had retired before my labour began. My baby was not born until the following evening, after 24 hours of intense suffering which an ignorant attendant did little to alleviate, assuring me at intervals that I should be much worse yet.[12]

Throughout the period, a majority of working class women gave birth at home with no pain relief, the common practice being to pull on a towel knotted round the end of the bed when the pains came. In 1917 qualified midwives in London charged 12/6d for first births and 10/- for subsequent ones; by the late 1930s this had risen to between 25/- and 50/- for first births and 21/- to 40/- for subsequent ones. A doctor would have charged at least twice as much. After 1911, women whose husbands were in insured employment received a maternity benefit of 30/- rising to £2 after World War I, which was completely absorbed by the cost of an attendant, leaving nothing for extra food and necessities for the mother and baby.[13] Poor women often 'made do', like Hannah Mitchell, with unqualified attendance, seeking a ticket from the Poor Law Relieving Officer for medical help in cases of emergency.

Poor, unmarried mothers resorted to the workhouse hospital;[14] 70 per cent of births in workhouses were illegitimate in 1907, and conditions in these hospitals varied considerably. In 1885 the lying-in ward in the Strand workhouse was located immediately above the female insane ward and despite the effort to reform workhouse nursing during the 1860s, elderly pauper women still acted as midwives and childminders. Prior to World War I, infant mortality rates in the workhouses were more than double the rate for the entire population.[15] Nevertheless, increasing numbers of poor women sought institutional care in both Poor Law and voluntary hospitals during the period, and after the local authorities took control of the Poor Law hospitals in 1929, the number of hospital births increased dramatically. This trend was welcomed by articulate working class women's groups such as the Women's Cooperative Guild, because of poor working class housing conditions and because they believed that working class wives needed a respite from the cares of managing a household. However, the Guild also asked for a comprehensive home-help service so that women would not worry about the welfare of younger children and husbands, but this was not forthcoming.

The legacy of childbearing was frequently one of impaired health. Marie Stopes found that amongst her first 10,000 birth control patients, 1,321 had slit cervixes, 335 serious prolapses, and 1,508 internal deformations.[16] As late as 1937 only 10 per cent of women were attending post-natal clinics, whereas 54 per cent received ante-natal care. One eminent obstetrician estimated in 1931 that 10 per cent of all pregnant women were disabled by the experience of childbirth.

The health and welfare of mothers suffered additionally because of the maldistribution of resources within the family. As Ellen Ross has observed, 'family socialism' operated only among women and children.[17] Many wives did not know what their husbands earned—as many as one-third of those surveyed in Middlesborough in 1907—and the vast majority of husbands kept back a proportion of their income for their own use.[18] In 1908 George Lansbury admonished working class men for not practising the economic equality at home that they preached in public, and noted that men who gave their wives 10/- to 12/- out of 30/- to 35/- felt that they had done enough.[19] It was not uncommon for men bringing home as small a wage as 18/- to keep back 2/- for themselves. In an early 1950s mining community, husbands kept their wives' allowances low so that they could skip a shift if they wished,[20] but few wives expected their husbands 'to work for nothing' and it is not difficult to find examples of wives exercising considerable control over all but the husband's pocket money. Mrs. Layton, a member of the Women's Cooperative Guild, made the decision to allow her husband the 1/6d to join the Cooperative Society in the first place.[21] As Anne Gray has pointed out, it is difficult to generalise about housekeeping systems.[22] Many husbands took responsibility for saving for such major items of expenditure as furniture or even boots out of the money they kept back for themselves. In 1899 one York wife responded to a question about the difficulties of providing footwear for her family in the following way:

> Well, as a rule . . . we 'ave to get it out of the food money and go short, but I never let Smith suffer—'e 'as to go to work, and must be kept up, yer know! When I want a new pair of shoes, or anythink, 'e 'elps me out of 'is pocket money, and we haven't to pinch the food so much.[23]

Thus housekeeping allowances might bear little relation to the portion of the husband's net income devoted to collective expenditure. However, it is interesting to note that during World War I, when soldiers' wives received dependants' allowances totalling a maximum of 17/6d in 1915 and 31/7d by 1918 for a wife and three children (the average male labourer's wage in 1918 was £2), the heights and weights of schoolchildren and the infant mortality rate both showed improvement, which would suggest that wives and children found themselves rather better off.

With the sum their husbands allowed them, wives organised the family budget, which in the first place involved solving the food/rent equation. Rent was a charge that had to be met first, although midnight 'flits' to avoid paying rent were common among the very poor and not unknown for the artisan in temporarily reduced circumstances.[24] Rowntree calculated that rent absorbed an average of 14 per cent of income in York in 1900. In fact the proportion spent on rent was inversely proportional to income. Thus a detailed examination of Birmingham families in the early 1880s found that those earning 27/6d paid 6/– rent (23.7 per cent of their income), while in London in the 1900s it was not uncommon to pay 8/- out of 24/- (33 per cent) for two rooms. Many families would therefore rent a four room house at ten or eleven shillings and let one room at two or three shillings. The rise in rents between 1848 and the late 1880s more or less matched the rise in real wages during the same period. When the rise in rents from 1912 onwards threatened to overwhelm the family economy it was women who protested and led rent strikes, for example in Leeds and, more famously, Glasgow, leading to the imposition of rent control in 1915. In London Sylvia Pankhurst coined the slogan 'No Vote No Rent'.[25] As a consumer protest based on the home, the rent strike was an important and relatively neglected form of working class direct action, which paralleled industrial unrest in the workplace during the late Edwardian period.

The task of household budgeting was an extremely difficult one and evoked harsh words from husbands if it was mismanaged, even though most husbands probably had little notion of how to manage on the sums they gave their wives. In one Lambeth family investigated by Mrs Pember Reeves, the expenditure on margarine doubled during the week the husband took over the family budgeting in the absence of his wife, simply because he allowed everyone to take as large a share as himself. The realistic appraisal by working class wives as to what was possible on a fixed budget was also shown in a study of savings conducted by Mass Observation during World War II. Twice as many men as women felt that it should be possible to save more out of the housekeeping allowance.[26]

Louise Jermy faced housekeeping on 13/- a week in the late nineteenth century with huge anxiety. It took her from 25 February to 30 June to save a shilling, but once she had accomplished that she was content that she could manage and 'never let it trouble me again'.[27] It was difficult to decide whether to spend more on better housing or food. Mrs Pember Reeves was ambivalent on the issue, commenting that it depended largely on whether the accommodation was above or below ground and on the absolute minimum that was allowed for food. During the inter-war period, when housing expectations among women were rising, one Medical Officer of Health found that mortality rates amongst families who had moved out of a slum area into new council houses actually rose, because correspondingly less was being spent on food. As to the amount left for food and clothing after rent and a more flexible sum for heat had been deducted, wives tended to act as the buffer against the needs of husbands and to a lesser extent children.[28]

Mrs Pember Reeves found that in Lambeth prior to World War I, the amount spent on food averaged 6d per head per day for men and 2½d per head per day for women and children. As Derek Oddy has commented, 'essentially the woman's diet was one of bread and tea, while almost all men consumed a main meal of meat or bacon or fish or potatoes'.[29] Mrs Pember Reeves described the diet of the family of a feather cleaner's assistant, earning 25/- a week. The father kept back 5/- for himself, out of which he bought his own clothes. He also had 6½d a day allowed to him for lunches at work and demanded that 1/1d a week be spent on 'relishes' for his breakfast and tea—usually consisting of an egg, a piece of bacon, or fish. At breakfast the father ate half the loaf and the mother and two children shared the rest. Mother and children spent 1/2d a week on lunches and all shared the Sunday joint, which provided suppers for two days in the week following. That apart, suppers closely resembled breakfast. Yet, as Mrs Pember Reeves observed, despite the inequitable division of resources and the apparent selfishness of the father, his diet did not seem overly luxurious for a working man.[30] During the inter-war period more sophisticated research into diet showed a clear relationship between haemoglobin deficiencies, iron and protein levels in diet, and family income. The Pilgrim Trust's survey of a sample of unemployed men included some 170,000 wives and it was calculated that these women ate only 70 per cent of the calories consumed by men, rather than the 85 per cent recommended by dieticians. Sample research also showed that the addition of special foods and milk to the diet of pregnant women caused a significant decline in the maternal mortality rate, which remained high until the mid-1930s. The ideal diet for a pregnant woman recommended by the Chief Medical Officer at the Ministry of Health included milk at a cost of 4/1d when the total allowance for the wife of an unemployed man was only 4/11d.[31]

These often poorly nourished women undertook hard physical labour in their homes. Very few husbands took on any household chores. In cotton textile workers' families, where there was a long tradition of married women's work, one night a week was usually set aside by husbands and wives as 'Mary-Ann night'. But if the woman cotton worker were married to a miner or an engineer, then the husband usually refused to do housework; his substantially higher earnings gave him breadwinner status and, notwithstanding his wife's employment, the right to leisure while at home.[32] The time-consuming tasks of keeping families clean and fed were for the most part carried out with wholly inadequate equipment in depressing surroundings. Provision of piped water and sanitary facilities varied widely from region to region and between different types of housing. Despite the poor conditions in many towns, Margery Loane, a health visitor, felt that the family of the pre-World War I urban labourer, earning 20/- a week and renting a small house or half a house, was better off than that of his rural counterpart, earning 13/- a week and living in a free, but often damp and usually overcrowded cottage. In Barrow each house had a water tap by the 1880s, but in Lancaster 475 houses shared a single tap as late as 1925 and in Manchester in 1931 there were 70,000 houses classified as 'unfit' with thirty to fifty people sharing a tap in a tenement building. Similar conditions prevailed in Shoreditch tenements during the 1930s, and Elizabeth Flint remembered that pre-World War I houses near Waterloo Station in London had one tap for the row. Very few working class houses had indoor lavatories before 1918 and at worst were provided with ash or midden privies. A 1914 Local Government Board return on 'scavenging' in urban districts showed that as many as 54 per cent of households in Hull and 15 per cent in Liverpool had ash privies. Midden privies were large uncovered receptacles sunk below ground level, but they were by no means watertight and often served two, four or more houses. Ash privies were an improvement, as they were built above ground level and cemented at the bottom; ash was thrown in at the front and the contents withdrawn through a door at the back. Alice Foley, growing up in Bolton during the 1890s, remembered the plague of houseflies emanating from the privies in summer.[33]

When overcrowding was added to poor sanitary conditions the battle with dirt was invariably lost. As Mrs Pember Reeves commented: 'To manage a husband and six children in three rooms on round about a pound a week needs, first and foremost, wisdom and loving kindness, and after that as much cleanliness and order as can be squeezed in'.[34] Wives whose husbands earned a regular wage would usually have a copper in which to heat water for washing, and by 1914, a mangle. Coppers were sometimes shared, which gave rise to disputes between neighbours, and mangles were sometimes rented to less fortunate families on the street at a ½d per load. Clothes were pounded in a 'dolly tub' and the whole process of washing was made harder by the high cost of soap: 2d worth had to suffice for clothes, floors and people for a week in 1913. Soda was much cheaper, if less effective, and was sometimes even used to wash the children's hair. As late as World War II, reception areas reported that between 8 and 35 per cent of children evacuated from London to escape the bombing had infested heads.[35]

By the end of World War I, working class women's groups, such as the Women's Labour League, were making three basic demands in terms of housing design: an indoor bathroom, a scullery/kitchen for cooking, and a front parlour. Middle class observers often complained that the parlour remained a showpiece in the respectable working class home, used only to house the piano and the aspidistra. But working class women fiercely defended their right to a room which expressed their pride in housewifery and which also afforded additional privacy, a scarce commodity in working class households. It was this desire for privacy that made the demands by some middle class feminists and leaders of the Women's Labour League for communal eating and washing facilities unpopular. The evidence on housing interiors given by the Women's Labour League to the Tudor Walters Committee on Housing Design at the end of the War proved influential, although housing policy generally was formulated more from a fear of unrest by working class men than with the needs of working class women in mind. The Committee approved the trend towards cooking in sculleries rather than on open fires in living rooms although the latter remained the only option for many families living in rooms until well into the inter-war period. By the 1930s gas was cheaper and gas ovens more common, which also saved the labour expended on black-leading the old kitchen ranges. (Prior to World War I, where gas had been available for cooking, it was often used only for the Sunday dinner.) Forty per cent of local authorities houses built to Tudor Walters' standards between the Wars had parlours, but later, in the inter-war years, economies were often effected by diminishing the size of parlours and sculleries and by not providing hot water for baths.[36] A bathroom was perhaps the item most prized by working class housewives after World War I, and there is ample evidence of wives planning moves up the housing hierarchy until one was acquired. The account given by an eminently respectable Bermondsey housewife to the compilers of the 1935 *Survey of London Life and Labour* illustrates this point well:

> We have a nice bath in this flat which makes one feel glad. I mean one can wash often when they have that convenience. I was in apartments for 10 years, and when one has lived under those conditions it makes one contented to know we can use plenty of water.[37]

However, working class wives living on the new housing estates of the inter-war period often had little but housework to occupy their days and, like many suburban middle class wives, tended to lead extremely isolated lives. Nella Last, the respectable wife of a joiner and shop fitter in Barrow, who kept a diary for Mass Observation during World War II, led what she termed a 'harem existence' during the inter-war years, which resulted in a nervous breakdown just before the outbreak of the War. Her wartime work for the Women's Voluntary Service and the Red Cross resulted in tremendous changes in her sense of self-worth, in her relationship with her husband and in her attitude towards housework. She refused to put up with her husband's moods, and commented at length on the ways in which her skill as a household manager had been undervalued in the past. She continued to record the details of almost every meal she cooked throughout the War but came to deplore the futility of her household routine:

> I thought of the stack of dirty crocks to tackle after tea, of pictures and furniture that were once polished every week, and now got done when I had the time. I wondered if people would ever go back to the old ways. I cannot see women settling to trivial ways—women who have done worthwhile things.[38]

In older working class communities, where neither housing conditions nor wages permitted such total devotion to housewifery, it nevertheless appeared that on the whole standards of housekeeping were high. The wives of better paid working class men played their part in the creation of a culture of respectability by the pride they took in their homes.[39] Freshly whitened steps signalled their status within the working class community and denoted the border of the respectable family's territory on the street. Middle class observers often expressed the opinion that working class housekeeping had grown sloppy and that the food budget could be better managed.[40] Porridge, for example, was always recommended as a cheap, nutritious food, but for a family cooking in a single pot on an open fire it was an impossible choice, primarily because it tended to stick to the bottom of the pan. Similarly, something like herrings, also cheap and nutritious, tended to add yet another offensive smell to poorly ventilated rooms and small houses. Wives coping in these conditions were more likely to patronise fried fish and ready-cooked meat shops than would housewives with ranges or gas stoves. There is also evidence that dietary customs, for example in the matter of baking bread, varied considerably from region to region. Moreover, as Anna Martin pointed out, what might be judged as sloppiness and poor management on the part of a well-to-do woman was not necessarily the case in a poor household. She quoted the example of a mother and daughter who habitually appeared 'with dishevelled hair and untidy blouses at 11 o'clock in the morning', and where dirty teacups rested on the breakfast table, but the fact was that both women stayed up until 4 am buttonholing, this being their only source of income.[41]

The daily routines of most working class wives left conspicuously little time for leisure. Rowntree commented that: 'No one can fail to be struck by the monotony which characterises the life of most married women of the working class',[42] especially the respectable poor who, by definition, did not gossip in courts and streets. In his book on working class leisure, Hugh Cunningham was able to find little evidence of any female pastimes.[43] Beatrice Webb recorded that she had been told by both a working class male school attendance officer and by the female manager of a block of 'model dwellings'[44] that working class women were not able to talk to their husbands, having little in their heads but household details.[45] Generally women had much less opportunity than men for either reading or exercise. Indeed, many women had no footwear suitable for walking beyond the local shops, boots always posing a major difficulty in household budgeting. During the more prosperous years of World War II, the Board of Trade reported an unsatisfied demand for shoes, which it explained by referring to a backlog of demand created by the inability of families to buy them during the 1930s. Increasing numbers of women went to cheap matinees at the cinema during the inter-war years, where 70 per cent of the weekly audiences in London comprised women and girls, and by 1939 the number of wirelesses had increased from 200,000 in 1923 to over 8.5 million.[46] But other opportunities for recreation remained few.

MOTHERHOOD AND THE STATE

During the early twentieth century a strong ideology of maternalism emerged, fuelled by eugenic concern about the quantity and quality of the race and the pronatalism induced by two World Wars. Policy makers sought to promote national health and welfare and it was considered to be in the nation's interest to extend child and maternal welfare services. As one prominent eugenicist put it, the state had 'neither womb nor breasts' and therefore needed to extend protection to those who had.[47] However, it was motherhood rather than the needs of individual mothers which evoked concern and relatively little attention was paid to the conditions faced by working class wives in their daily lives. Health for women was held to be synonymous with healthy motherhood. This had important implications for the debate over access to birth control information and abortion—rarely were demands for freer access to birth control information devoid of maternalist rhetoric. The protection extended to motherhood as a means of improving child and maternal welfare was rooted in particular moral and social mental maps. Working class women were encouraged to devote themselves to marriage and motherhood and to adopt middle class patterns of behaviour within their homes.

Between 1870 and 1918 it appeared to eugenicists concerned with finding ways of breeding a better race that the wrong class of people were using birth control. The Malthusian League had addressed its message to the working class, emphasising birth control as the only remedy for poverty, and had met with understandable hostility from leading (male) socialists. By the late 1930s, the rapidly falling birth rate made the quantity of population a more pressing issue than its 'quality'. In his 1935 budget speech, Neville Chamberlain, the Chancellor of the Exchequer, commented on the implications of a decreasing birth rate for an imperial power and appealed for more babies. Thus birth control groups during the inter-war period were careful to argue that the use of birth control would not necessarily lead to an increase in childlessness or very small families, but rather would result in better planned families and healthier mothers and children. The title Marie Stopes gave her birth control society—the Society for Constructive Birth Control and Racial Progress—was thus significant. Working class women's groups and the Workers' Birth Control Group, formed in 1924, which played a major part in the struggle for access to birth control information, also found it impossible to ignore the maternalist framework in their campaign. They argued for birth control primarily on the grounds that it would improve the health of the mother rather than on the grounds that women had the right to control their fertility. The Workers' Birth Control Group was anxious to show that women were not going to renege on motherhood if they were permitted easier access to birth control information: 'the committee of this organisation consists of married women who have children, and they are not in any way out to say it is a good thing not to have children'.[48] Limited gains were made in 1930 when the government agreed to make information available to sick women for whom pregnancy was deemed detrimental to health. In fact, only 95 of 423 maternal and child welfare centres had established birth control clinics by 1937. This policy was in line with the state's promotion of healthy motherhood, which did not encompass the right of individual mothers to choose whether they wished to bear children.

Access to abortion proved an even more difficult issue in relation to the state's desire to encourage motherhood. The Inter-Departmental Committee on Abortion reporting in 1939, feared that women might shirk their maternal responsibilities if legal abortion became more widely available. Nor did the Committee feel that birth control provided an acceptable alternative:

> A proposal that public money should be spent on a measure which is likely to aggravate this position (the low birth rate) by making contraception universally available on request and thereby to affect adversely the continuity of the state, is one which we feel we cannot endorse.[49].

On abortion, the Committee accepted the medical view that any abortion entailed danger to life and health and recommended only a clarification of the law to allow therapeutic abortion on health grounds. The Abortion Law Reform Association, founded in 1936 by seven women, of whom Dora Russell, Stella Browne and Frida Laski were particularly sympathetic to the labour movement, believed abortion to be safe, but called only for legal abortion to be made available on health grounds, using as their justification the way in which deaths due to abortion inflated the maternal mortality rate. Only Stella Browne, a socialist feminist, argued for abortion as an 'absolute right'.[50] Thus feminists prominent in the labour movement and leaders of middle class feminist groups, such as Eleanor Rathbone and Eva Hubback, were prepared to join anti-feminists in using the rhetoric of maternalism to promote the welfare of women. Their belief that it was possible for the individual to maintain a direct, unmediated relationship with the state made their position additionally vulnerable. As Sally Alexander has observed, they ran the risk of leaving the door 'wide open for all sorts of ideas equating the national interest with motherhood and children'.[51]

The truth of this becomes clear when particular initiatives involving the protection of motherhood and the welfare of children are considered. It was commonly held that the woman who worked outside the home could neither properly look after her child nor attend to her domestic duties. During the late nineteenth century, Medical Officers of Health, in particular, contended that women going out to work were responsible for raising the infant mortality rate because they tended to bottle-feed their infants and because, by carrying them out to nurse in the early morning, they exposed them to bronchitis. Women factory inspectors agreed that the less work women did in factories the better it would be for their home life and children's welfare, but they were also forced to admit that working women usually needed their earnings. It had not even proved possible to enforce the 1891 Factory Act, which obliged all women to take one month off after childbirth. Nevertheless, during the 1900s, John Burns, the President of the Local Government Board and of the Conference on Infant Mortality, continued to call for legal restrictions on married women's work. Women's work in sweated trades (defined with some difficulty by a Select Committee on the subject in 1890 as work carried on for inadequate wages and for excessive hours in insanitary conditions)[52], was also opposed because of the threat it posed to motherhood and the rearing of an imperial race. As A. G. Gardiner, the Chairman of the Anti-Sweating League, fulminated at the opening of the exhibition of sweated trades mounted by the *Daily News* in 1906:

> It was seen to be not an excrescence on the body politic, having no bearing upon its general health, but an organic disease... a running sore that affected the entire fabric of society, a morass exhaling a miasma that poisoned the healthy elements of industry.[53]

Mothers who were sweated workers were believed to produce physically and mentally enfeebled offspring which endangered the future of the race.

Ada Nield Chew, a working class mother, feminist and labour movement activist, was scornful in her assessment of the debate over the link between women's employment and infant mortality. She pointed out that while the infant mortality rate was high in Burnley, where a large proportion of women worked, housing conditions were also very poor. In Nelson, three miles away, an equal number of women went out to work, yet the infant mortality rate was lower than in John Burns' own constituency of Battersea.[54] However, working women generally were by no means in favour of the double burden of work at home and in the factory and Mary MacArthur may well have spoken for a majority when she said: 'We are all familiar with the old ideal that women's place is in the home, and I am sufficiently old fashioned to agree that there is something to be said for it'.[55] Women nevertheless defended their *right* to work; one wrote: 'If the Rt. Hon. John Burns will show me a way out of the difficulty [poverty] I shall be delighted, but it seems to me that until then I must work'.[56] Women supported the idea of compulsory leave from work as long as it was paid leave and called for the adoption of the International Labour Organisation's Washington Convention, which provided for six weeks maternity leave before and after childbirth. Britain never adopted the terms of the Convention because the Government Actuary considered that it threatened to usurp the husband's responsibility to provide for his family and because it would have resulted in the payment of higher National Health Insurance (NHI) contributions. Similar proposals put forward at the end of World War I, to provide financial support via NHI to women after childbirth, were rejected largely because it was felt that they would offer an inducement to married women to work.[57] But this meant that the costs of protecting motherhood continued to be borne by women. This was also true in respect to the regulation of homework, which followed the outcry about the sweated trades during the early twentieth century.

Homeworkers, who engaged in a wide variety of trades from matchbox-making to furpulling, did indeed suffer disproportionately from disease, particularly tuberculosis, and regulation was instigated not merely for the protection of the workers but also for the sake of the whole community. But again the penalty consequent on regulation fell on the workers. Mrs Layton described the unintended consequences of a small incident in her Bethnal Green childhood. A friend had plucked up courage to ask the Sisters of Mercy for food and the Sisters insisted on visiting the family, where they found women making matchboxes in a house infected with smallpox. As a result, the matchbox-making was stopped and the family's last remaining source of income disappeared.[58].

During both World Wars less was made of the effect of women's work on childbearing and childrearing. A report on women's work during World War I made the point that women's employment might be a lesser evil than poverty.[59] Dr Janet Campbell, who took charge of child and maternal welfare in the new Ministry of Health in 1919, believed that the dangers of underfeeding and anaemia were more acute than any danger resulting from the work itself, although fatigue was identified as a major problem.[60] (Paradoxically, married women tended to be put to work on many of the heaviest jobs, where welfare provision was least effective.) However, the fact that women's health was no longer used as a reason for limiting their paid employment did not mean that the belief in women's proper place being at home faded completely from view. Arthur Newsholme, the Chief Medical Officer to the Local Government Board, believed it would be 'folly' to infer from Campbell's report that 'the industrial occupation of mothers is not a most injurious element in our social life',[61] and in 1919 the Women's Employment Committee of the Ministry of Reconstruction, set up to advise on the opportunities for women's employment after the war, expressed the hope that 'every inducement, direct or indirect, will be given to keep mothers at home'. Similar attitudes were expressed during World War II, when the rapid decline in the birth rate gave additional force to the argument that married women should stay at home. Even when the demand for manpower was at its height, women with children under fourteen years old were never conscripted.[62]

The day nurseries opened during both wars were rapidly closed when the conflicts ended, and as Deborah Thom and Penelope Summerfield have convincingly argued, the amount of support offered to working mothers during both wars has been much exaggerated.[63] A survey carried out by the Medical Officer of Health for Sheffield in 1912 showed very few MOsH to be in favour of day nurseries.[64] Day-care provision also lacked the support of women trade unionists; Mary MacArthur declared that women had no desire to keep working in factories while trying to nurse their children in crèches. Feminist arguments in favour of day nurseries were also conspicuously absent.[65] Even during World War II, a very large proportion of child care (and the entire work of housework and shopping) remained the province of the women worker, subject to whatever private arrangements she could make with friends and relatives. Nursery schools, however, were generally supported because they were designed only to promote the health and education of children; their limited opening hours did not permit mothers to work. Rachel McMillan argued that nursery schools were necessary to compensate for the cultural deprivation suffered by working class children.[66] Prior to World War I, those interested in child and maternal welfare had urged that nurseries might both improve child welfare and set an example to mothers. The Department of Education had accepted criticisms of the provision made for young children in ordinary elementary schools and had phased out arrangements for under-threes by 1904 (in 1875 elementary schools accommodated 19,358 under-threes). It also cut the number of places for 3-5-year olds from 610,989 in 1901 to 332,888 in 1911, but the nursery schools advocated by its inspectors never materialised. The closure of elementary schools to young children made it much more difficult for mothers who needed to work to do so. In its post-World War II Circulars, the Department of Education stated explicitly that the children of working mothers were not to be given priority for nursery education.[67]

As well as attempting to limit the work of married women, policies to protect motherhood and enhance the welfare of children extended the direct surveillance of working class women in their homes. During the late nineteenth century, an army of middle class lady 'visitors' had brought the 'gospel of Godliness, cleanliness and needlework' to poor mothers.[68] Middle class women, including feminists, who deplored the idea of state employees entering working class homes regarded their own activities in this regard as right and proper. In his survey of London, published in 1889, Charles Booth commented on the overlapping territory of the various visitors from churches, the Charity Organisation Society, and other charitable organisations in Deptford: 'we hear of one woman busy at the washtub calling out [to a new visitor]: "you are the fifth this morning"'.[69] Some philanthropic workers, such as Octavia Hill, who trained numerous lady rent collectors, insisted on maintaining a business relationship with the poor, but the relationship between visitor and visited tended to be paternalistic rather than contractual. As Beatrice Webb pointed out, the visitors were a new breed of 'governing and guiding' women.[70] Octavia Hill laid down strict rules for her tenants including prompt payment of rent on pain of eviction. She considered this encouraged regular habits and represented a kindness to her tenants, but the policy could have made little sense to the working class woman managing on a tight and often irregular housekeeping allowance.[71]

The motive behind much late nineteenth-century visiting was to put the social classes back in touch with one another. As the Manchester Ladies' Health Society asked in 1893, who was 'more fitted to break this ground than women? Comparatively unfettered by the vexed relations between labour and capital, with their more ready sympathy and common interests with all other women, they would begin hopefully where men would have little chance'.[72] This Society aimed to popularise sanitary knowledge and thus to elevate the people physically, socially, morally and spiritually. The notion of friendship between classes also motivated organisations such as the Girls' Friendly Society and the Metropolitan Society for Befriending Young Servants. All visitors were exhorted to treat the poor courteously, but in general it was optimistically believed that women would be able to talk to women irrespective of social class: not until the 1900s were the difficulties of cross-class communication acknowledged more honestly.[73]

Given the nature of their mission, the visitors were invariably judgemental. Miss Mason, the Assistant Inspector responsible for children boarded out[74] under the auspices of the Poor Law during the late 1880s, was not in favour of working class women sitting on local, voluntary boarding-out committees because they would not be able to pass comment on the homes of their social equals.[75] Visitors were instructed to ask what time working class wives got up in the morning and to elicit a history of the way in which they organised their day's work. Charles Bosanquet assured his readers that 'the London poor are accustomed to the notion of being visited and more inclined to complain of being neglected than to look on a visitor as an intruder'.[76] But there is evidence that working class women bitterly resented what they regarded as middle class interference. Anna Martin spoke strongly of the necessity to avoid the attitude of 'Ladies from the West End come to do good' when organising mothers' meetings.[77] These meetings were originally suggested during the 1860s as a solution for visitors who could not manage to visit individual homes regularly enough. Mothers were expected to bring needlework and the meetings were usually noted for their deeply religious tone. Women's Cooperative Guild members also contrasted them unfavourably with their own more democratic Guild meetings, deploring the way in which 'ladies came and lectured on the domestic affairs in the workers' homes that it was impossible for them to understand'.[78]

Late nineteenth-century visitors were concerned to inculcate general principles of household management. As Mrs Bosanquet put it, 'The great problem with this class is how to bring them to regard life as anything but a huge chaos. The confusion which reigns in their minds is reflected in their worlds'.[79] During the early twentieth century a more focused attempt was made to instruct working class mothers in proper methods of infant care, in response to the concern about infant mortality. George Newman, Chief Medical Officer to the Board of Education, argued in 1906 that infant mortality was largely a 'question of motherhood' and that the most influential causal factor was domestic dirt and ignorance of infant care. The infant welfare movement, like the National Society for the Prevention of Cruelty to Children, whose inspectors also began to enter the working class home during the 1890s, too often interpreted lack of cleanliness as neglect. In coming to his conclusion, Newman ignored the available statistical evidence regarding environmental variables, which showed infant mortality to be primarily a problem of poor inner city areas, where sanitation was particularly bad. As Carol Dyhouse has pointed out, in concentrating their attention on mothercraft, medical experts tended to devalue women's knowledge regarding infant care, one doctor going so far as to label grandmothers as 'infanticide experts'.[80] The 'Schools for Mothers' and 'Babies' Welcomes', set up by volunteers from 1908 onwards, set out to teach women to breast feed their children, so as to avoid the problem of contaminated milk and unhygienic feeding bottles; to follow a strict feeding schedule; not to allow dummies; not to use inflammable flannelette clothing and not to permit the infant to sleep with its parents for fear of suffocating. Eugenicists, social purity campaigners and imperialists felt that strict schedules and regular habits would breed character in the child. Such advice did little to counter the practical problems of cost. Flannelette was the cheapest warm clothing available, and even the banana-box crib that was usually recommended cost 1/-, with blankets and mattresses, 1/8d, which put it beyond the budgets of the poor. Nevertheless, working class women could still filter out useful information from a visit to a School for Mothers, and as the local authorities increasingly came to take over the Schools and Babies' Welcomes and turn them into infant welfare centres, so they became more acceptable to working class women. Certainly Hannah Mitchell wished something of the kind had existed to give her advice on childrearing.[81]

The bedrock of the child welfare movement was still the visiting system however. Health visitors employed by local authorities in the 1900s were advised to show courtesy to their clients in much the same manner as their late nineteenth-century counterparts. Emelia Kanthack commented that she 'always approached my East End patients with my very best manners and extended the same little courteous considerations to them that I would have served towards a lady'.[82] But evidence suggests that these women, like other state-employed 'visitors', were often resented. Rebecca West referred in 1913 to health visitors as an 'inadequate and slightly offensive substitute offered to the poor woman for the skilled service the rich can command'.[83] And Somerset Maugham wrote in *Of Human Bondage* in 1915:

> The district visitor excited their bitter hatred. She came in without so much as a 'by your leave' or a 'with your leave' . . . she pushed her nose into corners, and if she didn't say the place was dirty you could see what she thought right enough.[84]

The Mother's Defence League, organised during the 1920s, opposed all intervention in the working class home on the grounds that it threatened to undermine the working class wife's responsibility for the welfare of her family and reduce her to a servant and drudge. This argument was closely related to that of Hilaire Belloc in his book *The Servile State*, which criticised the liberal welfare reforms of the period 1906–14 for sapping the independence of workers. The Mothers' Defence League was led by Ada Jones, the wife of Cecil Chesterton, Belloc's co-thinker. However, the sentiments the League expressed were probably more widely held. Anna Martin described the resistance of working class wives she knew to school meals, which they felt would undermine both their husbands' obligation to provide and their own role within the home.

> ... the women have a vague dread of being superseded and dethroned. Each of them knows perfectly well that the strength of her position in the home lies in the physical dependence of her husband and children upon her and she is suspicious of anything that would tend to undermine this. The feeling that she is the indispensable centre of her small world is, indeed, the joy and consolation of her life.[85]

Robert Roberts also recorded the objections of working class parents in Manchester to the preliminary investigations regarding elegibility for free school meals, which were made by the school attendance officers, 'men of little education and known authoritarianism'.[86] Distrust of the expert was also a feature of middle class women's attitudes towards the medical profession.[87] In the case of working class women, intervention by primarily middle class volunteers or state officials often served to increase their burdens by exacting higher standards of childcare and housekeeping—what Anna Martin called holding the mother to her task of making bricks without straw—and punishing her if she failed. With school attendance, for example, it was the working class mother who was visited by the school attendance officer if her child failed to attend school, whether through inability to pay the school fee charged prior to 1891, indiscipline, or because the child's services were needed at home. In the late nineteenth century it was also the mother who attended the School Board's hearing on the case and then, if necessary, appeared before the magistrate, despite the summons being invariably served on the father.[88] Later, under the 1907 provisions for the medical inspection of children, parents (and again the responsibility usually fell on the mother) were told what was wrong with their children but were left with the task of seeking and paying for treatment, dependants being excluded from the provisions of the 1911 National Health Insurance Act.

The protection of motherhood involved a series of measures designed to limit the scope of women's activities outside the home, and to make working class mothers more aware of their responsibilities within it. This assumed that women could afford to be economically dependent, which was rarely the case, and offered an individualist solution to what were complex environmental, social and economic problems.

NOTES

1. Richard M. Titmuss, *Essays on the Welfare State*, 1st edn. 1958 (Allen and Unwin, 1976), p. 91.
2. Edward Shorter, *A History of Women's Bodies* (New York: Basic Books, 1982).
3. Magdalen Stuart Pember Reeves, *Round about a Pound a Week* (G. Bell, 1913), p. 64.
4. Alva Myrdal and Viola Klein, *Women's Two Roles, Home and Work* (Routledge & Kagan Paul, 1956).
5. Margery Spring Rice, *Working Class Wives* 1st edn. 1939 (Virago, 1981).
6. Geoffrey Thomas, *Women and Industry. An Inquiry into the Problem of Recruiting Women for Industry* (HMSO, 1948), p. 20; and Stella Instone, 'The Welfare of the Housewife', *The Lancet*, 4 December 1948, pp. 899-907.
7. Margaret Llewellyn Davies, *Maternity: Letters from Working Women* (G. Bell, 1915).
8. Jane Lewis, *The Politics of Motherhood* (Croom Helm, 1980), p. 44.
9. PP., 'Report of the Departmental Committee on Sickness Benefit Claims under the National Insurance Act', Cd. 7687, 1914-16, XXX, 1, p. 79.
10. Spring Rice, *Working Class Wives*, p. 35.
11. Richard Board and Suzie Fleming, eds., *Nella Last's War*, 1st edn. 1981 (Sphere Books, 1983), pp. 227 and 255.
12. Hannah Mitchell, *The Hard Way Up*, 1st edn. 1968 (Virago, 1977), p. 101.
13. PP., 'Report of the Royal Commission on National Health Insurance', Cmd. 2596, 1929, XIV, 311, p. 147; and Lewis, *Politics of Motherhood*, pp. 140-164 (material not otherwise referenced in this section is taken from this work).
14. Prior to the 1946 Act setting up the National Health Service, some hospitals were run as charitable institutions, and until 1929, when they were taken over by the local authorities, some were administered under the Poor Law.
15. E. M. Ross, 'Women and Poor Law Administration 1857-1909', unpublished MA Diss. (LSE, 1956), pp. 158-9; and PP., 'Report of the Royal Commission on the Poor Laws and the Relief of Distress', Cd. 4499, 1909, XXXVII, 1, p. 781.
16. Marie Stopes, *Preliminary Notes on Various Technical Aspects of the Control of Conception Based on the Analysed Data from Ten Thousand Cases* (Mothers Clinic for Constructive Birth Control, 1930), p. 11.
17. Ellen Ross, '"Fierce Questions and Taunts": Married Life in Working Class London 1870-1914', *Feminist Studies* **8** (Fall 1982), p. 585.
18. Lady F. Bell, *At the Works: A Study of a Manufacturing Town*, 1st edn. 1907 (Thomas Nelson, 1911), p. 79; Margaret Llewellyn Davies ed., *Life as we Have Known it*, 1st edn. 1931 (Virago, 1977), p. 60; and Helen Bosanquet, *Rich and Poor* (Macmillan 1896), p. 106.
19. Sallie Heller Hogg, 'The Employment of Women in Great Britain, 1891-1921', unpublished D. Phil. Diss., Oxford University, 1967, p. 190.

20. N. Dennis, I. Henriques and C. Slaughter, *Coal is our Life: An Analysis of a Yorkshire Mining Community* (Tavistock, 1956), pp. 171-245.
21. Davies, *Life as We Have Known It*, p. 38.
22. A. M. Gray, 'The Working Class Family as an Economic Unit: An Enquiry into Attitudes affecting Earning, Spending and the Distribution of Income between Family Members', unpublished PhD. Diss., University of Edinburgh, 1973, pp. 226-7.
23. B. S. Rowntree, *Poverty: a Study of Town Life*, 1st edn., 1901 (Longman, 1922), p. 86.
24. See for example the autobiography of Alice Foley, *A Bolton Childhood* (Manchester: University of Manchester Extra Mural Dept., 1973), p. 1; and David Englander, *Landlord and Tenant in Urban Britain 1838-1918* (Clarendon 1983), p. 10.
25. John Burnett, *A Social History of Housing* (Newton Abbott: David and Charles, 1978), pp. 146-8; Standish Meacham, *A Life Apart: The English Working Class, 1890-1914* (Thames and Hudson, 1977), p. 75; Sean Damer, 'State, Class and Housing in Glasgow 1885–1919', in J. Melling ed., *Housing and Social Policy and the State* (Croom Helm, 1980), p. 73-112; and Englander, *Landlord and Tenant*, pp. 140-162 and 193-233.
26. D. Nield Chew, *Ada Nield Chew: The Life and Writings of a Working Woman* (Virago, 1982), p. 30; Reeves, *Round about a Pound*, p. 172; and Mass Observation, *A Savings Survey* (Mass Observation, 1941), p. 12.
27. Louise Jermy, *Memories of a Working Woman* (Norwich: Goose and Soon, 1934), p. 180.
28. Reeves, *Round about a Pound*, pp. 29, 181, 185; G.C.M. McGonigle and J. Kirby, *Poverty and Public Health* (Gollancz, 1936), pp. 108-26; and Laura Oren, 'The Welfare of Women in Labouring Families in England, 1860-1950', in *Clio's Consciousness Raised*, eds. Lois Banner and Mary Hartman (New York: Harper and Row, 1974), pp. 226-44.
29. Reeves, *Round about a Pound*, p. 140; and Derek Oddy, 'Working Class Diets in Late Nineteenth Century Britain', *Economic History Review* XXIII (1970), p. 321.
30. Reeves, *Round about a Pound*, p. 124.
31. The Pilgrim Trust, *Men Without Work* (Cambridge: Cambridge University Press, 1938), p. 140; and Charles Webster, 'Healthy or Hungry Thirties?'. *History Workshop Journal* No. 13 (Spring 1982), pp. 110-129.
32. Susan Bruley, 'Socialism and Feminism in the Communist Party of Great Britain, 1920-39', unpublished PhD. Diss., LSE, 1980, pp. 203-4.
33. Margery Loane, *From Their Point of View* (Edward Arnold, 1908), pp. 248-9; E. A. Roberts, 'The Working Class Family in Barrow and Lancaster 1890-1930', unpublished PhD. Diss., University of Lancaster, 1978, pp. 237 and 260; Burnett, *Social History of Housing*, p. 237; Women's Group on Public Welfare, *Our Towns: A Close-Up* (Oxford: Oxford University Press, 1943), p. 88; Elizabeth Flint, *Hot Bread and Chips* (Museum Press, 1963); Foley, *A Bolton Childhood*, p. 17.
34. Reeves, *Round about a Pound*, p. 19.
35. Flint, *Hot Bread and Chips*; Reeves, *Round about a Pound*, p. 61; and Richard M. Titmuss, *Problems of Social Policy*, 1st edn. 1950 (HMSO, 1976), p. 125.
36. A. D. Sanderson Furniss, *The Working Woman's House* (Swarthmore Press 1919);

Caroline Rowan, 'Women in the Labour Party 1906–20', *Feminist Review* No. 12 (1982), pp. 87–9; Mark Swenarton, *Homes Fit for Heroes* (Heinemann, 1981), p. 22; and Burnett, *Social History of Housing* pp. 219–223.

37. H. Llewellyn Smith ed., *The New Survey of London Life and Labour* Vol. IX (P. S. King, 1935), p. 423. See also Leonora Eyles, *The Woman in the Little House* (Grant Richards, 1922), p. 52.
38. Broad and Fleming eds., *Nella Last's War*, pp. 174 and 289.
39. Geoffrey Crossick, *An Artisan Elite in Victorian Society. Kentish London 1840-1880* (Croom Helm, 1978), p. 119; R. W. Gray, *The Labour Aristocracy in Edinburgh* (Oxford: Clarendon, 1976), pp. 99–100; Meacham, *A Life Apart*, p. 28; and Ross, '"Fierce Questions and Taunts"', p. 583.
40. These opinions are accepted uncritically by Peter Steans, 'Working Class Women in Britain 1890–1914', in *Suffer and be Still*, ed. Martha Vicinus (Bloomington: Indiana University Press, 1973) pp. 100–120; and Margaret Hewitt, *Wives and Mothers in Victorian Industry* (Rockcliff Press, 1958).
41 Eyles, *Woman in the Little House*, pp. 37–48; Women's Group on Public Welfare, *Our Towns*, p. 41; Roberts, 'The Working Class Family', p. 180; and Anna Martin, *Married Working Women* (NUWSS, 1911), p. 11.
42. Rowntree, *Poverty: A Study of Town Life*, p. 108.
43. Hugh Cunningham, *Leisure in the Industrial Revolution* (Croom Helm, 1980).
44. Blocks of flats built during the mid- and late nineteenth century by philanthropists. These enterprises assured investors of a moderate rate of return and usually charged rents that made them inaccessible to any but the regularly employed. *See* J. Tarn, *Five per cent Philanthropy: An Account of Housing in Urban Areas between 1840 and 1914* (Cambridge: Cambridge University Press, 1973).
45. Beatrice Webb's Diary, TS, 8 May 1887, BLPES.
46. Bell, *At the Works*, p 128; Reeves, *Round about a Pound*, 164; and Smith ed., *New Survey of London* Vol. IX, pp. 45–6.
47. C. W. Saleeby, *Parenthood and Race Culture* (Cassell, 1909), p. 170. On motives behind the introduction of health policies during the period before World War I, see Pat Thane, *Foundations of the Welfare State* (Longman, 1983); John McNicol, *The Movement for Family Allowances* (Heinmann, 1981), p. 44; and R. A. Pinker, *The Idea of Welfare* (Heinemann, 1979).
48. Angus McLaren, *Birth Control in Nineteenth Century England* (Croom Helm, 1978); and Linda Ward, 'The Right to Choose. A Study of Women's Fight for Birth Control Provisions', unpublished PhD. Diss., Bristol University, 1981, p. 289.
49. Ministry of Health and Home Office, *Report on the Inter-Departmental Committee on Abortion* (HMSO, 1939), p. 66.
50. Barbara Brookes, 'Abortion in England 1919-1939. Legal Theory and Social Practice', unpublished PhD. Diss., Bryn Mawr University, 1982, p. 117; and Sheila Rowbotham, *A New World for Women. Stella Brown Socialist Feminist* (Pluto, 1977), p. 67.
51. Sally Alexander, Introduction to *Round about a Pound a Week* by M.S. Pember Reeves, 1st edn. 1913 (Virago, 1979),p. xix.
52. PP., 'Fifth Report of the Select Committee of the House of Lords on the Sweating System', (169), 1890, XVII, 257, p. xlii.
53. Clementina Black, *Sweated Industry and the Minimum Wage* (Duckworth, 1907), p.x; see also Constance Smith, *The Case for Wages Boards* (National Anti-

Sweating League, 1907).

54. Chew, *Ada Nield Chew*, p. 212.
55. Mary MacArthur, 'The Woman Trade Unionist's Point of View', in *Women in the Labour Party*, ed. Marion Phillips (Headley Bros, 1917),p. 18.
56. *Reynold's News*, 25 April 1909, Tuckwell Papers, file 23, TUC Archives.
57. PRO., ACT 1/65, A. Watson to M. Nathan, 19 November 1918.
58. Davies, *Life as we have Known It*, p. 11.
59. PP., 'Report of the War Cabinet Committee on Women in Industry', Cmd. 135, 1919 XXXI, 241, pp. 228 and 246.
60. Deborah Thom, 'The Ideology of Women's Work 1914–24, with special reference to the National Federation of Women Workers and other Trade Unions', unpublished PhD. Diss., Thames Polytechnic, 1982, p. 151.
61. Lewis, *Politics of Motherhood*, p. 79.
62. PP., 'Report of the Women's Employment Committee of the Ministry of Reconstruction', Cd. 9239, 1918, XIV, 783, p. 5; and Margaret Allen, 'Women's Place and World War II', unpublished M.A. Diss., University of Essex, 1979, pp. 42-50.
63. Thom, 'The Ideology of Women's Work'; and Penelope Summerfield, 'Women Workers in the Second World War. A Study of the Interplay in Official Policy between the Need to Mobilise Women for War and Conventional Expectations about their Roles at Work and at Home in the Period 1939-45', unpublished PhD. Diss., University of Sussex, 1982.
64. Marion Kosak, 'Women Munition Workers during the First World War', unpublished PhD. Diss., University of Hull, 1976, p. 249.
65. MacArthur, 'Woman Trade Unionists' Point of View', pp. 18–19; and Denise Riley, 'War in the Nursery', *Feminist Review*, No. 2 (1979), p. 105.
66. Rachel McMillan, *Education Through Imagination*, 1st edn. 1904 (Allen and Unwin, 1923), pp. 47 and 50.
67. N. Whitbread, *The Evolution of the Nursery—Infant School* (Routledge & Kegan Paul, 1972), pp. 64 and 50; and N. Fonda and Peter Moss, 'Current Entitlements and Provisions: A Critical Review', in *Mothers in Employment*, eds. N. Fonda and P. Moss (Uxbridge: Brunel University, 1976), p. 46.
68. Frank K. Prochaska, *Women and Philanthropy in Nineteenth Century England* (Oxford: Clarendon Press, 1980), p. 145.
69. Gareth Stedman Jones, 'Working Class Culture and Working Class Politics in London, 1870-1900', *Journal of Social History* **7** (1974), p. 471.
70. Beatrice Webb's Diary, TS, 7 August 1885.
71. Anthony S. Wohl, 'Octavia Hill and the Homes of the London Poor', *Journal of British Studies* (May, 1971), pp. 105-131; and Nancy Boyd, *Josephine Butler, Octavia Hill and Florence Nightingale* (Macmillan, 1982).
72. *The Ladies Health Society of Manchester and Salford* (Manchester: Richard Bell, 1893), p. 5; on charity more generally see Gareth Stedman Jones, *Outcast London*, 1st edn. 1971 (Harmondsworth: Penguin, 1976).
73. Octavia Hill, *Homes of the London Poor* (Macmillan, 1883), p. 42; and R. McKibbin, 'Social Class and Social Observation in Edwardian England', *Transactions of the Royal Historical Society* **28** (1978), pp. 175–199.
74. The modern expression would be 'children in care'.
75. Ross, 'Women and Poor Law Administration', p. 90.

76. C. B. Bosanquet, *A Handy Book for Visitors of the Poor in London* (Longman, 1874), p. 15; and Henrietta O.W. Barnett, *The Work of the Lady Visitor* (Council of the Metropolitan Association for Befriending Young Servants, 1881).
77. Martin, *Married Working Women*, p. 8; and on mothers meetings, Mrs. M. Bayly, *Ragged Homes and how to Mend Them* (J. Nisbet, 1860).
78. Davies, *Life as We Have Known It*, p. 73.
79. Bosanquet, *Rich and Poor*, p. 60.
80 Carol Dyhouse, 'Working Class Mothers and Infant Mortality in England 1895-1914', in *Biology, Medicine and Society, 1840-1940*, ed. Charles Webster (Cambridge: Cambridge University Press, 1981), pp. 96-7; and on the NSPCC see George Behlmer, *Child Abuse and Moral Reform in England, 1870-1908* (Stanford: Stanford University Press, 1982).
81. Mitchell, *The Hard Way Up*, p. 102. On the infant welfare movement see Lewis, *Politics of Motherhood*, pp. 61-116; Anna Davin, 'Imperialism and Motherhood', *History Workshop Journal* No. 5 (Spring 1978), pp. 9-65; and Carol Dyhouse, 'Social Darwinistic Ideas and the Development of Women's Education in England, 1880-1920', *History of Education* **5** (February 1976), pp. 41-8; and 'Good Wives and Little Mothers: Social Anxieties and the Schoolgirls' Curriculum, 1880-1920', *Oxford Review of Education* **3** (1977), pp. 21-36.
82. Emelia Kanthack, *The Preservation of Infant Life* (H. K. Lewis, 1907), p. 2.
83. Jane Marcus ed., *The Young Rebecca: Writings of Rebecca West, 1911-17* (Virago, 1983), p. 200.
84. Quoted in Davin, 'Imperialism and Motherhood', p. 32.
85. Martin, *Married Working Women*, pp. 29-30. On the Mother's Defence League see Martin Durham, 'The Mother's Defence League, 1920-21: a Case Study in Class, Patriarchy and the State', paper given to the History Workshop Conference, Sheffield, 1982.
86. Robert Roberts, *The Classic Slum* (Manchester: The University Press, 1971), p. 92.
87. See p. ?
88. Jane Lewis, 'Parents, Children, School Fees and the London School Board, 1870-1890', *History of Education* **11** (December 1982), pp. 291-312.

The Family Economy

A FAMILY WAGE?

Policy makers and social investigators assumed that all married women would be dependent on their husbands for financial support. The reasons for such an assumption were made quite clear during the late nineteenth and early twentieth centuries. Dr William Ogle explained to the Royal Statistical Society that,

> There are men who toil because work is a pleasure to them and there are others who toil because work is a duty; but the great majority of men are only stimulated to labour that in amount or character is distasteful to them, by the hope that they may be able, in the first place, to maintain themselves, and secondly to marry and maintain a family... If therefore, the well-being of a state consists in the mature well-being of the people, a country is then most flourishing when the largest proportion of its population is able to satisfy these two natural desires.[1]

The bourgeois family model with its breadwinning husband and dependent wife and children was thus believed to secure male work incentives. Moreover, preservation of this family model was seen as crucial to the stability of the state and throughout the period fears regarding family disintegration were repeatedly expressed. As one social purity advocate put it in 1949: 'the family is the yardstick to measure values by... and the stability of the family unit is of major importance to the health and welfare of the community'.[2]

Ideally, the roles of husband and wife were to be complementary, the husband earning the wage and the wife acting as 'chancellor of the family exchequer' and spending it wisely. Middle class commentators went to some pains to emphasise the importance of the wife's role. As a result of his comparison of household budgets in 1893, Henry Higgs commented that good housekeeping was the crucial variable which could actually 'turn the balance of comfort in favour of one workman whose wages are much below those of another'. Higgs believed that the services of a working man's wife were more valuable economically when they were employed at home than in the labour market. Both Charles Booth and Helen Bosanquet felt that the majority of working class wives were too ill-trained to command a decent wage outside the home and that they should stop struggling to do two jobs, thereby also reducing the amount of un- and under-employment among men.[3]

Social investigators assumed that in the private sphere of the family altruism prevailed, and tended to ignore the possibility that resources within the family might not be shared equally. Herbert Spencer, a leading nineteenth-century social theorist, crystallised this view when he wrote: 'The welfare of a society requires that the ethics of the Family and the ethics of the State shall be kept distinct. Under the one the greatest benefits must be given where the merits are the smallest, under the other the benefits must be proportioned to the merits'.[4] However, middle class observers were sensitive to the possibility that the working class husband might *not* provide; after all, the bourgeois family model was favoured because of the work incentive it provided for working class men, which presupposed that such an incentive was necessary.

In general, the working class wife evinced more sympathy than the working class husband. Lady Bell and Anna Martin both stressed the wisdom and foresight needed to plan the family budget. Social investigators were also ready to criticise the management of the household economy and were particularly concerned to establish the degree to which thriftlessness on the part of the wife contributed to poverty. Charles Booth included a category labelled 'Drunken or thriftless wife', quite separate from the general category of 'Drink', in his list of nine causes of poverty. Similarly, during World War I, fears were expressed that servicemen's wives would spend their dependants' allowances on drink.[5] But generally it was felt that mothers could be relied upon to exert themselves on behalf of their children and that mismanagement resulted more from ignorance than from vice.

The behaviour of the working class husband was by no means as charitably assessed. The belief that working class men would choose idleness if at all possible and that married women's work provided them with the opportunity was particularly strong during the late nineteenth and early twentieth centuries. As the authors of a 1906 investigation of 6000 women workers in Birmingham put it, either 'women are compelled to work because their husbands are unsteady, drunken or idle, or the husbands develop bad habits because their wives remove the burden of responsibility from them'. Mass unemployment during the 1920s and 1930s modified opinion somewhat, although the economist F. Y. Edgeworth opposed the idea of family allowances in 1922 on the grounds that they would encourage male idleness and quoted approvingly the comment of a social worker in 1908, who said 'if the husband got out of work the only thing that the wife should do is sit down and cry, because if she did anything else he would remain out of work'. But by 1937, J. C. Pringle, the head of the Charity Organisation Society (COS), was prepared to admit that married women's paid employment did not necessarily have an adverse effect on the family economy, something that 'could not have been said with anything like the same confidence 25 years ago'.[6]

The possibility that husbands might fail to provide altogether caused some soul-searching during the late nineteenth century. If the husband did not fulfil his obligation to maintain, then on balance it was considered preferable for the wife to go out and earn than for the whole family to become chargeable to the Poor Law. Thus there was a certain ambivalence in attitudes towards wage-earning wives. In 1870 the first Married Women's Property Act was passed, primarily in order to give working class women control over any earnings they might make. A factory owner, A. J. Mundella, viewed the legislation as part of the same protective impulse that prompted the Factory Acts, which placed restrictions on the place and hours of women's labour.[7] The assumption was that women would be working because of their husband's fecklessness and would therefore need legal protection for their earnings. As the Rev. Septimus Hansard, the Rector of Bethnal Green, testified to the Select Committee on the issue: 'I think that it [the Married Women's Property Bill] would raise the social condition of the wife considerably in the eyes of her husband; as she is, practically, the great educator of the working classes, I think it would do a great deal to raise her'.[8] Similarly, the National Association for the Promotion of Social Science considered that if legal protection was given to the married woman's earnings, she and her family would benefit: 'is it likely that a wife and mother will be less solicitous for the well-being... of her household? We think probably the reverse is the case, and we feel certain that if the industrious factory woman were able to deposit in the savings bank a portion of her earnings in her own name, the school pence for her children would be very seldom withheld'.[9]

Suspicions regarding the character of the working class husband were fuelled during the 1870s by revelations concerning wife-beating and the propaganda campaign mounted by Frances Power Cobbe, a leading middle class feminist, over what she called 'wife torture'. It was in response to what Lord Penzance called 'sensational cases of cruelty'[10] that the first law giving working class wives an opportunity to sue for separation and maintenance was passed in 1878. Many more women sought separations after the passing of the 1886 Act, which allowed them to do so on grounds of the husband's unwillingness or inability to maintain, although in practice the legislation provided them with little material assistance. Magistrates usually granted both a separation order and maintenance, yet as evidence to the 1912 Royal Commission on Divorce showed, between 50 and 80 per cent of couples were reconciled when the husband's financial position improved. This suggested that the fundamental problem of many working class families was one of scarce resources. In cases where the husband's finances did not improve, there was little hope of maintenance anyway and wives and children were usually forced onto the Poor Law.[11] As Claud Mullins, a London magistrate, commented on the plight of separated women in 1935: 'Day by day as I watch the women who come into court on summonses for arrears—probably the least attractive of all Police Court work—I sometimes wonder whether after all many of them would not have done better to put up with the ills they had, rather than to have placed their faith in court orders'.[12]

Middle class legislators failed to confront the fact that large numbers of industrious working class men did not earn enough to keep a wife and children. Charles Booth's 1889 survey of London showed that 30 per cent of the population were unable to rely on a man's wage alone. Rowntree made a similar discovery in York some ten years later and also showed how poverty dogged the course of the individual life cycle, being most acute in infancy, at the point of family formation and again in old age. He calculated the subsistence wage for a male breadwinner with a wife and three children to be 21/8d, and in 1908 Edward Cadbury calculated it to be 25/-. The 1906 Wages Census showed that in the cotton industry 27.2 per cent of male workers earned below 22/-per week and 41.6 per cent less than 25/-. In the metal, engineering and shipbuilding trades, which accounted for 12 per cent of the male workforce, 20 per cent of all men over the age of twenty earned less than 22/- and 30.6 per cent less than 25/-, while the notoriously poorly paid male agricultural labourer received an average of 18/4d a week.[13] In 1921 Bowley estimated that only 41 per cent of working class families could depend on a man's wage and of the families drawing public assistance during the 1930s fewer than one half depended on only one wage earner.[14] Anna Martin vividly described the plight of the wives of low-paid men:

> 'I've only just found out something' said Mrs H., a tidy, respectable young woman with a husband in regular work, though with small wages. 'Now the children are getting bigger I find they eat all the dinner and there is none left for me. Looking back, I remember that we children never expected mother to have any dinner. She always took a bit of bread. Now it has come to my own turn and I don't like it.'[15]

Nor did early twentieth-century state welfare provision do much to alleviate the position of working class wives because it too assumed the existence of the bourgeois family model and a family wage. Married women found themselves either excluded entirely from, or treated very poorly by, a whole range of measures designed to work through the labour market. The pillar of the British social security system was national insurance, introduced in 1911, but health insurance did not cover dependants, and married women could only join the scheme if they were insured workers in their own right. As the Fabian Women's Group (FWG) pointed out, contributory insurance was bound to reflect the existing economic position of women and divide them into those living as their husbands' dependants and those living as economically independent individuals. The Women's Industrial Council (a group of primarily middle class women who devoted themselves to the investigation of working women's problems) went so far as to suggest that such a form of provision was inappropriate for women and merely intensified the 'regrettable tendency to consider the work of a wife and mother in her home of no money value'.[16] But as was later made explicit, married women were considered too great an insurable risk if they were not themselves employed.[17] Beveridge aimed to correct this situation in the 1940s by refusing to call housewives dependants and by referring to marriage as an equal partnership. He proposed to give wives a separate insurance status and spoke of the recognition that was due to their 'vital work in ensuring the adequate continuance of the British race and British ideals in the world'. But in fact married women remained totally dependent on their husbands' contributions and the benefits husbands received on their behalf.[18]

Women workers who were covered by national insurance found that they tended to be submitted to strict surveillance by national health insurance visitors because of the unexpectedly large number of sickness claims. Alice Foley found this to be the one disagreeable aspect of her work as a sickness visitor. She was expected to knock and enter the insured person's house without waiting for a reply, something that would not have been possible at the door of a middle class household.[19] Married women were thought to be particularly likely to abuse the system because of the temptation to stay at home to catch up with housework. Pregnancy also posed difficulties to those administering health insurance, and this showed how difficult it was for state welfare policies to treat women as both workers *and* wives and mothers. Because pregnancy was a natural physiological process and not a disease, many of the approved societies administering health insurance benefits felt that women 'disabled' by pregnancy alone were not entitled to sickness benefit.[20] Married women were always treated as a class apart for insurance purposes and in 1932 they found their health insurance benefits cut because of the high risk they represented, even though no other group with excessive claims (for example miners) was singled out for similar treatment. Men, on the other hand, were granted dependants' benefits under national insurance in 1922, plus the married man's tax allowance from 1919, on the assumption that a man supporting a wife needed additional tax relief (in fact the allowance was paid to all men regardless of whether or not their wives worked).

The idea of a family wage was strongly promoted within the labour movement. Even in Lancashire, where in Blackburn, Preston and Burnley as many as one-third of women continued to work after marriage, the *Cotton Factory Times* could print a piece of verse which to all intents and purposes ignored married women's double role: 'How Sweet it is when toil is o'er/To sit upon the hearth once more/To whistle, sing and sweet converse/With the sweetest queen in universe/In homely way'.[21] By the 1890s the wives of skilled men did not usually work, for the ability to keep a wife had become a measure of working class male respectability. An Independent Labour Party pamphlet of 1900 declared that true freedom for women lay in not having to earn 'any wage under *any* conditions'.[22] Male trade unionists also felt that the employment of married women depressed their wages; and thus their struggle for a family wage also entailed opposition to married women as workers. As a male chainworker commented to a Commissioner on the Factory Acts in 1876: 'I should advocate their [women's] time should be so limited as neither to interfere with their own health and morals or with our wages'. The case of the chainmaking trade was particularly acute because of the large numbers of women who entered it during the late 1870s from nailmaking. In 1889 a Select

Committee heard another plea from a male trade unionist for the restriction of married women's work on the grounds that 'when the married women turn into the domestic workshops they become competitors against their own husbands and it requires a man and his wife to earn what the man alone would earn if she were not in the shop'. He added for good measure: 'During the time she is in the shop her domestic duties are being neglected'.[23]

During the inter-war period what trade union support there was for family allowances (generally it was feared that allowances would lead to a wholesale reduction in wages and reduce the bargaining power of male workers), was based on the hope that they would lead to a withdrawal of married women from the workforce. However, there may well have been other pressures on working class men as individuals, causing them to oppose the work of their wives. In a piece she wrote in 1913, Ada Nield Chew constructed an imaginary discussion between a Cockney and a Lancashire couple on women's work and the vote, in which the London husband says: 'It wouldn't do for a man in my position to have a wife going out to work. I'm just a counterman, and if my boss knew my wife worked I should get the sack, because people would think he didn't pay me enough'.[24]

Women in the labour movement also tended to favour the idea of a family wage. Very few took the position of Ada Nield Chew, who saw clearly how the position of working wives was complicated by their reproductive function, and who believed that women's sole responsibility for home and children represented the chief impediment to self-fulfilment. On the whole, women trade unionists agreed that the withdrawal of female labour would benefit male wages with the additional advantage that working class homes would be better ordered and managed. In 1894 Gertrude Tuckwell (Secretary and later President of the Women's Trade Union League) advocated 'the gradual extension of labour protection to the point where mothers will be prohibited from working until their children have reached an age at which they can care for themselves', and the Women's Labour League agreed that mothers with children under five should not be employed.[25] Mary MacArthur spoke in defence of married women's high sickness claims to the Departmental Committee on National Health Insurance in 1914, but she still feared that any improvement respecting their position under the scheme would 'discriminate in favour of the wage-earning woman as against her uninsured sister, whose need is often as great, [and] will result in a State premium on the industrial employment of married women'.[26]

Most working women's groups accepted that the respectable woman's place was in the home, emphasising women's contribution as wives and mothers and the need to bring the 'mother spirit into politics'. The Women's Cooperative Guild (WCG) was founded in 1884 with a view to helping women become better housewives and cooperators and to take their role as consumers seriously. At their first venture into the male Cooperative Congress in Edinburgh in 1884, it was decided that there should be 'no platform speaking, no advertising, no going out of women's place'. Both the WCG and the Women's Labour League (WLL) continued to play a subordinate role to their 'parent' bodies. The WCG mounted spirited campaigns on the issues of maternity and easier divorce—the latter in opposition to the Cooperative movement as a whole—but women continued to play only a minor role in the central decision-making bodies of the Cooperative Society and the Labour Party.[27] Nevertheless, the Guild succeeded in imbuing its members with a firm sense of self-worth and purpose.

Many leaders of working class women's groups agreed that women's paid work had a bad effect on the father's willingness to earn. Mrs J. Ramsay MacDonald believed that while a prohibition on married women's work would cause distress in the short term, in the long run it would ensure that men provided for their families.[28] The Women's Labour League, of which Mrs MacDonald was a leading member, took the same view, seeing in paid work the additional disadvantage that a woman had less opportunity to 'give thought and companionship to her husband'. The WLL gave priority to the new Labour Party's Right to Work Bill, introduced into the House of Commons every year between 1906 and 1908, which they believed would provide a charter of the 'Right to Leisure and Home Comfort' for working men's wives.[29] There is limited evidence to suggest that working class women were also convinced of the danger their contributions to the family economy posed to their husbands' work incentives. Among North Kensington laundresses, the local maxim was 'the best ironer gets the worst husband', although within the local community it would appear that husbands and wives adjusted to the often superior earning power of the wife, and in at least one suburban district the custom prevailed whereby husbands remained responsible only for a sum which covered rent, the baker's bill and boots for the family. Other women, however, seem to have been anxious to maintain their husbands' position of economic dominance, even when they were not the chief breadwinners. Thus one Nottingham woman, whose husband earned only 10/- a week as a framework knitter in the 1900s, gave him money so that he could continue to give the children their pocket money.[30]

Anna Martin showed that some working class women also distrusted state intervention, not on principle, as was the case with middle class feminists, but because they feared its effects on their husbands' incentives to work and on their own pivotal position in the family. However, leaders of working class women's groups showed no awareness of this anxiety regarding the role of the state. Women active within the labour movement, particularly members of the Fabian Women's Group, were concerned that women's economic dependence had a detrimental effect on the status of the wife and mother and proposed the state endowment of motherhood, which was intended to give the married woman a degree of economic independence without undermining her role as a wife and mother. Mrs Pember Reeves, a member of the FWG, asserted that 'the woman who shrinks from the feeling that her wifehood is a means of livelihood will proudly acknowledge that her motherhood is a service to the state'. Anna Martin preferred the approach of feminists such as Clementina Black, a former President of the Women's Industrial Council and the head of its Investigation Committee, who argued that women should have a legal right to a certain portion of their husband's wage. After World War I, Eleanor Rathbone, President of the National Union of Societies for Equal Citizenship (NUSEC—formerly Millicent Garret Fawcett's constitutional suffrage society) campaigned for a family allowance that would provide a 'wage' for the mother as well as an allowance for the children, hoping that this proposal would unite women of all social classes. Similarly, in an effort to reach an accommodation with women trade unionists, the NUSEC rejected the traditional nineteenth-century feminist opposition to protective legislation, pledging to work for the extension of such legislation to men rather than opposing it for women.[31] But when family allowances were finally introduced in 1945, it was with the primary intention of holding down wages and hence inflation.[32] By 1950 the idea of part-time work for married women had become a solution to the problem of married women's status for feminists such as Eva Hubback, for policy makers anxious to preserve male work incentives, and for trade unionists concerned about the right to bargain for a family wage.

Economic Strategies of Working Class Wives

The main strategy of the working class wife faced with the responsibility of managing the family economy and the problem of scarce resources was always to augment the family income by her own efforts, the most important of which was the sale of her own labour power. Recourse was also made to kin and neighbours, to sources of credit and in the final event to charities and the Poor Law. The range of income-supplementing strategies open to women was probably greater prior to World War I, as was the need, poverty being more widespread. In such circumstances, as Jill Liddington and Jill Norris have remarked, the role of the domestic 'chancellor of the exchequer' became more exacting than exalted. Small debts could rapidly mount up and begin to exert intolerable pressure on the relationship between husband and wife.[33]

1. Credit, Neighbours and Kin Many women made use of various forms of credit. Magistrates and solicitors in the 1870s and 1880s painted a picture of working class wives falling prey to the tallyman or 'scotch hawker' selling inferior and expensive goods, and called for a law to limit the power of the married woman to pledge her husband's credit in such circumstances.[34] In an 1884 case, the Divisional Court held that an artisan whose wife had bought blankets at the door for 22/6d when he had given her permission to spend but 17/6d, could not be held liable for the extra sum.[35] Here protection was being offered to the husband, but also to the wife against her apparently uncontrollable consumerism. In fact, credit systems were often used by wives without their husbands' knowledge as part of their routine management of the family economy.

The reasons why the poor resorted to credit did not go unrecognised. Mrs Bosanquet remarked that some saw the pawnshop as 'an efficient and legitimate way of equalising the [irregular] income and the claims made upon it'. However, in the manner of all philanthropists, she believed thrift to be the more correct solution.[36] But in the fragile family economy of the poor, tallymen, pawnshops, goose clubs (to provide the Christmas dinner) and ticket clubs were an essential part of household management, some being more respectable than others. Ticket clubs were often used to purchase boots: in Middlesborough a shilling a week was paid to a store on an 18/- ticket until the sum of 21/-had been paid back, the advantage being that the store offered more choice of goods than the tallyman. One woman told Elizabeth Roberts that she had resorted to taking her wedding ring to the pawnbrokers' three times: 'each time I was caught with babies'. The depression of 1884 was marked by a large increase in the number of wedding rings pawned. Many other families pawned a bundle regularly each Monday, retrieving it on Friday. In 1907 George Sims, a journalist, wrote of women in London's East End: 'From home to the pawnshop and from pawnshop to the public house is the conventional Monday morning trip of a vast number of poor married women... The women meet their neighbours at the pawnshop and adjourn to the public house for a glass and a gossip'.[37]

Least respectable of all was moneylending. A World War I study found that those with a clean rent book would borrow a lump sum of about a pound from which between 1/6d and 5/- would be deducted in interest; the very poor might borrow one or two shillings on which they paid a penny in the shilling weekly interest. The first loan was often sought to escape a pauper funeral, to keep the children off the school meals list, to pay for boots, or to tide the family over the illness of the breadwinner. But the spiral of indebtedness then proved hard to check.[38] The 1927 Moneylenders Act provided that all moneylenders must possess a license costing £15 and that interest should not exceed 48 per cent a year. But it appears that the law was often broken. In the 1940s, the weekly interest rate for loans was still 1/8d in the pound or 1d in the shilling: 433 per cent a year. By the late 1930s, hire purchase payments, a more respectable form of credit which increased twenty-fold between 1918 and 1938, often totalled 3/- a week in the budget of a labourer earning about £2. And on the new council estates of the inter-war period, the isolated housewife tended to make much more use of door-to-door salesmen. Forms of credit other than hire purchase were largely neighbourhood based. Local women often acted as pawnbrokers' touts, collecting clothing and other items for 7.5 to 15 per cent of the takings. The moneylender dealing in small sums was also often 'a poor woman, who lets us have money when we needs it'; the 1917 survey found that these were sometimes soldiers' wives lending their separation allowances, bigger sums being lent by men.[39]

The neighbourhood provided an important support network in ways other than those associated with the supply of credit. Mrs Pember Reeves found that housewives in Lambeth were reluctant to move away and forego the help they knew to be available in times of need, for neighbourliness implied reciprocity.[40] When social investigators and philanthropists condemned women for gossiping and deplored the excitement of the street life, striving to bring order and a respect for quiet to the lives of the poor, they were in fact often attacking the sources of neighbourly communication and mutual aid.

Some needs were not met by neighbours. In Barrow and Lancaster, for example, neighbours did not bring up orphans, or take in the old, although Bethnal Green residents would apparently adopt children. Usually, however, the day-to-day care of the elderly in particular, was a matter for the kin group. By the early twentieth century this was undoubtedly less of a calculative relationship than Michael Anderson has described for the middle decades of the nineteenth century. Elizabeth Roberts found that sons and daughters helped because 'it was the thing to do' and because of the all-pervasive fear of the workhouse. In her study of Chilvers Coton, a ribbon-making village, Jill Quadagno found more elderly men and women living with their children in 1901 than in 1851.[41] Elderly women were more likely to find a home with the children than were elderly men, doubtless because they were more useful as babysitters and in doing odd bits of sewing. Indeed women's earning power in old age was as great or greater than men's, but women lacked the collateral resources possessed by men, in the form of savings and union or Friendly Society benefits.[42]

Until 1948, the Poor Law required children to maintain their parents and the law was implemented with varying degrees of rigour from district to district. In 1909, in Faversham, the old were permitted to live with their children in the summer, doing fieldwork and babysitting chores, but had to return to the workhouse in winter.[43] Charles Booth argued, probably correctly, that old age pensions would encourage children to take in elderly parents. The 5/- a week given in 1908 to those aged over seventy would have made a significant contribution to the pre-war family economy, but the Standing Joint Committee of Industrial Women's Organisations and members of the Fabian Women's Group felt that this should be weighed against the increased friction caused by an old person coming into an already overcrowded home, pointing out that elderly people's ideas of hygiene and childrearing might not be desirable, an argument that appealed to the infant welfare movement.[44]

During the 1930s the imposition of the household means test on those drawing public assistance benefits led to greater reluctance to take in elderly relatives. The same household means test extended the liability of families to support the able-bodied unemployed. Anyone resident in a house could be held liable for the support of other household members, which meant that a wage-earning son or daughter often moved out of the home in order not to diminish the unemployed parents' entitlement to benefit. Leo Abse commented on the effects this legislation had on kinship ties when he recorded the support given by people in South Wales to his efforts to reform the divorce law during the 1960s: 'Welshmen who had endured the depression had no time for the unctuous pleas for the need at all costs to maintain the unity of family life'.[45] Just as the Depression, followed by the dislocation of World War II, broke up many families, so also were many working class neighbourhoods transformed. For example, the experimental Peckham Health Centre (opened in 1926 in the London suburb of Peckham as a community centre dedicated to the study and maintenance of the conditions necessary for health) found that when it re-opened after the War only about half the original members' families remained in the area.

2. Casual Work Many women found it necessary either to supplement the wages of their husbands or to become breadwinners themselves. Full-time married women workers formed about 10 per cent of the labour force between 1911 and the outbreak of World War II, and the experience of these women will be considered in Part II. A literally incalculable number of wives, ex-wives, widows and children were also engaged in casual work which is not recorded by the census, and it is this kind of employment, usually undertaken at the dictates of the family economy, that will be considered briefly here.

A substantial number of women in the late nineteenth and early twentieth centuries were homeworkers engaged in a wide variety of tasks, including the making of matchboxes, shirts, artificial flowers, umbrellas, brushes, carding buttons, furpulling, bending safety pins and covering tennis balls. Some of these trades, like boxmaking, would have been learned in factories before marriage and some, like sewing, were occupations women tended to turn to in old age. Homeworkers also worked in what remained essentially family industries; many of the chainmakers in the Midlands fitted this description. The 1908 Select Committee did not, however, include a discussion of these workers in its report on homework, classifying families working together at home under the category of domestic workshops.[46] Finally, women engaged in what Shelley Pennington has called 'extended homework': washing, charring, babysitting and lodging-house keeping.[47] An 1894 survey by the Women's Cooperative Guild showed that 50 per cent of working mothers left their children with grandmothers or other kin (whom they usually paid), while the remainder used neighbours as childminders. The importance of these earnings to elderly kin and to neighbours was a major factor accounting for working class women's apparent lack of interest in crèches.[48]

Children were expected to make a contribution to the family economy as soon as they were able. Very young children of four or five were put to work making matchboxes; Lady Dilke, leader of the Women's Protective and Provident League (which became the Women's Trade Union League in 1889) reported hearing a mother in Shoreditch saying 'Of course we cheat the School Board. . . It's hard on the little ones, but then their fingers is so quick they that has most of 'em is best off'. Girls of seven undertook babysitting chores, cleaned steps and ran errands, sometimes bringing in as much as 1/6d to 2/- a week.[49] A Women's Industrial Council investigation of 10,000 girls during the 1890s found that 5 per cent spent an hour at midday and between two and four hours after school, as well as Saturdays, thus employed. A much larger number helped at home or in the homes of neighbours and kin: 'At one school, where only twelve are returned as regular wage-earners, "nearly all" are said to be employed. . .'. Girls of seven or eight could mind the baby, one of the most frequent excuses that parents offered to the school attendance officers for the absence of girl children. The 'baby difficulty', as one attendance officer called it, led to many late nineteenth-century state elementary schools opening crèches. Mrs Burgwin, headmistress of the Orange Street School in Southwark, told the Royal Commission which reported on elementary school education in 1888 that:

> the girls of my school have to take the place entirely of the mother of the family; the families are generally large; the woman goes out in the morning, she works in a pickle house, if she is a better class woman she goes out charring, or she goes out step cleaning during the day and the little girl takes the place of the mother of the family. We were obliged to open a crèche because we found girls staying at home to look after the babies.[50]

Crèches were abandoned in the early twentieth century partly for reasons of economy and partly as a result of the pressure exerted by the infant welfare movement on mothers to stay at home with their children. In agricultural districts school attendance registers showed poor attendance at harvest time when girls of ten or eleven were set to work picking up stones in the fields. Rural girl children worked full-time in the fields or as servants by the age of 15.[51]

Poor mothers were often anxious for their daughters 'to get their feet under someone else's table' as soon as possible. In 1881 as many as one in three girls aged between fifteen and twenty had entered domestic service. Flora Thompson described girls leaving a North Oxfordshire railway station for service, 'the girl in her best, would-be fashionable clothes and the mother carrying the baby of the family, rolled in its shawl'.[52] These young girls, who often travelled long distances to their first position, frequently endured agonies of loneliness and bewilderment. A member of the Women's Cooperative Guild remembered working as a nursemaid to a doctor's family at the age of nine in 1867, and being unable to read or write, could not let her parents know about the unkind treatment she received. As late as the inter-war years, one young girl felt 'cut in half' on leaving her Gloucestershire village at fourteen. Employed in a maisonette in a London suburb, she ate by herself and slept in the junk room, enduring agonies of loneliness and misery. During the Depression years mothers often called at the better-off houses in the neighbourhood to try and find places for their daughters and one woman recalled employing a succession of unemployed miners' daughters to whom she paid 5/- a week.[53] Young servant girls paid whatever they could out of their often scanty wages to their families. Flora Thompson recalled one Oxfordshire girl leaving her new best dress behind for her sister after her visit home.

Girls in Lancashire, like their brothers, became half-timers in the mill rather than servants. The minimum age for half-time attendance at school was ten in the 1880s and 1890s and twelve in the 1900s. During the early 1890s one child in every two in the appropriate age group was a half-timer in Lancashire. Alice Foley remembered that her family was able to move into a better house as soon as her sister started work in the mill.[54] Children could leave school entirely at thirteen on possession of the 'labour certificate', which required either a minimum attendance record or the passing of Standard VII, although it seems that the certificate was rarely if ever refused and 10 per cent of 10–15-year-old girls were fully employed as late as 1911.[55]

Adult women could often turn their hand to more than one form of casual employment. Lodging-house landladies regularly did their lodgers' washing for a small extra charge—Lady Bell found this to be a common practice among the one-third of Middlesborough wives who took in lodgers. Many London families went 'hopping' in the summer months; Margaret Wynne Nevinson recalled that when working as a rent collector (with Beatrice Webb) for the Dwellings Improvement Company in the East End, she found many flats empty in August and September for this reason. Charles Booth also made reference to the large-scale absenteeism in London schools at the time of the hop harvest. During the remainder of the year, the wife might turn to sewing, boxmaking or mangling, as required.[56]

Much of the casual work women did at home was categorised as 'sweated'. Sweated workers were not necessarily homeworkers, but also included outworkers (usually engaged in contract work and employed mainly in unregulated workshops or hired workrooms), and some workers in unionised factory premises.[57] In all cases, a majority of sweated workers were female. The main reason why women took up such work was undoubtedly poverty, resulting chiefly from either the low wages, sickness, unemployment or absence of the male breadwinner. However, as Clementiha Black pointed out at the end of her inquiry into married women's work for the Women's Industrial Council, some women worked when the family income was already adequate, because they prized their independence: 'A shilling of your own is worth two that he gives you'. An investigation of 300 boxmakers in 1915 (of whom 78 per cent were married women and 16 per cent widowed) found that one-third were totally dependent on their earnings, one-third partly dependent, and one-third worked only for 'pin money'; but a much larger study of Birmingham workers in 1906 had found that 52 per cent of outworkers (a category including those employed in small workshops and homeworkers) were married with husbands earning small or irregular wages, 46 per cent were widows or deserted wives and only 0.4 per cent worked for pocket money.[58] Large numbers of casual women workers were found in areas where men's wages were low (as in the Eastern counties) or irregular (as in dockland areas), or where there was little alternative work for women. As R. H. Tawney remarked, homework did not exist in the northern textile towns where the largest percentages of married women were employed full-time in factories. In a 1907 study of West Ham, 53 per cent of the 520 women homeworkers investigated were the wives of casual labourers, or men on short time. One reason why women in London took up washing was that it tended to be a seasonal trade, the peaks in the availability of the work (during the London season) coinciding with the troughs in the male employment cycle in the gas and building trades.[59]

The tendency in the historical literature has been to dismiss the number of homeworkers during the 1900s as insignificant,[60] but the numbers of women employed in casual tasks are extremely difficult to estimate. The Royal Commission on Labour reported in 1894 that much of the cheaper work for Bristol clothiers was done by a female labour force at home, and the 1901 Census returns recorded one-third of women employed in the clothing trade as homeworkers.[61] But much of the casual work done by women was probably never reported to census enumerators; the number of wives recorded as lodging-house keepers or washerwomen, for example, was probably very inaccurate, largely because of the difficulty census enumerators experienced in classifying women's domestic labour. The Factory Acts of 1891 and 1895 made provision for the regulation of homework, but the numbers remained hard to calculate. Employers were supposed to give a list of their homeworkers' addresses to local authorities, but in 1907 two investigators found that in West Ham only 520 homeworkers on a list of 1,786 could be successfully traced and concluded that the Acts (and therefore the inspection of homework premises) were a dead letter.[62] MPs were reluctant to pass legislation that would result in government officials inspecting homes and there was also the widespread belief that the home was perhaps the most appropriate place for women to work. After the establishment in 1909 of a minimum wage in certain sweated trades, including tailoring and boxmaking, the number of homeworkers decreased. Some employers introduced 'speed-up' for their factory hands, resulting in less work for homeworkers, while others gave the best paying work to their indoor hands and gave out only the inferior grades of work which required the most time spent on it to houses where the inspectors were unlikely to penetrate.[63] The 1911 National Insurance Act undoubtedly reduced the number of homeworkers still further. The fourth report on homework in the series edited by Tawney estimated that in 1914 between 11 and 16 per cent of workers in the tailoring trade and 7 per cent of all boxmakers were homeworkers.[64]

Sweated trades have traditionally been seen as a residual sector, and in some traditional women's occupations this was undoubtedly the case. The often elderly 'dustwomen', who sieved refuse at rubbish tips and sorted out rags, bottles and paper, were a diminishing group of workers, as were the strawplaiters and lacemakers.[65] But some forms of technological change resulted both in new forms of homework (the retailing revolution, for example, brought changes in the way goods were packaged, giving rise to the homework trade of boxmaking), and a greater demand for certain traditional tasks performed by homeworkers, for while parts of a particular trade might become subject to large scale organisation, other aspects of the same trade not uncommonly remained the province of homeworkers. Thus as the Leeds tailoring business became more advanced, with up to forty sewing machines grouped together in workshops (compared to London's eight or ten), so the amount of work for the lowly 'finisher', usually a homeworker and often a widow, also increased.[66] Contemporaries often failed to realise that homework was thus an integral part of a trade or industry. An exchange between a finisher and members of the 1888 House of Lords Select Committee on Sweating showed the difficulties of politicians and policy makers in understanding the nature of homework and their tendency to assume that such a worker did her work by hand only because she was too inefficient to do otherwise:

I forgot to ask you whether you use a sewing machine in your work?
—No
Why not?
—I do not use a sewing machine; I am a finisher.
Do you mean that a sewing machine could not be used in finishing?
—Of course it can be, but I am too old to do it now.
Other finishers use a machine?
—Oh yes, there are some that can finish and machine together.

The witness was subsequently recalled and it was established that her particular work (presumably some form of basting or binding) could not be accomplished by machine.[67]

All homeworkers supplied their own heat, light and materials—glue or paste or thread—and sometimes also paid an initial premium for the supply of work: this was particularly common in dressmaking and did not die out until the growth of the ready-made trade in the 1920s. Dressmakers also had to meet the cost of hiring a sewing machine at 1/6d to 2/6d a week. Women usually had to call for their work and were often kept waiting in all weathers. Some London women could not afford the appropriate clothing for a trip to the City, where the better paid work was to be found. Moreover, when the home became a workshop, poor living conditions rapidly became worse. Furpulling was among the most noxious occupations and one of the most injurious to health:

> they are scantily clothed in rough, sacking-like dresses, open for the most part at the throat . . . The women work and eat and sleep in an atmosphere thick with impalpable hairs and tainted with the sickly smell of the skins . . . the average daily earnings are 1/1d. From this a deduction has to be made for knife sharpening and shields, about 4d a week . . . the women suffer greatly from chronic asthma . . . and by the acids with which the Colonial skins are cleaned.[68]

The isolation of such workers was often intense. In 1897, the social investigator E. F. Hogg reported the case of a furpuller who had not left home for weeks. The monotony and laboriousness of the tasks women often performed day in, day out for a pittance was well-illustrated in Clementina Black's meticulous description of a matchbox-maker:

> At first sight it is a pretty enough spectacle to see a matchbox made; one motion of the hands bends into shape the notched frame of the case, another surrounds it with the ready-pasted strip of painted wrapper, which, by long practice is fitted instinctively without a wrinkle, then the sandpaper or phosphorous paper, pasted ready beforehand, is applied and pressed on so that it sticks fast. A pretty high average of neatness and finish is demanded by most employers, and readers who will pass their matchboxes in review will seldom find a wrinkle or a loose corner of paper. The finished case is thrown upon the floor; the long narrow strip which is to form the frame of the drawer is laid upon the bright strip of ready-pasted paper, then bent together and joined by an overlapping bit of paper; the edges of paper below are bent flat, the ready-cut bottom is dropped in and pressed down and before the fingers are withdrawn they fold over the upper edges of the paper inside the top. Now the drawer, too, is cast on the floor to dry. All this, besides the preliminary pasting of the wrapper, coloured paper and sandpaper had to be done 144 times for 2¼d, and even this is not all, for every drawer and case have to be fitted together, and the packets tied up with hemp.[69]

Women worked extremely long hours when the exigencies of the family economy demanded it. Mrs Layton remembered washing until 4 am when her husband was temporarily unemployed, and this was physically arduous work. Louise Jermy's health was permanently impaired by the long hours she spent helping her mother mangle clothes, and Kathleen Woodward recalled her mother's bitter complaints about washing: 'Wash wash wash; it's like washing your guts away. Stand stand stand. I want six pairs of feet and then I'd have to stand on my head to give them a rest'.[70] Furpulling, matchbox-making and washing ranked low in the status hierarchy of homework. Other work was less messy, easier and sometimes better paid. Women so engaged would therefore consider themselves rather more respectable. One Birmingham woman was able to keep her button-carding work in her bedroom, which was important because she considered that it looked 'so poverty' to be seen doing it downstairs.[71]

Women homeworkers' earnings were extremely low and there is some evidence that they were actually declining during the late nineteenth and early twentieth centuries. A woman with an 'afflicted' husband told the 1888 Select Committee on Sweating that she 'finished' four pairs of trousers a day, for which she made at most 1/2d, that her wages were 4d per day less than four years previously, and that after paying her rent, she had 5/- a week on which to keep her three children, her husband and herself.[72] Finishing and matchbox-making were amongst the worst paid homework trades. Clara Collet, by her own admission, differed from other observers in her belief that the number of 'hard cases' was small, accounting for perhaps 10 to 20 per cent of the total in her experience.[73] Differences in earnings depended on a wide variety of factors: wages varied from region to region, employers paid different amounts for the same work, and their practices regarding fines differed. Many employers forced workers to buy damaged articles themselves. Better quality work did not necessarily pay better; for instance, a worker generally earned more by making plain blouses than ones with collars, cuffs and tucks. Some workers deliberately took less well-paid work because employers gave it out in the particular quantity they desired.[74]

Informed observers generally agreed that, contrary to popular belief, the worst paid workers were those who needed the money most—widows and deserted wives, in particular—rather than the respectable married women earning 'pin money': in other words, the latter were not responsible for dragging down wages. One investigator suggested that this was because women whose husbands were in work were better nourished, less strained and therefore more efficient workers.[75] Widows and deserted wives, on the other hand, may well have been forced to supplement their meagre earnings by resorting to the Poor Law. Official sources were divided on this. A survey carried out for the 1909 Royal Commission on the Poor Laws found that subsidised pauper wage-earners made up only 0.5 per cent of the female population in the sixteen areas investigated, though an 1898 report by a woman factory inspector in Glasgow had considered that a substantial amount of poor relief went in aid of wages.[76] Kathleen Woodward recalled that when the washing trade was slack her mother sought relief from the Guardians. Ordinarily a 'deserving' widow might have sought the aid of various charities first, but apparently Mrs Woodward's lack of deference made this impossible.[77] Even after the passing of minimum-wage legislation in 1909, as many as 42 per cent of the homeworkers in the trades covered by the Acts found that they could not earn the statutory minimum.[78] Because women homeworkers' wages tended to be small and because it is not clear either how many 'hard cases' there were, or how large the homeworking sector was, historians have tended to regard this area of women's employment as being of slight importance.[79] However, in the context of the fragile family economy of the very poor in the years before World War I, it should be remembered that if a wife earned only 1/6d a week it meant that she could feed her family for two days.[80]

The opportunities for women to pick up casual earnings, particularly through homeworking, probably shrank during the inter-war period. Investigations by factory inspectors in 1925 and 1932 reported that the number of homeworkers had diminished in all but tailoring, and that few women were entering homework. The *New Survey of London Life and Labour* agreed with this assessment and reported that whereas in the 1880s homework had been done primarily to supplement wages, in the 1930s women tended to work in order to buy extras, reflecting the greater regularity of men's employment, together with a more efficient social security system for the families of the unemployed. One sanitary inspector reported that 'far from being carried on in the poorer types of dwelling, outwork was taken to supplement their resources by many people whose names one would never expect to find on an outworkers list'. The inspector expressed his wish 'that some of the poorer types would take on homework, as it would indicate some desire on their part to improve their circumstances' and give him an opportunity of trying to improve the sanitary conditions of their dwellings.[81] Some forms of extended domestic work, particularly lodging-house keeping, also declined during the inter-war period. Rising real wages made subletting as a means of supplementing income less essential and, among the unemployed, the household means test made letting rooms a more difficult proposition. However, charring in both private homes and institutions probably increased: in his survey of Merseyside in 1934, Caradog-Jones found cases of hospital chars working 84–99 hours a week.[82]

3. Poor Relief When all else failed there was the Poor Law. In particular, women who found themselves without a source of male economic support—widows, deserted wives and unmarried mothers—tended to end up drawing poor relief. The 1834 Poor Law Amendment Act had said little about women. Only the unmarried mother was given specific mention; for the rest it was assumed that women would follow their husbands.[83] During the 1900s feminists began to protest this assumption. Margaret Wynne Nevinson's play *In the Workhouse* was prompted by the case of a woman detained with her children in the workhouse because her husband was a drunkard, despite her desire to earn her living as a dressmaker. The 'baffling problems' of the widow, the deserted wife, the wife of the absentee soldier or sailor, the wife of a husband resident in another parish or county, in each case with or without children, were ignored altogether by the 1834 Act.[84] The Poor Law was intended to deter the able-bodied from seeking relief. Widows, deserted wives and unmarried mothers were usually able-bodied, but were often responsible for the care of dependent children. Thus the authorities faced a similar problem to the wife whose husband was unwilling or unable to provide: whether to treat the woman as a mother or worker. Should a mother be encouraged to work, in which case her children might have to be taken into the workhouse, or should she and the children be given outdoor relief? The latter course kept the family together, a consideration which became increasingly important during the first half of the twentieth century, but which was believed to be open to abuse unless the state assumed the role of the male breadwinner and insisted on good household management and sexual fidelity.

In an effort to tighten up the administration of poor relief the Local Government Board issued a circular in 1871 to the effect that outdoor relief should not be granted to the able-bodied widow with one child. In cases involving more than one child, the circular advised that it might be better for the local Board of Guardians to test the widow's need by offering to take the children into the workhouse rather than give her outdoor relief. Deserted wives were regarded with even more suspicion than widows, and in their case the circular advised that outdoor relief should be denied for twelve months, to ensure that they were not colluding with their husbands to defraud the authorities.[85] In practice, the treatment of widows and deserted wives varied considerably from region to region. The 1909 Royal Commission on the Poor Laws found that for widows the first recommendation of 1871 was generally observed, some Boards of Guardians going further and insisting that the widow maintain two children by herself before any relief was given, while others refused relief to healthy able-bodied widows no matter how many children they had. But neither the second 1871 recommendation regarding widows, nor the order respecting deserted wives were generally implemented, as outdoor relief was found to be cheaper than taking children into the workhouse. Nevertheless, the numbers of women receiving outdoor relief decreased from 166,407 on 1 January 1871 to 53,371 on 1 January 1892, and the numbers of widows in the same category fell from 53,502 on 1 January 1873 to 36,627 on 1 January 1892.[86]

Rates of relief varied from 1/6d to 2/6d for the mother herself, with 1/6d usually added for each child. Some relief was often given in kind, although as Eleanor Rathbone reported, most women resented the ignominy of 'fetching the parish' and the fatigue of a journey to claim the usually stale and monotonous food. Deductions were often made if it was considered that the widow had overspent on her husband's funeral, or if mothers were not keeping their houses sufficiently clean.[87] If a widow had an illegitimate child, outdoor relief was likely to be stopped altogether. There was considerable confusion as to whether the relief of widows was to be considered independently of either their late husbands' failure to provide for them, or of the needs of their children. For example, the Chairman of the Board of Guardians for St Giles in the East London considered that widows must be held in part responsible for their own condition: 'After the lapse of a certain number of years, when a widow has had the opportunity of showing providence on her own account, I think you may separate her from her late husband, but not immediately after his death'. The Relieving Officer for East Greenwich, however, favoured giving relief to widows for the first few weeks after their husband's death, but after that he believed some of the children should be taken into the workhouse, because he considered that an able-bodied widow should work.[88]

The rules regarding outdoor relief for widows were significantly relaxed in 1911. Nevertheless a 1914 government report cited the case of a woman found guilty of cruelty for locking her children up in one room while she went out to work for 10/- a week. She had feared that if she made a claim for poor relief it would have meant the break-up of her family.[89] Acute hardship persisted until widows' pensions—granted in 1925—ameliorated the problem, but even then ambivalent feelings on the part of the authorities about the proper place of the able-bodied widow persisted. During the 1940s and 1950s, when the concept of 'maternal deprivation' was growing in popularity and links were being made between it and juvenile delinquency, Professor Zweig still found National Assistance[90] officials ready to label the widow with school-age children who did not go out to work as an 'inferior type' and a 'professional' widow.[91]

The problem of the unmarried mother was considered even more intractable because of the danger posed by her immoral behaviour. The 1834 Act had made the mother wholly responsible for her illegitimate child so that the privileges of marriage would not be extended to the undeserving. A proposal put forward by Mona Wilson, a feminist employed at the Ministry of Reconstruction during World War I, to make provision for all one-parent families outside the Poor Law, failed because, in the view of the Government Actuary, first it was too expensive and, secondly, by abandoning the principles of the 1834 Act, he feared that it would lead to an increase in illegitimacy.[92]

The options for the single, pregnant woman were few. Some women managed to keep their condition secret and in the late nineteenth century it was probably these women who were responsible for many of the infanticide cases. In 1870, 264 dead infants were found in London's metropolitan and city police districts.[93] During the late nineteenth and early twentieth centuries, there was also the possibility of informal adoption. Most local newspapers contained numerous advertisements for and by people wanting children to nurse. Usually the mother offered and the prospective adoptive parents requested either a weekly sum or, more commonly, a premium or lump sum of anything between £5 and £100. Many of these advertisements were undoubtedly genuine, but during the late nineteenth century attention was drawn to several court cases involving 'baby-farming' for profit, which had resulted in the death of the infants concerned. Legislation requiring the registration of houses taking children for adoption followed,[94] but respectable working class women resented this inspection, especially when it was carried out by the Poor Law Relieving Officer.[95] Middle class feminists also objected to this increasing 'officialism, police interference and espionage',[96] just as they objected to other aspects of state intervention in the working class family and to protective legislation for women workers. Adoption was not made a legal procedure until 1926.

The majority of unmarried mothers were forced to enter the workhouse hospital for their confinements, where they were virtually imprisoned for a two-week period.[97] Together with 'fallen women', unmarried mothers were more likely than other women to be employed on the unpleasant task of picking oakum, and were also more likely to be deprived of Sunday outings to church, despite the fact that previous behaviour was not supposed to influence the treatment meted out inside the workhouse.[98] Workhouse visiting committees composed of middle class ladies tried to place unmarried mothers as domestic servants and increasingly strove to keep mother and child together, but, as Mrs Hardie of the Manchester Ladies' Health Society commented, their task was difficult: a mistress usually feared the presence of a young woman of immoral character in her family.[99]

During World War I, attitudes towards 'war babies' and their mothers briefly relaxed largely as a result of the efforts of the Council for the Unmarried Mother and her Child (founded in 1917), and greater concern was expressed about the high infant mortality rate amongst illegitimate children. One Conservative MP was prepared to advocate temporary relaxation of the bastardy laws in order to ease the path of children of men fighting in the war.[100] Between the wars unmarried mothers were more rigorously classified. Voluntary organisations took mainly 'first offenders' and tried to place them in domestic service. The National Vigilance Association (NVA) played an active role in putting single pregnant girls in touch with charities. For example, they arranged an adoption for Lily O'Connell, a nurse, in the mid-1920s. The premium charged by the Roman Catholic church orphanage was nearly £50 and Lily was required to pay it back at 10/- a month until, in 1931, she was finally released from the burden of payment. The NVA representative who wrote to tell her of the decision explained that although he must have 'seemed unsympathetic in the past', it had been for her own good.[101] Most of the voluntary organisations considered it their duty to inculcate a proper sense of shame in their charges, until World War II brought about the first intimation that unmarried mothers were beginning to avoid the hostels run by charitable institutions for that very reason.[102]

The Poor Law authorities took 'repeaters' and from 1927 had sweeping powers to detain girls who were classified as mentally defective and who were in receipt of poor relief at the time of their child's birth. (During the late nineteenth century, single pregnant women were sometimes assumed to be insane and were confined to the workhouse under the 1890 Lunacy Act.) The 1927 powers of detention were conferred at a time of enormous concern about the high birth rate of mental defectives and the supposed decline in the 'national intelligence'. Present-day writers are generally in agreement that the position of the unmarried mother under the Poor Law showed remarkably little change before World War II.[103]

It is hard to generalise about the quality of the family experience of working class women. Commentators throughout the period made much of the working class woman's limited horizons and passivity. Lady Bell wrote of women in Middlesborough in 1907 being 'curiously devoid of public spirit or interest in outside affairs', and some 40 years later, Slater and Woodside described their female respondents as looking out on the world from their homes 'as from a beleagured fortress'.[104] Historians have commented on working women's fatalism in respect to childbirth and the material conditions of their lives. No one has yet argued that the attitudes of nineteenth-century working class wives 'modernised', although such a case has been made for both young, single working class women and middle class wives.[105]

Much of the discussion in this section has conveyed a picture of relentless toil, but this is not the whole story. As Elizabeth Roberts has remarked, older women will refer to the hardness of their lot as young wives and in the same breath claim that 'they were good times'. The key to this paradox, she suggests, is that in general these women led lives of purpose.[106] The welfare of their families depended on their budgeting and management skills, and in the closely-knit working class communities the talents of skilful housewives were readily acknowledged. Quite possibly this sense of self-worth was lost by the relatively isolated suburban wife of the regularly employed man during the inter-war period.

It is also difficult to assess the quality of husband/wife relationships. Accounts which present a picture of brutal, sexually segregated relationships being gradually transformed into the 'symmetrical' family of the post-World War II years are certainly inadequate.[107] Relations between working class husbands and wives never lacked affection and it may well be that the poor, early twentieth century working class wife derived as great a satisfaction from the mix of activities she undertook to sustain her family as her modern counterpart does from, typically, a part-time job and the performance of less arduous domestic tasks (with varying degrees of help from her husband). But what are we to make of the evidence which suggests that working class wives rarely knew what their husbands earned, or enjoyed sex, or of the probably greater incidence of violence between spouses? Descriptions of late-nineteenth-and early-twentieth-century working class family life as crude and brutal usually attribute the blame to the husband in a manner similar to that of the politicians and policy makers, who so mistrusted his commitment to work and hence to provide. There is, however, plenty of evidence from contemporaries, as well as from historians, that not all husbands were drunken brutes and that many would willingly take a hand at quietening the baby for an hour or two after a long working day, or take tea up to their wives before leaving for work.[108] Research on East Anglian fishermen and on working class families in Barrow, Lancaster and London has revealed that a deeply home-based culture was established by the early twentieth century.[109]

Yet the economic and sexual dependency of wives cannot be overlooked. It has been argued that the sexual division of labour between husband and wife may be interpreted as the best way of maximising the welfare of the working class family, and certainly the struggle for a family wage benefited working class families to the extent that it raised the wages of the male breadwinner.[110] However, the struggle was conducted at the expense of the woman worker and, within the family, the family wage system benefited men disproportionately, because they gained the full-time household services of their wives. Eleanor Rathbone identified the power that husbands derived from their breadwinner status as the 'Turk Complex' which she described in a biting passage:

> A man likes to feel that he has 'dependants'. He looks in the glass and sees himself as perhaps others see him—physically negligible, mentally ill-equipped, poor, unimportant, unsuccessful. He looks in the mirror he keeps in his mind, and sees his wife clinging to his arm and the children clustered round her skirts; all looking up at him, as that giver of all good gifts, the wage-earner. The picture is very alluring.[111]

Moreover, to the extent that the family wage was never realised, women shouldered the double burden of household and paid employment and received little assistance from government welfare legislation, which assumed female economic dependency to be the norm.

Leonora Eyles characterised the position of working class wives during the 1920s as that of 'privileged servants'.[112] Time and again the complaint from articulate working class women's groups about husbands was not of ill-treatment or economic neglect, but rather of lack of sympathy and understanding. In the 1940s wives were still bitterly resentful of the fact that their husbands did not seem to realise that they needed leisure.[113] The Women's Cooperative Guild and other groups translated such feelings into a call for measures to improve the status of working class wives, whether through divorce law reform, health services or an assured income. For individuals, it took immense determination, on the part of an Ada Nield Chew or Hannah Mitchell, for example, to change the pattern of their lives and make time for the political work they held dear. In neither case did their husbands fully understand their aspirations and the nature of their difficulties which meant that the burdens of domestic work and childcare went largely unrelieved. Chew and Mitchell paid for their awareness and involvement with the unresolved tension between their own ambitions and the constraints of poverty and male expectations. Many working class women did, however, participate in Women's Cooperative Guild meetings and campaigns, and as Jill Liddington and Jill Norris have shown, large numbers of working class women in Lancashire actively supported the suffrage movement, albeit with 'one hand tied behind them', as for all these women any cause was something that had to be fitted in 'between dinner and tea'.[114]

NOTES

1. William Ogle, 'On Marriage Rates and Marriage Ages with Special Reference to the Growth of Population', *Journal of the Royal Statistical Society* **53** (June 1980) pp. 253-280
2. Sir J. Spence, *The Purpose and Practice of Medicine* (Oxford: Oxford University Press, 1960); and S. Neville Rolfe, *Social Biology and Welfare* (Allen and Unwin, 1949), p. 54.
3. H. Higgs, 'Workmen's Budgets', *Journal of the Royal Statistical Society* **56** (June 1893), pp. 255-285; Charles Booth, *London Life and Labour* Vol. I (Williams and Norgate, 1889), p. 199; and Helen Bosanquet, *Rich and Poor* (Macmillan, 1896), p. 155.
4. Susan Sleeth Mosedale, 'Science Corrupted: Victorian Biologists Consider "The Woman Question"', *Journal of the History of Biology* **11** (Spring 1978), p. 13.
5. Lady F. Bell, *At the Works*. 1st edn. 1907 (Thomas Nelson, 1911), p. 98; Anna Martin, *The Married Working Woman* (NUWSS, 1911), p. 12; Booth, *London Life and Labour*, Vol. I, p. 147; and E. Sylvia Pankhurst, *The Home Front* (Hutchinson, 1932).
6. Edward Cadbury, Cecile M. Matheson, and George Shann, *Women's Work and Wages* (T. Fisher Unwin, 1906), p. 216; F. Y. Edgeworth, 'Equal Pay to Men and Women for Equal Work', *Economic Journal* **32** (December 1922), p. 453; and J. C. Pringle, *Mothers of Britain: An Estimate of their Efficiency* (COS, 1937), p. 70.
7. House of Commons, Debates, CCXX, Col. 317.
8. PP., 'Special Report from the Select Committee on the Married Women's Property Bill' (441), 1867-8, VII, 339, Q. 1154.
9. NAPSS, *Laws Relating to the Property of Married Women* (NAPSS, 1868).
10. Debates, House of Lords, 1878, 239, col. 191; and Frances Power Cobbe, *Life of Frances Power Cobbe*, Vol. I (NP, 1894), p. 22. See also PP., 'Reports to the Secretary of State for the Home Department on the State of the Law Relating to Brutal Assaults etc.', C.1138, 1875, LXI, 29.
11. PP., 'Report of the Royal Commission on Divorce and Matrimonial Causes', Cd. 6487, 1912-13, XVIII, 143, p. 68; and Iris Minor, 'Working Class Women and Matrimonial Law Reform, 1890-1914', in *Ideology and the Labour Movement*, eds. David E. Martin and David Rubinstein (Croom Helm, 1979), pp. 103-124.
12. Claud Mullins, *Wife Versus Husband in the Courts* (Allen and Unwin, 1935), p. 16.
13. Jenny Morris, 'The Sweated Trades, Women Workers and the Trade Boards Act of 1909: An Exercise in Social Control', unpublished PhD. Diss., LSE, 1982, pp. 97-8.
14. Hilary Land, 'The Family Wage', *Feminist Review* No. 6 (1980), pp. 55-76.
15. Anna Martin, *The Mother and Social Reform* (NUWSS, 1913), pp. 15-16.
16. Fabian Women's Group, *How the National Insurance Bill Affects Women* (FWG, 1911), p. 24; and Women's Industrial Council, 'Memo on the National Insurance Bill as it affects Women', TS, 1911, BLPES.
17. PRO., ACT 1/448, Memo by the Government Actuary, 19 January 1932.
18. PP., 'Report by Sir William Beveridge on Social Insurance and Allied Services', Cmd. 6404, 1942-3, VI, p. 53; see also Jane Lewis, 'Dealing with Dependency: State Practices and Social Realities, 1870-1945', in *Women's Welfare/Women's Rights*, ed. Jane Lewis (Croom Helm, 1983), pp. 17-37.

19. Alice Foley, *A Bolton Childhood* (Manchester: University of Manchester Extra Mural Dept., 1973), p. 77.
20. PP., 'Report of the Departmental Committee on Sickness Benefit Claims under the National Insurance Act', Cd. 7687, 1914–16, XXX, 1, pp. 48–49.
21. Jill Liddington and Jill Norris, *One Hand Tied Behind Us: The Rise of the Suffrage Movement* (Virago, 1978), p. 53.
22. Quoted in Standish Meacham, *A Life Apart: The English Working Class, 1890-1914* (Thames and Hudson, 1977), p. 111.
23. PP., 'Report of the Commissioners Appointed to Inquire into the Working of the Factory and Workshop Acts with a view to their Consolidation and Amendment', C. 1443, 1876, XXIX, 1, p. cxvi; and 'Third Report of the Select Committee of the House of Lords on the Sweating System' (165), 1889, XIII, 1, Q. 18010.
24. Doris Nield Chew, *Ada Nield Chew; The Life and Writings of a Working Woman* (Virago, 1982), p. 211.
25. Gertrude Tuckwell, *The State and its Children* (Methuen, 1894), p. 161; and Mrs. J. R. MacDonald, Mrs. Player, Dr. Ethel Betham, Dr. Olive Claydon, Mrs. F. S. Donaldson and Mrs. G. H. Wood, *Wage Earning Mothers* (Women's Labour League, nd).
26. Cd. 7687, p. 80.
27. Caroline Rowan, 'Women in the Labour Party, 1906–20', *Feminist Review*, No. 12 (1982), pp. 74-91; and Jean Gaffin, 'Women and Cooperation', in *Women in the Labour Movement*, ed. Lucy Middleton (Croom Helm, 1977), p. 114.
28. PP., 'Minutes of Evidence taken before the Royal Commission on the Poor Law', Cd. 5066, 1910, XLVIII, 1, Q. 82604–5.
29. MacDonald et. al., *Wage Earning Mothers*. On the Right to Work Bill see K. D. Brown, *Labour and Unemployment, 1910-1914* (Newton Abbot: David and Charles, 1971).
30. Patricia E. Malcolmson, 'Laundresses and the Laundry Trade in Victorian England', *Victorian Studies* **24** (Summer, 1981), p. 459; and Thea Thompson, *Edwardian Childhoods* (Routledge & Kegan Paul, 1981), pp. 65–7.
31. On family endowment see M. Atkinson, *The Economic Foundations of the Women's Movement*, Fabian Tract No. 175 (1914); and the Fabian Women's Group, *Summary of Eight Papers and Discussions upon the Disabilities of Mothers as Workers* (FWG, 1910), p. 5. On women's right to a portion of the husband's wage see Clementina Black, *Married Women's Work. Report of an Enquiry by the Women's Industrial Council* (G. Bell, 1915), p. 14; Anna Martin, *The Mother and Social Reform* (NUWSS, 1913), pp. 60–61; and Lady McLaren, *The Women's Charter of Rights and Liberties* (np, 1909). On inter-war feminism and family allowances see Jane Lewis, 'Beyond Suffrage: English Feminism in the 1920s', *Maryland Historian* VI (Spring 1975), pp. 1-17.
32. John McNicol, *The Movement for Family Allowances* (Heinemann, 1981), pp. 169-202.
33. Liddington and Norris, *One Hand Tied Behind Us*, p. 32. On the effects of the spiral of working class indebtedness see the fictional account by Robert Tressall, *The Ragged Trousered Philanthropists*, 1st edn. 1914 (Lawrence and Wishart, 1955).
34. PP., 'Report of the Select Committee on Imprisonment for Debt' (348), 1873,

XV, 1, Q. 3472-3.

35. Walter V. Aldridge, 1884, 1 TLR 138.
36. Bosanquet, *Rich and Poor*, p. 98.
37. Bell, *At the Works*, pp. 110-11; E. A. Roberts, 'The Working Class Family in Barrow and Lancaster 1890-1930', unpublished PhD. Diss., University of Lancaster, 1978, p. 206; Melanie Tebutt, *Making Ends Meet: Pawnbroking and Working Class Credit* (Leicester: Leicester University Press, 1983), p. 26; and Ellen Ross, 'Survival Networks: Women's Neighbourhood Sharing in London before World War I', *History Workshop Journal* No. 15 (Spring, 1983), p. 11.
38. M. E. Bulkley and V. de Vessilitsky, 'Moneylending Among the London Poor', *Sociological Review* **9** (Autumn, 1917), pp. 129-138.
39. Women's Group on Public Welfare, *Our Towns: A Close Up* (Oxford: Oxford University Press, 1943), p. 18; Tebbutt, *Making Ends Meet*, pp. 193 and 180; Margery Spring Rice, *Working Class Wives*, 1st edn. 1939 (Virago, 1981, p. 149; Shelley Pennington, 'Women as Homeworkers—An Analysis of the Homework Labour Force in England from 1850 to the present Day', unpublished PhD. Diss., University of Essex, 1980, p. 135; and Bulkley and Vessilitsky, 'Moneylending', p. 130.
40. Magdalen Stuart Pember Reeves, *Round About a Pound a Week* (G. Bell, 1913), p. 39.
41. Roberts, 'The Working Class Family', pp. 93 and 103; Ellen Ross, 'Survival Networks', p. 13; Michael Anderson, *Family Structure in Nineteenth Century Lancashire* (Cambridge: Cambridge University Press, 1971); and Jill Quadagno, *Aging in Early Industrial Society: Work, Family and Social Policy in Nineteenth Century England* (Academic Press, 1982), pp. 80-89.
42. PP., 'Report of the Royal Commission on the Poor Laws and the Relief of Distress', Cd. 4499, 1909, XXXVII, 1, p. 19; and Janet Roebuck, 'When does Old Age Begin?', *Journal of Social History* **12** (Spring, 1979), p. 108.
43. Michael Anderson, 'The Impact on the Family Relationships of the Elderly of Changes since Victorian Times in Governmental Income-Maintenance Provision', in *Family Bureaucracy and the Elderly*, eds. Ethel Shanas and Martin B. Sussman (Durham, NC: Duke University Press, 1977), p. 54.
44. Charles Booth, *Old Age Pensions and the Aged Poor: A Proposal* (Macmillan, 1899). (See also Pat Thane, 'Non-contributory versus Insurance Pensions', in *Origins of the Welfare State*, ed. Pat Thane (Croom Helm, 1978), pp. 84–106.) PP., 'Appendix to the Report of the Departmental Committee on Old Age Pensions', Cmd. 411, 1919, XXVII, 229.
45. Leo Abse, *Private Member* (Macdonald, 1973), p. 15. On the family obligation to maintain generally see Anne Crowther, 'Family Responsibility and State Responsibility in Britain before the Welfare State', *Historical Journal* **25** (March 1982), pp. 131–46.
46. PP., 'Report from the Select Committee on Home Work' (246), 1908, VIII, 1.
47. Pennington, 'Women as Homeworkers', p. 129.
48. Liddington and Norris, *One Hand Tied Behind Us*, p. 59; and Margaret Hewitt, *Wives and Mothers in Victorian Industry* (Rockliff, 1958), p. 166.
49. Lady Dilke, *The Industrial Position of Women* (WTUL, nd), p. 6; and Hewitt, *Wives and Mothers*, pp. 62-3.
50. E. F. Hogg, 'School Children as Wage Earners', *Nineteenth Century* (August

1897), p. 238; and Jane Lewis, 'Parents, Children, School Fees and the London School Board 1870-1890', *History of Education* **11** (December, 1982), p. 303.

51. Richard Jefferies, *Toilers of the Field* (Longman, 1894), p. 126; David Hoseason Morgan, *Harvesters and Harvesting, 1840-1900. A Study of the Rural Proletariat* (Croom Helm, 1982), p. 64; Mary Chamberlain, *Fenwomen. A Portrait of Women in an English Village*, 1st edn. 1975 (Routledge & Kegan Paul, 1983), p. 34. See also Jennie Kitteringham, 'Country Work Girls in Nineteenth Century England', in *Village Life and Labour*, ed. Raphael Samuel (Routledge & Kegan Paul, 1975), pp. 73-138.
52. Quoted in Pamela Horn, *The Rise and Fall of the Victorian Servant* (New York: St. Martin's Press, 1975), p. 47.
53. Pam Taylor, 'Daughters and Mothers—Maids and Mistresses: Domestic Service between the Wars', in *Working Class Culture*, ed. John Clarke, Chas Critcher and Richard Johnson (Hutchinson, 1979), p. 131. See also Taylor, 'Women Domestic Servants 1919-39. The Final Phase', unpublished M.A. Diss., University of Birmingham, 1978; and Frank Dawes, *Not in Front of the Servants* (Wayland Ltd., 1973), pp. 107 and 111.
54. M. Cruikshank, *Children and Industry* (Manchester: Manchester University Press, 1981), p. 96; and Foley, *A Bolton Childhood*, p. 44.
55. Joanna Bornat, 'Home and Work. A New Context for Trade Union History', *Radical America* **12** (September-October 1978), pp. 54-56.
56. Leonore Davidoff, 'The Separation of Home and Work. Landladies and Lodgers in the Nineteenth and Twentieth Centuries', in *Fit Work for Women*, ed. Sandra Burman (Croom Helm, 1979), pp. 64-97; Margaret Wynne Nevinson, *Life's Fitful Fever* (A & C Black, 1926), p. 86; and Lewis, 'Parents, Children and School Fees', p. 299.
57. The definition of homework and outwork is a matter of debate: Jenny Morris, 'State Reform and the Local Economy', and James Smiechen, 'State Reform and the Local Economy: A Reply', *Economic History Review* XXXV (May 1982), pp. 292-305.
58. Black, *Married Women's Work*, p. 4; M. E. Bulkley, *The Establishment of Legal Minimum Rates in the Box Making Industry* (G. Bell, 1915), p. 67; and Cadbury et. al., *Women, Work and Wages*, p. 147.
59. Pennington, 'Women as Homeworkers', p. 81; R. H. Tawney, *The Establishment of Minimum Rates in the Tailoring Industry* (G. Bell, 1915), p. 185; E. G. Howarth and Mona Wilson, *West Ham: A Study in Social and Industrial Problems* (J. M. Dent, 1907), p. 258; and Patricia E. Malcolmson, 'Laundresses and the Laundry Trade in Victorian England', *Victorian Studies* **24** (Summer 1981), pp. 439-462.
60. Duncan Bythell, *The Sweated Trades* (Batsford, 1978), p. 148.
61. PP., 'Final Report of the Royal Commission on Labour', C. 7421-1, 1894, XXXV, 9, p. 484; and Pennington, 'Women Homeworkers', p. 96.
62. Howarth and Wilson, *West Ham*, pp. 156-7.
63. V. de Vessilitsky, *The Homeworker and her Outlook* (G. Bell, 1916), pp. 56 and 82.
64. R. H. Tawney, *The Establishment of Minimum Rates in the Tailoring Industry* (G. Bell, 1915), p. 214.
65. Emily Hobhouse, 'Dustwomen', *Economic Journal* **10** (September 1900), pp. 411-420.
66. Bythell, *Sweated Trades*, p. 138; Morris, 'The Sweated Trades, Women Workers

and the Trade Boards Act', p. 51; and Vessilitsky, *The Homeworker*, p. 30.
67. PP., 'First Report of the House of Lords on the Sweating System' (361), 1888, XX, 1, Qs. 1610-14 and 1655-62.
68. Women's Industrial Council, *Home Industries of Women in London* (WIC, 1897), p. 19.
69. Pennington, 'Women as Homeworkers', p. 250; and Clementina Black, *Sweated Industry and the Minimum Wage* (Duckworth, 1907), p. 4.
70. Margaret Llewelyn Davies ed., *Life as We Have Known It*, 1st edn. 1931 (Virago, 1977), p. 37; Louise Jermy, *The Memories of a Working Woman* (Norwich: Goose and Son, 1934), pp. 28-9; and Kathleen Woodward, *Jipping Street* (Longman, 1928), p. 12.
71. Cadbury, *et. al.*, *Women Work and Wages*, p. 156.
72. House of Lords Select Committee (361), Qs 1520-62.
73. PP., 'Report of the Select Committee on Homework. Minutes of Evidence' (290), 1907, VI, 55, Q. 776.
74. Constance Smith, *The Case for Wages Boards* (National Anti-Sweating League, 1908), pp. 22-4; R. H. Tawney, *The Establishment of Minimum Rates in the Tailoring Industry* (G. Bell, 1915), pp. 110-12; Howarth and Wilson, *West Ham*, p. 285; Booth, *London Life and Labour*, Vol. I, p. 495.
75. Vessilitsky, *The Homeworker and Her Outlook*, p. 19.
76. PP., 'Report by Miss Constance Williams and Mr. Thomas Jones on the effect of Outdoor Relief on Wages and the Conditions of Employment'; Cd. 4690, 1909, XLIII, 1, p. 155; Pat Thane, 'Women and the Poor Law in Victorian and Edwardian England', *History Workshop Journal* No. 6 (Autumn 1978), p. 43; and Morris, 'The Sweated Trades', p. 36.
77. Woodward, *Jipping Street*, p. 17.
78. Bulkley, *The Establishment of Legal Minimum Rates in the Box Making Industry*, p. 71; and Vessilitsky, *The Homeworker and her Outlook*, p. 45.
79. E. H. Hunt, *Regional Wage Variations in Britain 1850-1914* (Oxford: Clarendon Press, 1977), p. 109.
80. Roberts, 'The Working Class Family', p. 49.
81. D. Sells, *British Wages Boards* (Washington DC: Brookings Institute, 1939), p. 305; and PP., 'Annual Report of the Chief Inspector of Factories and Workshops for 1925', Cmd. 2714, 1926, X, 467, pp. 59 and 60-61.
82. Davidoff, 'The Separation of Home and Work', p. 88; and Pennington, 'Women as Homeworkers', p. 148.
83. Thane, 'Women and the Poor Law', p. 31.
84. Nevinson, *Life's Fitful Fever*, pp. 222-5; Sidney and Beatrice Webb, *English Poor Law Policy* (Longman, 1910), p. 7.
85. Thane, 'Women and the Poor Law', p. 35.
86. PP., 'Report of the Royal Commission on the Poor Laws and the Relief of Distress', Cd. 4499, 1909, XXXVII, 1, p. 154; and Thane, 'Women and the Poor Law', p. 40.
87. Cd. 4499, p. 171; Eleanor Rathbone, *Report on the Condition of Widows under the Poor Law in Liverpool* (Women's Industrial Council, 1913), p. 8; and Thane, 'Women and the Poor Law', pp. 41-2.
88. PP., 'Minutes of Evidence taken before the Royal Commission on the Poor Laws', Cd. 4684, 1909, XL, 1, Qs 17765 and 19774.

89. PP, 'Survey of Relief to Widows and Children', Cmd. 774, 1920, XXXVII, 129, p. 3.
90. The Poor Law was finally dismantled with the passing of the National Assistance Act in 1948. National Assistance was the forerunner of Supplementary Benefit.
91. Quoted in Simon Yudkin and Anthea Holme, *Working Mothers and their Children* (Michael Joseph, 1963), p. 70.
92. PRO., ACT 1/66, Report by the Government Actuary on Mother's Pensions, 17 January 1919.
93. PP., 'Report from the Select Committee on the Protection of Infant Life', 1871 (372), VII, 607, p. iv.
94. George Behlmer, *Child Abuse and Moral Reform in England, 1870-1908* (Stanford: Stanford University Press, 1982), pp. 26-33.
95. PP., 'Report from the Select Committee on Infant Life Protection', (99) 1908, LX, 147, Q. 1080.
96. Behlmer, *Child Abuse*, pp. 33–4.
97. John Gillis, 'Servants, Sexual Relations and the Risks of Illegitimacy in London, 1901-1900', *Feminist Studies* **5** (Spring, 1979), p. 166.
98. Thane, 'Women and the Poor Law', p. 72; and E. M. Ross, 'Women and Poor Law Administration 1857-1909', unpublished M.A. Diss., LSE, 1956, p. 161.
99. PP., 'Report from the Select Committee of the House of Lords on the Infant Life Protection Bill and Safety of Nurse Children Bill' (343), 1896, X, 225, Q. 2735.
100. Pankhurst, *Home Front*, p. 175.
101. Box 115, NVA Files, Fawcett Library, City of London Polytechnic.
102 Sheila Ferguson and Hilde Fitzgerald, *Studies in the Social Services* (HMSO, 1954), p. 95.
103. Nigel Middleton, *When Family Failed* (Gollancz, 1971), p. 284 and 294; and PP., 'Report of the Committee on One-Parent Families', Cmnd. 5629-I, 1974, XVI, 1113, Appendix 5, p. 128. On the concern about mental deficiency see R. Cattell, *The Fight for our National Intelligence* (P. S. King, 1937); and G. R. Searle, 'Eugenics and Politics in Britain in the 1930s', *Annals of Science* **36** (1979), pp. 159-169.
104. Bell, *At the Works*, p. 232; and E. Slater and M. Woodside, *Patterns of Marriage* (Cassell and Co., 1951), p. 91.
105. On fatalism see Peter Stearns, 'Working Class Women in Britain, 1890-1914', in *Suffer and Be Still*, ed. Martha Vicinus (Bloomington: Indiana University Press, 1973), pp. 100-120; on modernisation see Edward Shorter, 'Illegitimacy, Sexual Revolution, and Social Change in Modern Europe', *Journal of Interdisciplinary History* **2** (Winter 1972), pp. 237-261; and Patricia Branca, *Silent Sisterhood: Middle Class Women in the Victorian Home* (Croom Helm, 1975).
106. Elizabeth Roberts, 'Working Wives and their Families', in *Population and Society in Britain, 1850-1980*, eds. T. Barker and M. Drake (Batsford Academic Press, 1982), p. 162.
107. Michael Young and Peter Wilmott, *The Symmetrical Family* (New York: Pantheon Books, 1973).
108. Margery Loane, *From their Point of View* (Edward Arnold, 1908), pp. 26, 108, 145.
109. Trevor Lummis, 'The Historical Dimension of Fatherhood. A Case Study', in

The Father Figure, ed. L. McKee and M. O'Brien (Tavistock, 1982), pp. 1-25; Roberts, 'The Working Class Family'; Gareth Stedman Jones, 'Working Class Culture and Working Class Politics in London, 1870-1900', *Journal of Social History* **7** (1974), pp. 460-508.

110. Jane Humphries, 'Class Struggle and the Resistance of the Working Class Family', *Cambridge Journal of Economics* **1** (September 1977), pp. 241-258 has argued this strongly.
111. Eleanor Rathbone, 'Changes in Public Life', in *Our Freedom and its Results*, ed. Ray Strachey (Gollancz, 1936), p. 58.
112. Leonore Eyles, *The Woman in the Little House* (Grant Richards, 1922), p. 147.
113. Spring Rice, *Working Class Wives*, p. 104.
114. Liddington and Norris, *One Hand Tied Behind Us*.

3 Middle Class Women

Introduction

The separation of spheres was much more rigid for middle class women than for working class women, for although both were excluded from the public sector in terms of political citizenship and legal rights, working class women did engage in paid employment and there was a certain ambivalence on the part of politicians and policy makers as to their behaviour in this respect. No such ambivalent feelings characterised the firm belief—sanctioned by Victorian science and medicine—that the place of the middle class woman was in the home.

Lydia Becker, a leading Victorian feminist, compared the position of middle class women unfavourably with that of working class women: 'What I most desire, is to see married women of the *middle classes* stand on the same terms of equality as prevail in the working classes and the highest aristocracy. A *great lady* or a *factory woman* are independent persons—personages—the women of the middle classes are nobodies, and if they act for themselves they lose caste!.[1] The comparison was naive in its failure to recognise the burden borne by working class wives, but Becker was rebelling primarily against the idea that the middle class woman should be 'kept', if not by a husband then by a father, brother, or other male relative.

During the late nineteenth century considerable correspondence was conducted in the daily newspapers and periodical press on 'the proper time to marry', prudence and postponement being the key words in the discussion. A prospective husband had to be able to afford a wife, children and their educational expenses, and the trappings of domestic life. W. R. Greg, a statistician, suggested that one reason for the 'surplus' of women (which particularly afflicted the middle classes) was the 'self indulgence of the bachelor's career' and Henry Fawcett, the political economist, agreed:

> The majority of men are accustomed to some particular style of living, and they generally refrain from marriage, if the increased expenses of married life would compel them to live in a manner which would not give them what has been aptly termed their historical standard of comfort.[2]

Throughout the late nineteenth and early twentieth centuries, middle class women faced a choice between marriage and motherhood, and a career. In the early part of the period there was little choice as it was unusual even for young, single women to engage in paid employment unless family circumstances demanded it. In particular, the gradual decline of the small private family business and the growing importance of jobs for men as managers in large companies, in government and in the professions wrought substantial changes in the position of many middle class women within the family. (As will be seen in the second part of the book, the same changes opened up new jobs for working and lower middle class girls as shop assistants and teachers.) Kinship networks in business became less important and by the end of the century, middle class wives and daughters no longer played an active role in the management of the small family business or shop. Articulate women, anxious to lead purposeful lives, found it impossible to dismiss the idea, supported as it was by scientific theories of sexual difference, that their proper place was in the home. They were, however successful in arguing that charitable endeavour represented an acceptable extension of women's domestic work, and many late nineteenth- and early twentieth-century middle class mothers and daughters became active voluntary social workers.

For a minority of educated, ambitious women the choice they were forced to make between marriage and work was an agonising one. The young Beatrice Webb was convinced of the importance of family life for women and during the 1880s desperately desired an intimate relationship with the leading politician, Joseph Chamberlain, yet she knew that to marry him would cut her off for ever from the purposeful life of work that she also wanted. In many ways the life of a great political hostess was very attractive to her, which only made her feel more guilty, but she knew that she could not tolerate a life of subordination and absolute dependency. Her decision was extremely painful, for Beatrice believed (as it happened incorrectly) that she was committing herself to a celibate life for ever:

> I must check those feelings which are the expression of physical instinct craving for satisfaction, but God knows celibacy is as painful to women (even from the physical standpoint) as it is to men—could not be more painful than it is to a woman.

She observed two of the leading women philanthropists of the day, Ella Pycroft and Octavia Hill, both of whom had remained single, and recorded her opinion that both 'might have been more' with a happy family life, which only served to increase her anguish.[3]

During the whole period, a conscious decision to remain unmarried signified a revolt against the prescribed feminine role, but only sometimes was this revolt consciously feminist. Often there was little sympathy with the position of women, but rather a strong commitment to a cause or an ideal; this was the case with Florence Nightingale and the leading women educationalists, Miss Beale and Miss Buss, both of whom turned down offers of marriage. Many feminists also rejected the 'scramble for husbands', induced by the need of middle class women for someone to maintain them financially. Andrew Rosen has shown that the overwhelming majority of the members of the leading suffragette organisation, the Women's Social and

Political Union, were single.[4] C. P. Gilman's (the American feminist) late nineteenth-century lament that 'wealth, power, social distinction, fame... home and happiness, reputation, ease and pleasure, her bread and butter—all must come to her thro' a small gold ring', was echoed by the English writer, Cicely Hamilton, in her book *Marriage as a Trade* (1909). Margaret Wynne Nevinson, an active suffragist, rebelled against the way 'marriage was dinned into me from morning till night... from a business and commercial standpoint'. As a result she developed a 'repulsion' to men and to her mother's creed that 'a bad husband is better than none'.[5]

While marriage represented the only means to a livelihood for a majority of middle class women, most of whom were but poorly educated, it was nevertheless not 'done' for a young woman to solicit male attention. In 1897 Mona Caird vividly outlined the social dilemma of the woman forced to marry for a living:

> People think women who do not want to marry unfeminine, people think women who *do* want to marry immodest—people combine both opinions by regarding it as unfeminine for women not to look forward longingly to wifehood as the hope and purpose of their lives, and ridiculing and condemning any individual woman of their acquaintance whom they suspect of entertaining such a longing. They must wish and not wish; they must by no means give and they must certainly not withhold encouragement—and so it goes on, each precept cancelling the last, and most of them negative.[6]

Women who did not deliberately choose to remain single out of conviction or because they wished to pursue a career, but who nevertheless 'got left on the shelf', were often made to feel that they were failures. Beatrice Webb wrote feelingly that the position of the unmarried daughter at home was 'an unhappy one even for a strong woman'.[7] By the early twentieth century this situation had improved slightly, due in part to an expansion in the range of occupations open to young middle class women. Cicely Hamilton commented in the course of a debate with G. K. Chesterton at Queen's Hall in 1919: 'Do you suppose that forty or fifty years ago a woman would have dared to stand up on a platform and say, without the slightest shame, that she was over thirty and unmarried? She could not do it. That is past'.[8] There was, however, little change in the rigid separation of spheres between the male world of work and the world of home and family experienced by adult women. For after World War I, the ideology of separate spheres was substantially reinforced by the imposition of a 'marriage bar' on women pursuing professional careers.

Nevertheless, considerable changes did take place in regard to the nature of marriage. The Victorian image of a woman as the 'angel in the house', passive, sexually innocent and dependent, gave way to the ideal of a companionate marriage. As late as 1913, the anti-feminist surgeon, Sir

Almroth Wright, continued to applaud what was undoubtedly an extreme form of the traditional patriarchal marriage, whereby the husband promised to do his wife reverence, to protect and to serve her as long as she did not jettison personal refinement, act in an ungrateful manner or put an extravagantly high estimate on her intellectual powers.[9] As J. S. Mill recognised in his essay *On the Subjection of Women* (1869), this degree of inequality was by no means true of all Victorian marriages, but the idea of the wife as a 'natural' subordinate was widely accepted. Such a view differed markedly from Beveridge's characterisation of marriage as a 'partnership' of equals with different but complementary talents.

This shift in the meaning of marriage was accompanied by changes in married women's property rights and in the grounds women could use to sue for divorce, both of which benefited primarily middle class women. These legal advances must also be related to long-term changes in the nature of property-holding among the middle class and to changes in the ideology of domesticity.[10] As land gradually ceased to be the major source of middle class wealth, and as salaries became more important, so marriage ceased to be an essentially dynastic settlement between two kin groups and it became possible to grant women more freedom, both emotional (to marry whom they wished) and legal, within marriage. The Married Women's Property Acts of the 1870s and 1880s permitted women to control their own property, although married women were not given the same capacity as single women to acquire, hold and dispose of property until 1935. Nor did the Acts change the right of landed families to make settlements on their daughters in order to protect the family property from the rapacity of sons-in-law and from any action of the daughter herself which might prove contrary to the family interest. The importance of these settlements died away only slowly. The reform of both property and divorce law modernised and rationalised the institution of marriage and brought it into line with new kinds of family wealth and relationships. The debate over the inequality in the divorce laws (men could divorce on a simple charge of adultery but women could not) also began during the late nineteenth century, and revision of the laws was recommended by the Royal Commission on Divorce in 1912. Legislation was not brought in until 1923, however, largely because any attempt at reform was regarded as an attack on the sanctity of marriage, despite the Royal Commission's argument (repeated by all later proponents of divorce law reform) that relaxation would in fact strengthen rather than weaken it. Extension of the grounds for divorce took even longer to enact and was not achieved until 1937.

By the inter-war years married women were no longer regarded primarily as ornamental and sexually innocent creatures; the ideal companionate marriage also involved an expectation of sexual harmony. The sexes no longer led the uncommunicative, separate lives, which is perhaps the most striking characteristic of middle class Victorian autobiographies and popular literature such as Mrs Henry Wood's *East Lynne* (1861). However, the emphasis on companionship and sexual harmony was not altogether compatible with the sanctity of marriage, and the contradiction between the importance attached to the quality of the sexual act and the celebration of family life continued to deepen in the years following World War II.[11] From women's point of view, changes in the occupational structure which gave young women in the twentieth century more opportunity for a career also reduced the need to marry out of pure economic necessity, which in turn increased the importance of companionship within marriage. The unanimous condemnation of marriage as a trade by the feminist movement may also have made a significant contribution to the new emphasis on marriage as a partnership.[12] However, none of these changes affected the sexual division of labour within the home, and the equality of tasks and responsibilities that began to be envisioned for husbands and wives after World War II was in practice often associated with subordinate and superior status. 'Peterborough', the *Daily Telegraph*'s columnist, was probably not alone in ridiculing the 1942 Beveridge Report's idea of marriage as a partnership, which he referred to as 'Cupid's team'.[13] Nor was the sense of isolation experienced by so many married middle class women in any way lessened.

NOTES

1. Andrew Rosen, *Rise Up, Women!* (Routledge & Kegan Paul, 1974), p. 8.
2. J. A. Banks, *Prosperity and Parenthood* (Routledge & Kegan Paul, 1954), p. 36; *Victorian Values. Secularism and the Size of Families* (Routledge & Kegan Paul, 1981), p. 67; and Peter Cominos, 'Late Victorian Sexual Respectability and the Social System', *International Review of Social History* **8** (1963) Pt. 1, p. 28.
3. Barbara Caine, 'Beatrice Webb and the Woman Question', *History Workshop Journal* **14** (Autumn 1982), p. 28; and Jane Lewis, 'Re-reading Beatrice Webb's Diary', *History Workshop Journal* **16** (Autumn 1983), pp. 143–146.
4. Rosen, *Rise Up, Women!*, pp. 210–11.
5. C. P. Gilman, *Women and Economics*, 1st. edn. 1898 (New York: Harper Torchbook: 1966), p. 71; Cicely Hamilton, *Marriage as a Trade* (Chapman and Hall, 1909); and Margaret Wynne Nevinson, *Life's Fitful Fever* (A & C Black, 1926), p. 44.
6. Mona Caird, *The Morality of Marriage and Other Essays on the Status and Destiny of Women* (George Redway, 1897), p. 103.
7. Beatrice Webb's Diary, TS, 1 January 1886, BPLES.
8. *The Vote* 3, 15 April 1911, p. 295.
9. Constance Rover, *Love Morals and the Feminists* (Routledge & Kegan Paul, 1970), p. 150.
10. These ideas are explored by Tim Murphy, 'Female Shadow, Male Substance, Women and Property in Nineteenth Century England', unpublished paper,

1983; and Albie Sachs and Joan Hoff Wilson, *Sexism and the Law* (Oxford: Martin Robertson, 1978).

11. Jeffrey Weeks, *Sex Politics and Society. The Regulation of Sexuality since 1800* (Longman, 1981), pp. 212 and 238.
12. Ellen Key, *The Woman Movement* (G. P. Putnams, 1912), p. 86, certainly thought this.
13. *Daily Telegraph*, 2 December 1942, p. 4. I am grateful to Marjorie Ferguson for this reference.

Role Prescriptions and the Articulate Woman's Response

Literature giving women guidance as to their proper behaviour and place was more profuse and inflexible for middle than for working class women. Women were told unequivocally that they should confine themselves to the sphere of home and family; the middle class husband unlike his working class counterpart, could be safely relied upon to provide.

The circumstances of women within the middle class varied widely. Patricia Branca has reminded us that in the Victorian household where the man earned between £100 and £300 a year, an income range which excluded the highly skilled manual worker and included as many as 42 per cent of the middle class, there was only enough money available for the employment of one or at most two domestic servants and very little at all for the rest of the 'paraphernalia of gentility' desired by the aspiring middle class household.[1] While crucial to an assessment of the *reality* of middle class women's experience, these differences in income and status within the middle class did not affect the prescriptions meted out to middle class women, which were fundamentally rooted in theories of sexual difference and the idea of separate spheres.

While arguments regarding biologically-based sexual differences applied to all women, the Victorian scientists who developed them built up their theories on the basis of assumptions regarding the behaviour of women in their own class, and, as Elizabeth Fee has pointed out, there was therefore an essential circularity in their reasoning. Scientists used their own society as the model from which they formulated their ideas, which in turn justified the position of women as they found it. Having stopped women acquiring certain capacities, science provided the justification for refusing rights on the grounds that those capacities were 'naturally' absent. Within an evolutionary framework it could be argued that the work working class women did outside the home was an anachronistic survival and that society was in fact progressing towards a position whereby all women would be able to stay at home.[2] (The argument was similar to the one used by economists when discussing homework.) This view accorded with the idealisation of married love in the work of Ruskin, Coventry Patmore and a range of writers on the domestic duties of wives and mothers, who believed that women's fundamental task was to create a haven of peace, beauty and emotional security for their husbands and children. The home was to be a sanctuary in which the wife reigned as guardian 'angel' in the words of Patmore, or as a 'Queen' in Ruskin's imagery. During the mid- and late nineteenth centuries, the wife and mother at home became doubly important as a moral force because evolutionary ideas had shaken the religious faith of so many. The hearth itself became sacred, and the chief prop of a moral order no longer buttressed by belief.[3]

Scientific theories of biologically-based sexual difference were important, for as the status of scientific explanation increased, so the arguments became harder to refute.[4] By the late nineteenth century it was already necessary to demonstrate a scientific approach in order to gain full recognition: the Charity Organisation Society, for example, made much of its promise to organise charity on 'scientific principles'. The use of biological analogy, in particular, proved very popular in explaining all kinds of social problems. Nineteenth-century Liberals used the idea of society as a biological organism to draw attention to the need for competition (as between species), while twentieth-century Liberals argued the reverse to justify greater collective provision, stressing not competition but the harmonious working of the organism as a whole. Early twentieth-century sociologists also drew parallels between the workings of biological and social systems, some of which were extremely crude.[5] Above all, social Darwinistic ideas achieved enormous popularity. For instance, in an 1897 novel, *The Typewriter Girl*, the heroine comments on finding a job: 'I had justified myself before the impartial tribunal of political economy. . . I had proved myself the fittest by the mere fact of survival. The sole remaining question was could I adapt myself to my environment? If so I had fulfilled the whole gospel of Darwinism'.[6]

The idea that there was a 'natural' basis for sexual difference, as opposed to patently artificial class differences, was powerful and long-lived. As the eminent physician Henry Maudsley put it in 1874, 'sex is fundamental, lies deeper than culture, [and] cannot be ignored or defied with impunity'.[7] Moreover, the nature of the evidence adduced and the tone of the argument shifted over time, serving to justify the changing nature of sexual divisions in society (the 'typewriter girl' was herself a product of changes in the occupational distribution of women workers). The theme running through Victorian Darwinistic science was that women were merely vehicles for reproduction and were thus nearer nature (and the lower animals) than men, but towards the end of the century a more positive view of motherhood emerged, largely as a result of eugenic concern about the quality of the race. The essential role prescription of wife and motherhood did not change, but, in theory at least, the importance of the work performed by mothers was recognised.

It was impossible for middle class feminists to attack theories of sexual difference directly because of their purported scientific authenticity. Moreover, to those women long accustomed to playing a complementary role to their husbands in running a family business, the idea of natural sexual differences appeared both sensible and acceptable. Thus the ideas formulated by scientists and mediated by the medical profession formed the framework within which all women, including active feminists (most of whom were middle class), had to work.

SEXUAL DIFFERENCE AND SEPARATE SPHERES IN THE NINETEENTH CENTURY

Darwinistic Victorian science derived psychological and cultural difference between men and women—such as women's stereotypically greater tenderness, generosity and intuition—from male and female biology. The tone of Darwin's *The Descent of Man*, published in 1871, was mild. He outlined a process of sexual selection whereby males competed for females, who initially remained passive, but eventually exercised power of choice; vigorous females preferring vigorous males. Later, eugenicists stressed the importance of teaching women the criteria by which to choose a mate. In the process of sexual selection, certain males were said to develop characteristics that gave them the edge over other males in the competition for females. Over generations secondary sexual characteristics caused males in general to differ more and more from females. The differences in male and female secondary characteristics listed by Darwin shaded into intellect; women were referred to as more intuitive and more 'capable of rapid perception and perhaps of imitation'. Darwin considered that male traits were strengthened by use and were transmitted in greater amounts to male offspring. He thought it fortunate that improvements in male characteristics were passed on in some measure to women, otherwise the man would have become as superior in mental endowment to women as the peacock is in plumage to the peahen. Women might be trained to exercise her reason and imagination to help reduce the inequality, but Darwin insisted that children of both sexes were more like adult women than men, and within an evolutionary doctrine, the implication was that women were less completely evolved.[8]

This was also the independent conclusion of Herbert Spencer, perhaps the most influential late nineteenth-century writer on sexual difference on both sides of the Atlantic. In his early writings, published between 1850 and 1861, Spencer echoed the opinion of the pro-feminist, J. S. Mill, in his belief that convention had stifled women's academic achievement, and while he believed that there would be 'natural' limits on women's achievements he saw no harm in educating them. But his *Principles of Biology* (1867) and his *Principles of Society* (1876) showed the impact of evolutionary thought on his idea of sexual difference. Spencer argued that sexual difference was a product of mankind's successful adaptation to social survival and that it should be understood in terms of women's individual evolution being arrested earlier than men's to permit the conservation of their energies for reproduction. The more highly developed the society, the greater the differentiation in sex roles, and the more able women would be to produce superior offspring. Spencer thus condemned any attempt to change women's position in society, just as he opposed any state intervention to safeguard the position of the poor and weak. Both would interfere with the natural process of evolution and natural selection which ensured social progress. In particular, he feared that higher education would render women incapable of breast feeding their children and probably also infertile. Thus when biological ideas were applied to society by Spencer and by social Darwinists, they were allied to the powerful notion of human progress, which was not a part of Darwin's evolutionary theory. In Spencer's formulation, sexual divisions were a hallmark of social progress and a reflection of organic law. Thus woman's sphere had to be limited for the sake of the race.[9] Karl Pearson, a leading social Darwinist, wrote in 1885: 'If childbearing women be intellectually handicapped, then the penalty to be paid for race predominance is the subjection of women'.[10]

The theory of women's arrested development was taken up in the debate over women's inferior mental ability. George Romanes, the evolutionist, physiologist and early comparative psychologist, declared in 1887 that 'we must look the fact in the face... it must take many centuries for heredity to produce the missing five ounces of the female brain'. When it was realised that, in proportion to body weight, women's brains were in fact heavier than those of men, scientists began to search for other measures of difference. (Nancy Stepan has documented similar shifts in the measurement of skulls designed to support the idea of racial difference.) In the event, women's proportionately larger brain was taken as evidence of their childlike physiology, just as in a similar manner women's recognised capacity to read faster and remember more was interpreted as shallowness.[11]

Ideas of sexual difference were mediated by medical doctors, whose female patients consisted largely of middle class women in the late nineteenth and early twentieth centuries. As Frances Power Cobbe, a leading Victorian feminist, perceived, the medical profession occupied 'with strangely close analogy the position of the priesthood of former times, it assumes the same airs of authority ... and enters every family with a latch key of private information'.[12] Doctors concentrated on the best way of achieving the healthy development of women's reproductive systems and in so doing elevated women's capacity for reproduction into a moral and social duty. 'The gigantic power and influence of the ovaries over the whole animal economy of woman', as Dr Bliss put it in 1870, meant that women's constitutions were believed to be inherently unstable throughout the lifecycle. Doctors believed that the development of girls' reproductive systems took place primarily at the time of menstruation and, in keeping with Spencer's belief in the need to conserve energy in order to ensure healthy reproductive development, advised rest for teenage girls. Maudsley wrote graphically of the dangers facing a fifteen-year-old girl working hard to pass school examinations:

> For a time all seems to go well with her studies; she triumphs over male and female competitors ... But in the long run nature, which cannot be ignored or defied with impunity, asserts its power; ...health fails ... [she] leaves college a good scholar but a delicate and ailing woman ... the special functions which have relation to her future

offices as a woman, and the full and perfect accomplishment of which is essential to sexual completeness, have been deranged at a critical time.[13]

Thus doctors agreed with scientists that for the sake of the welfare of the race, women's intellectual development and range of activities should be severely curtailed.

After adolescence, women faced the danger of puerperal insanity following childbirth and finally the 'climacteric paroxysms' of menopause.[14] Otto Weininger, gynaecologist and polemicist, wrote in 1906 that 'man possesses sexual organs; her sexual organs possess woman'.[15] As a result, women were held to be psychologically unstable. But whereas middle class women were described as physiologically weak and in need of treatment, working class women were considered physiologically strong and potentially polluting. Such an analysis paralleled the belief that middle class women were more highly evolved and that working class women were nearer 'nature' and the lower animal passions and behaviour. Medical diagnosis therefore tended to vary according to the social class of the patient. Chlorosis, which was described as an anaemia and commonly referred to as the 'green sickness' because of the appearance of its victims, was regarded by doctors as a middle class ailment, contracted by women who led an idle, self-indulgent life. In reality it was also very much a working woman's disease, but this fact was generally ignored by physicians.[16] Similarly, aberrant sexual behaviour was more likely to be treated as organic malfunction in middle class women and insanity in working class women.

In a period when a rigid separation of spheres prevailed between men and women, the physician's approach to female illness exemplified the strong influence of theories of sexual difference and the nature of their implications for the position of women in society. By the 1880s nearly all female disorders were ascribed to uterine malfunction, in accordance with medical and scientific preoccupations with the over-riding importance of female biology. Moreover, female well-being was defined in terms congruent with both women's reproductive function and ideal feminine behaviour. Thus, 'simple hysterical mania' was frequently diagnosed in women exhibiting any uncommon behaviour. One leading physician described such sufferers as becoming 'rapidly less and less conventional. Thus a lady will smoke, talk slang, or be extravagant in dress; and will declare her intention of doing as she likes'. According to the obstetrician, Isaac Barker Brown, female insanity went through eight stages, beginning with hysteria, and was largely due to 'failure of nervous power ... produced by peripheral irritation arising in the branches of the pudic nerve, more particularly the incident nerve supplying the clitoris'. For Barker Brown and many other gynaecologists and obstetricians of the period, clitorectomy was the solution. Brown himself was expelled from the Obstetrical Society in 1867 for failing to obtain the consent of his patients and their husbands to the operation, rather than for his methods *per se*. The vote against him was taken after the Secretary of the Society explained that 'we have constituted ourselves as it were the guardians of their [women's] interests and in many cases ... the custodians of their honour ... We are in fact, the strong and they the weaker. They are obliged to believe all that we tell them'.[17] It was therefore doubly important that the physician did not deceive his patients. Like legislators, doctors set themselves up as women's protectors and the preoccupation with women's reproductive systems as the source of their illness and weakness led them to assume the role of moral guardian. Female well-being was classically associated with passivity, a love of home, children and domestic duties and, in the mid- and late nineteenth century, sexual innocence and absence of sexual feelings. Healthy development in women was thus signified by an attachment to their prescribed sphere and by the manifestation of moral virtue.

The female patient/doctor relationship is particularly difficult to interpret during the late nineteenth century. As Frances Power Cobbe observed, the doctor assumed a position of great importance in the middle class household and was indeed one of the very few men of her own class that the married middle class woman dealt with directly; while to doctors, middle class female patients represented a lucrative source of income. Moreover, because of their physical and mental weakness women were clearly incapable of qualifying as doctors themselves.[18] But it is not sufficient to characterise the relationship between doctors and their female middle class patients as one of simple economics or misogyny. The extent to which the medical prescriptions regarding women's role were mediated and/or resisted by middle class women is difficult to assess, but it would be wrong to characterise women simply as victims either in their relationship with their physicians or in respect to theories of sexual difference generally. Jacques Donzelot has argued that women actively colluded with doctors because of the new-found status that accrued to them within the family as educators of their children and as medical auxiliaries.[19] While it is true that by the turn of the century both middle and working class women were profoundly affected by the gospel of maternalism preached by the medical profession, imperialists and politicians, it is also possible to find examples of straightforward resistance to physicians both on the grounds that they encouraged middle class women to lead idle lives and that they posed a threat to female modesty. Frances Power Cobbe deplored the approval doctors gave to what she considered to be an essentially unhealthy lifestyle; she had little faith in medical expertise and liked to recall the case of a women friend who, on deciding to stop seeing her doctor and carry on normally, promptly recovered.[20]

It is nevertheless likely that more middle class women accepted than resisted the experts' view of their physiology and psychology, though they may also have passed those views through their own filter. One feminist, Mrs Wolstenholme-Elmy (who as a young woman determined to follow Mary

Wollstonecraft's example and live with her lover, until on becoming pregnant she took the advice of fellow suffragists and married) accepted the idea that menstruation was essentially pathological, although she also argued that it was caused by men's brutality.[21] Josephine Butler, a feminist who led the fight against the Contagious Diseases Acts during the 1860s and 1870s, accepted the desirability of female moral purity and sexual innocence, but also registered her vehement objection to the medical profession. She was appalled that women should be attended by male doctors, and of male attendance in childbirth she wrote:

> Is it desirable that the finest and most sensitive part of a woman—that which God gave her, should on the one hand be wounded with such a wound as no proud and gentle nature ever recovers from, or else should on the other hand be deadened so that the woman becomes only half herself, and this is what the tyranny of the medical profession has accomplished.

Similar sentiments led Butler to label the use of the speculum by doctors inspecting prostitutes for venereal disease under the Contagious Diseases Acts as 'instrumental rape'.[22] Such a stand was also shaped by the essentially libertarian ideas of the mainstream feminist movement, which included opposition to state intervention of all kinds (including protective legislation and the inspection of homes under the Infant Life Protection Acts), and by the more general movement for moral reform, which comprised an interlocking nexus of feminist, social purity, temperance, anti-vaccination, and animal welfare societies.[23]

In the long run it may be correct to argue, as Patricia Branca has done, that doctors were 'the logical answer to the middle class woman's increasing desire for self-improvement and self-control',[24] but evidence suggests that medical and scientific expertise set the basic framework for discussion and action within which women tended to respond—albeit not always in an anticipated manner—rather than initiate. This was especially true of the late nineteenth century, when ideas of sexual difference condemned women to a position of inferiority, but the pattern remained substantially the same throughout the period. For example, middle class women were as convinced as working class women by the medical profession's call for hospitalised childbirth, although just as working class women wanted what they regarded as the additional bonus of hospital rest, so middle class women also saw the availability of anaesthesia as a major reason for welcoming the trend to hospital births.[25]

The complicated nature of women's response to doctors' views about their role also characterised the way in which women dealt with the whole area of sexual difference and its implications for their position in terms of both the separation of spheres and of female dependency within the private sphere of home and family. The pervasive belief in the natural, biological difference between male and female characteristics formed a framework within which feminists and non-feminists alike thought and lived. Spencerian analysis not only assigned women a narrow and subordinate role, but also stressed that this was necessary if human progress was to be sustained. In an 1897 article, the eminent lawyer, journalist and essayist Walter Bagehot agreed that any attempt by women to escape what he regarded as their biological destiny was anti-evolutionary.[26] Scientists and social theorists assumed that the ethics of family and state were entirely separate, and politicians of all persuasions felt justified in using familial language—in which men became benevolent protectors and women childlike—to describe the subordinate position of women (and 'primitive' peoples), for within the family subordination was considered legitimate.[27] Unlike the doctor's authority, scientific theories of sexual difference could not be directly challenged; rather, women found ways of circumventing or reinterpreting them.

In challenging the idea of a natural separation of spheres, the nineteenth-century feminist movement took up two major positions: first, that women wishing to enter the public sphere should be able to do so on the same terms as men, and second, that women's domestic talents and virtues should be extended to the wider sphere beyond the home. Feminists adopting the first position demanded equal rights to men in respect to property, education and employment opportunities, and the vote. In so doing, they inevitably rejected the idea of innate sexual difference, laying much greater emphasis on what would today be called patterns of socialisation. Thus J. S. Mill, the leading theoretician of liberal feminism, stressed that it was impossible to know what women's true capacities were because of their inferior education. He nevertheless accepted the idea that there would probably be 'natural' limitations on their development, and envisaged that the vast majority of women would remain wives and mothers after legal emancipation. Only a few exceptional women were likely to take advantage of equal education opportunities, though on grounds of utility alone, Mill argued that it was important for this small pool of female talent to be permitted free choice of occupation so that it might contribute to human development. In this way, Spencer's argument about the conditions necessary for human progress was neatly turned on its head.[28]

Yet feminists who made women's right to enter the public sphere a priority never really addressed the issue of women's role as wives and mothers, which late nineteenth-century doctors and scientists held to be the chief and necessary constraint on women's achievements. They acknowledged the importance of motherhood: Mill wrote of wives 'naturally' running a household and teaching their children, and of women's 'naturally' greater elegance and taste.[29] To all intents and purposes, however, they *ignored* the implications of their demand to enter the public sphere for the role of women in the private sphere of home and family, and chose not to confront the emphasis doctors and scientists placed on the latter. Instead, they focused their main arguments on the position of women who did not marry, using the individualistic framework of nineteenth-century liberalism and political economy to argue for a 'fair field and no favour' and the removal of all barriers that hindered single women from earning a decent living. In particular, they supported their case by invoking the plight of the 'surplus' women, who, through no fault of their own, found themselves either reliant on the good offices of a male relative or obliged to earn their own living. An increasing number of late nineteenth- and early twentieth-century feminists, such as Theresa Billington Greig and Cicely Hamilton, advocated the deliberate choice of spinsterhood as the only means to intellectual fulfilment and a successful career.

The other main strand in nineteenth-century feminism accepted the idea of women as the natural guardians of the moral order. It stressed the importance of women's domestic role and sought to expand it. The language feminists used to make this appeal was steeped in the evangelical tradition, which in the early and mid-nineteenth century had proved as successful as science in containing women, but which in the later part of the century was used by feminists to argue for an extension of maternal influence beyond the home. Thus Josephine Butler spoke of the home as the 'nursery of all virtue', and of the need to re-establish ideal family life, both by improving the position of women as wives and mothers and by extending domestic values to the world beyond the home.[30] In Butler's case this led to a radical campaign against the Contagious Diseases (CD) Acts of the 1860s (under which prostitutes were subject to compulsory medical inspection and detained if found to have venereal disease), which she saw as part of the double moral standard oppressing all women and debasing family life.

The two strands in feminist thought were by no means separate.[31] Elizabeth Wolstenholme-Elmy, for example, was associated with the suffrage movement, Butler's campaign against the CD Acts, and the campaign for the Married Women's Property Acts, while Millicent Fawcett, though withholding public support for Butler because she feared it would bring the suffrage movement into disrepute, in fact wholeheartedly approved of her work. Women's domestic virtues comprised an important part of most feminists' argument for the vote. Both Fawcett and Frances Power Cobbe argued that women's virtue, tenderness and eye for detail—in short the special qualities they developed as wives and mothers—were necessary to complete man-made legislation and male-supervised charitable endeavours.[32] As Rosalind Rosenberg has pointed out, arguments based on female uniqueness paradoxically 'provided the biological affirmation that anti-feminists needed to oppose change and that feminists relied on to defuse the threat of change'.[33]

Theresa Billington Greig, who broke away from the Pankhursts' suffragette organisation, the Women's Social and Political Union, over the issue of militant action, was virtually alone in criticising suffragists and suffragettes who regarded the home 'as an exemplar of what ought to be in the political world'. Her condemnation of the home and family as the source of women's subjection and inferiority, and her assertion that 'any woman who is really a rebel longs to destroy the conventions which bind her in the home as much as those which bind her in the state',[34] has a modern ring, although in practice her solution, like that of Florence Nightingale, amounted to a complete rejection of family life rather than a demand for its restructuring. Most late nineteenth-century feminists saw feminism primarily as a movement for moral reform, which would of necessity bring in its wake desirable political and social change.

In accepting that the world occupied by a majority of adult women would be different from that of men, feminists distinguished themselves from the mainstream of opinion only by their refusal to accept that women's role was thereby rendered inferior. The difficulties they experienced in arguing this are clearly visible in Emily Pfeiffer's attempt to counter the case made by doctors and scientists against more rigorous schooling for adolescent girls. Pfeiffer's claim to equality was remarkably convoluted: 'The equality I would claim is not as things at present stand, not *de facto*, but in original capacity, and even so, an equality in difference, and to some extent of compensation'.[35] Education provided a good example of the accommodation feminists had to make in regard to scientific theories of sexual difference and the ambivalence many of them felt about the whole issue. Those who, like Emily Davies, wished to give middle class girls exactly the same educational opportunities as boys in terms of curriculum and examinations, had to deal with opposition arising from the view that adolescent girls needed to conserve their energies for reproduction. Elizabeth Garrett Anderson, one of the few qualified women physicians, replied to Maudsley on this point, acknowledging that pubescent girls were severely taxed, but arguing that the quiet routine of school afforded them adequate protection. She maintained that the reproductive organs were formed in girls at birth and not newly created in adolescence as Maudsley claimed, and while agreeing that women stored nutrient in reserve for childbearing, argued that it was not in finite supply and could safely be drawn upon in adolescence. She did not deny female weakness and invalidism, merely suggesting that the physical condition of girls could be improved. Many of the new middle class girls' schools sought to show that they took the problem of adolescent development seriously by appointing doctors to safeguard the welfare of their charges, and until well into the twentieth century pupils attending the Girls' Public Day School Trust schools, the first of which opened in 1872, went to school only in the mornings so that they should avoid strain and be allowed to be at home with their mothers in the afternoons.[36]

Feminists were also considerably divided over what constitued an appropriate curriculum for girls. Many pioneers of women's education made it quite clear that they did not accept Emily Davies' view that girls might be trained in the same way as boys, and argued that they should be given an opportunity, by way of, for example, domestic science classes, to prepare for the lives a majority of them would lead as wives and mothers. Dorothea Beale, the Principal of the first proprietary girls' school in England, Cheltenham Ladies College, was firmly committed to a separate curriculum for girls and declared that her aim was to train 'girls so that they may best perform that subordinate part in the world to which, I believe, they have been called'.[37] Just as working class girls were included in the state provision of elementary education in 1870 and provided with an education which emphasised the virtues of good housewifery and domestic management, so the increased attention paid to the education of middle class girls during the late Victorian period—by male bureaucrats as well as female pioneers—may be seen as being as much a result of the general educational reform initiative of the period as of feminist ambition.[38] Nevertheless, in terms of their effects, the new endowed and proprietary girls' schools, of which there were two hundred by 1894, provided girls with different role models, access to a peer group, and also succeeded in loosening family ties.[39]

It was generally accepted that the role of wife and mother was incompatible with a career, not only because of the time and energy required, but also because of the very different qualities and characteristics it demanded. It is interesting that both Mrs Pankhurst and Millicent Fawcett only entered public life as feminists after their husbands' deaths. Emily Davies was one of the few to argue that housekeeping took up little time and that women could in fact combine work and marriage, and Elizabeth Garrett Anderson belonged to an even more select band who put this advice into practice. Moreover, when nineteenth-century feminists demanded equal education and employment opportunities for single women, they did not ask for any special consideration to be extended to women on account of their reproductive role. On the contrary, middle class feminists asked for the repeal of all protective legislation because they believed it to represent one of the barriers to female employment. By the late 1880s, however, they found themselves in open conflict with the women's trade union movement on this point. In 1890, Beatrice Webb referred caustically to 'individualists, reinforced by a batch of excellent ladies (eager for the Right of Woman to work at all hours of the day and night with the minimum space and sanitation)'[40] who opposed any attempt to regulate conditions in workshops and the homework trades.

For mothers, feminists claimed only the right to extend their domestic influence beyond the home, and to practise what was later termed 'social' or 'civic maternalism'. Nineteenth-century feminists did not demand measures to improve the status and conditions of wives and mothers other than to campaign for the equal right of married women to control their own property. A significant number of feminists concerned primarily with rights in the public sphere rejected the confines of the middle class family altogether, while promoters of maternal influence beyond the home did so on the basis of women's unique qualities as wives and mothers. The problem of establishing the appropriate limits of social maternalism remained. Public support was forthcoming for philanthropic work, such as visiting the homes of the poor, but not for permitting mothers to elect Members of Parliament. Philanthropy provided women with an acceptable bridge to the public world of work and citizenship, even though, as Anne Summers has argued, it involved a fundamental contradiction, whereby women left their own homes in order to tell working class women to stay in theirs.[41]

SOCIAL MATERNALISM

The majority of middle class women who engaged in philanthropic work, volunteering their services to tend the sick and children in institutions, and to visit the homes of the poor, were not feminists, though they too stressed the unique contribution that women could make by virtue of their particular qualities of caring and sympathy. Thus while philanthropic work was for some integral to their feminist beliefs, for others it represented merely a diversion from household cares, a sublimation of other desires, or, and this was probably the most common motivation, a socially acceptable way for both married women and their daughters to engage in purposeful work. Charitable work was also something that daughters could do without prejudicing their chances in the marriage market.

Beatrice Webb's admiration for the philanthropic work of Mary Booth rested on the way in which the latter expressed 'gentle and loving contempt for any *special* work outside the ordinary sphere of a woman's life, [and] her high standard of excellence which should discourage any vain attempt to leave the beaten track of a woman's duty'. Beatrice was anxious not to follow what she regarded as the purposeless social round of the society wife and felt that the 'governing and guiding' work performed by women philanthropists was much less likely to 'unsex' women than academic work or the 'push and severity' demanded of a professional woman such as the hospital matron. Her notion of duty was perhaps the most important factor in her own decision to pursue voluntary social work.[42] Many women with no desire to reject the social round and daily duties expected of middle class wives, but who still deplored idleness as the antithesis of duty, often made an explicit link between their idea of duty and their spiritual responsibilities.[43]

Women used their supposedly greater spirituality as a further justification for transcending the confines of the private sphere. The retreat into other-worldliness on the part of some women may be interpreted as a form of escapism by those who found their ideas unacceptable to society as a whole,[44] not that this made their religious faith any less genuine or deep. Both Josephine Butler, who was happily married and a strong feminist, and

Florence Nightingale, who decided to reject middle class family life entirely and was scornful of feminism, were convinced of the possibilities of women's spiritual leadership. For Nightingale, self-giving and service provided the key to spiritual growth, while Butler couched her appeal on behalf of prostitutes as a call to the justice and equality announced by Christ. It is clear that the latter found in her religious faith the strength necessary to undertake a public campaign on the taboo subjects of prostitution and venereal disease.[45] Both women stressed the idea of service, which Butler saw as an outgrowth of women's role in the home, while neither envisaged impinging on men's work. Nightingale rejected Mill's criticism that her *Notes on Nursing* restricted women's opportunities in the medical world by saying that feminism urged 'women to do all men do including the medical and other professions, merely because men do it, and without regard to whether this is the best women can do'.[46]

Women who were inspired neither by feminism nor revulsion against the prescribed role of the middle class wife and mother, but who nevertheless found a sense of purpose in philanthropy, often wrote of their work with a cloying sentimentality and in terms that reveal a strange mixture of humility (expressed in religious terms); insecurity, class superiority and a grim determination to do God's will. Marianne Farningham, who remained single, adopted an air of benevolent maternalism towards her girls' Bible class and her sense of complacency, like that of most middle class philanthropic women, could be punctured only from within. Farningham described one of her most fearsome lessons in humility as follows:

> One Sunday evening I went into the vestry to speak to a number of my girls who were about to take their first communion. I was very happy; but I am sure that I needed a sharp lesson in humility and I received it. As I walked through the chapel to my pew, a strange thick darkness came upon me, and encompassed my soul. I was suddenly filled with fear and doubt. Something whispered to me that I have never myself been converted! . . .[I was] so oppressed by a sense of sin that I felt almost as if I should die![47]

Women who engaged in charitable work tended to confine themselves to particular activities; principally fund raising, and visiting the homes of the poor and institutions. Men continued to run the executive committees of charitable societies and to fill the paid positions in workhouses and prisons. Female visitors were cheap, a point in their favour which continued to be emphasised as late as 1920, when the Local Government Board considered the possibility of using them to inspect the homes of widows drawing poor relief. When in 1861 Louisa Twining proposed to a government Select Committee that women should be allowed to stand for election as Poor Law Guardians, she agreed that they should not interfere in the male province of finance and administration, and should not have any say over the treatment of male paupers.[48]

Philanthropic work, like workhouse visiting, inevitably raised the question of women's representation on public bodies at the local level. The first female Poor Law Guardian was elected in Kensington in 1875 and immediately appointed to a district relief committee and to the workhouse visiting committee, having the special responsibility of supervising the female scrubbers and washers. The first married female guardian was elected in 1881 and in 1908 a Women's Local Government Society survey of 837 female Guardians showed 405 to be married. By 1910 there were 1,655 female Guardians, although there remained 234 boards with no female representatives. Generally the social standing of female Guardians was higher than male Guardians. Despite the fear that they would prove sentimental and spendthrift, women were inclined to favour the strict administration of outdoor relief, although they sought substantial improvements in matters such as diet and the provision of clean sheets and underclothing inside the workhouse.[49]

Women also sat on school boards (which were responsible for state elementary schools prior to 1902), and the first generation of such women —elected during the 1870s—was particularly active. They took a special interest in the girls' curriculum and, in keeping with the 'equal but different' philosophy, tended to promote the study of domestic subjects. In London, Helen Taylor played a leading part in the fight to abolish school fees and provide school meals, and there is also some evidence that women school-board members took an interest in the pay and conditions of women teachers. When the Boards were abolished in 1902, the Women's Local Government Society fought to have women elected to the County and Borough Councils, which became the new Local Education Authorities (LEAs). They were partially successful in 1907, when unmarried women ratepayers were allowed to stand as candidates.[50] Women ratepayers, married or unmarried, had long been permitted to sit on urban and rural district councils and parish councils, so that during the late 1890s the number of women holding elected office in local government (including Poor Law and school board work) may well have exceeded the number holding office today.[51]

Local politics were considered to be an extension of philanthropic work, and were seen as an extension of women's domestic sphere. But the larger and more important the elected body, the more likely it was that women's suitability—and especially married women's suitability—would be called into question. At the national level, women's political participation was confined to the ladies auxiliaries of the Conservative and Liberal parties, which were formed during the 1880s and 1890s as a means of making use of women's formidable political energies and of siphoning off potential protest.

Marianne Farningham became a member of the Northampton School Board in the mid-1880s, but she declined to canvass or address meetings, preferring to send a printed letter round to electors, though this ladylike course of action did not prevent her heading the poll. She found her male colleagues courteous, although she was 'not at all sure' that they were all glad to have her there. Margaret Wynne Nevinson, an active feminist, who was a member of a school management committee for twenty-five years and who also served as a Poor Law Guardian, found her fellow male Guardians actively hostile.[52] Many women, feminist, non-feminist and anti-feminist, who played a prominent part in public life between the Wars initially served in local government. Mary Stocks, for example, helped her mother with her visiting for the Charity Organisation Society, and on leaving school became the honorary secretary of an elementary school care committee. Similarly, Violet Markham served first on a school management committee and later as a member of Chesterfield LEA.[53]

Women who entered voluntary work during the inter-war years did so largely because it provided them with a diversion from household routine. This was particularly important in view of the fact that women were often forced to give up paid work on marriage. Voluntary work was no longer seen as either a stepping stone to bigger and better things or as a part of a women's mission, but rather as the exclusive province of married women. Young, single middle class women were by this time engaging in paid work outside the home. In the nineteenth century, many middle class women devoted considerable time to philanthropic work and local politics; a single woman such as Louisa Twining worked five days a week as a Poor Law Guardian between 1884 and 1890. This level of activity stands in marked contrast to that of the very few working class women who qualified under local government franchises (although increasing numbers became Guardians after 1894, when the property qualification was abolished), who squeezed in two or three hours Poor Law work on a Saturday between household chores.[54]

It was possible to argue for an infinite extension of social motherhood. Josephine Butler, for example, argued that women's powers of guidance, their spiritual wisdom and maternal qualities should be represented in Parliament. Similarly, in an 1894 speech, Millicent Fawcett pressed for the vote on the grounds that she 'wished to strengthen true womanliness in women, and because I want to see the womanly and domestic side of things weigh more and count for more in all public concerns'. She assured the women she addressed that suffragists did not want them to give up 'one jot or tittle of your womanliness, your love for children, your care for the sick, your gentleness, your self-control, your obedience to conscience and duty'.[55] These were the very qualities required in the political arena. While there was very little dispute about the incompatibility of marriage with a career (even at the end of the century only a very few radical feminist theorists, such as Olive Schreiner, were prepared to argue that all adult women should be engaged in regular paid employment), the vote proved a much more contentious issue for feminists as well as non-feminists, because it required such a substantial re-drawing of the boundaries between male and female spheres. Married women's inability to hold property (the basis of the nineteenth-century franchise) and lack of a legal personality made the task of achieving social citizenship additionally difficult. Chiefly for tactical reasons, a clause was inserted in the women's suffrage bills of 1870 and 1874 expressly excluding married women. This manoeuvre caused dissension within feminist ranks, however, and in 1889 a small group of women, including Mrs Pankhurst and Josephine Butler, formed the Women's Franchise League, in reaction to what they perceived as a preoccupation with the cause of spinsters and widows. The League emphasised the rights of married women to the vote and to equal divorce and inheritance laws.[56]

The famous 1889 'Appeal' against women's suffrage, signed by 104 women, viewed women's direct participation in national politics as impossible 'either by the disabilities of sex, or by strong formations of custom and habit *resting ultimately upon physical difference against which it is useless to contend*' (my italics).[57] Pamphlets written by men who opposed the vote for women also stressed that sexual difference was fundamental to their argument. A. V. Dicey, the prominent nineteenth-century jurist and by no means an extreme anti-feminist, considered that while distinctions of rights founded on sex often gave rise to injustice 'they have this in their favour—they rest upon a difference not created by social conventions or by human prejudice and selfishness, or by accidental circumstances... which split society into classes, but by the nature of things'. Sex difference unlike class difference was believed to be natural and immutable. Francis Latham put the point yet more clearly: 'women are physiologically disqualified from contention with men in the political arena, not by virtue of any tyrannical law of man's devising, but by reason of fixed and irrevocable decrees of nature which may not be violated with impunity'.[58]

The argument that an imperial power needed physically strong and virile rulers convinced many female anti-suffragists. Violet Markham, for example, recalled in her autobiography that her antagonism to the vote was closely associated with her imperialism, even though as a Liberal she often felt herself to be siding with a 'hotbed of reactionaries'. Some male anti-suffragists used a more hostile and demeaning picture of women's place reminiscent of Spencerian Darwinism to justify their arguments. Harold Owen, a playwright, and Sir Almroth Wright, a surgeon, stressed that women's prime purpose was reproduction and emphasised the need for their proper dependence on men. Owen saw as one of the chief evils of the suffrage movement its apparent disrespect for men. A latent violence—which also surfaced in police treatment of suffragettes—pervaded the work of Belfort Bax, a leading socialist, who warned that suffragists had foregone the right to male protection and should be treated accordingly.[59]

The signatories of the Appeal argued that women had adequate opportunity to make their influence felt in local government. Florence Nightingale, for example, believed that the vote had no relevance to women's work. As Brian Harrison has remarked, one of the main reasons for the bitterness of the suffrage struggle was that so many on both sides had roots in the philanthropic world. To be anti-suffrage was not necessarily to be anti-feminist; many opponents of the suffrage, men and women, campaigned for better educational opportunities for women and supported their work at the local level. Beatrice Webb signed the Appeal, although as she recorded in her diary for 1889, she was impressed by a reply she received from a woman who complained that her lodger could vote but she could not, and that while she could vote for her parish council and her local Poor Law Guardians, she could not do so for an MP. However, the diary makes it quite clear that Beatrice did not want to be associated with what she viewed as primarily a celibate woman's cause.[60]

Underlying the suffrage struggle was a set of attitudes which dictated that women's natural sphere was the home, that their full development came only with motherhood and that a 'womanly woman' would not be interested in or want the vote. It is interesting that when Asquith, the Liberal Prime Minister, eventually agreed to receive a suffrage deputation, he called in representatives of Sylvia Pankhurst's East London Federation, which was composed chiefly of working class women.[61] The separation of spheres was less rigidly prescribed for working class women and it appears that working class suffragists aroused less ire on the part of politicians than did middle class women. When Beatrice Webb publicly renounced her stand against the suffrage in 1906, she explained in a letter to Millicent Garrett Fawcett that: 'The raising of children, the advancement of learning and the promotion of the spiritual—which I regard as the particular obligations of women—are, it is clear, more and more becoming the main preoccupations of the community as a whole'.[62] Because of her involvement in politics and close knowledge of major social issues, Webb was among the first of those anti-suffragists who rested their case on the fact that local politics provided a sufficient outlet for maternal influence to recognise that the huge divide between local and national issues in politics was ceasing to exist. But male opponents of women's suffrage, who based their case primarily on sexual difference, showed very little inclination to change their views. The women's victory in 1918 was unspectacular and came about primarily because the government had to update the electoral register to include those serving in the armed forces. The Parliamentary majority in favour of including women was still small and as Martin Pugh has commented, 'when one remembers that the 1918 Act actually enfranchised boys of nineteen if they had served in the forces, the limit on women [to those of thirty years of age or over] was almost an insult'.[63]

WOMAN'S SPHERE IN THE TWENTIETH CENTURY

The turn of the century brought an important change in attitudes towards women's role as mothers: a strengthening ideology of motherhood, accompanied by changes in theories of sexual difference, resulted in a shift in emphasis away from the negative constraints imposed by female biology towards the importance of healthy and intelligent motherhood to an imperial nation. After all, as Havelock Ellis remarked: 'the breeding of men lies largely in the hands of women'.[64] The tenets of the evolutionary model of sexual difference also began to crumble, parallelling the movement in Liberal thought away from the brutal competition of Spencerian individualism towards the possibilities of harmonious cooperation.[65] The two major causes of this were first, increasing doubts about the validity of Darwin's ideas of natural and sexual selection (Darwin had failed to produce a satisfactory theory of heredity), and second, new empirical research findings and observable changes in the position of women, particularly the increasing numbers of single women in the labour force.[66]

Some of the empirical research which demolished aspects of late nineteenth-century ideas regarding sexual difference was in fact performed by women. Karl Pearson, for example, employed two unmarried women researchers at University College (largely because they were cheap). They were Ethel Elderton (who conducted the study of the English birth rate), and Alice Lee, who investigated the relationship between skull capacity and intellectual ability in both men and women. She recorded the cranial measurements of 35 male anatomists attending the Anatomical Society meeting in Dublin in 1898, 30 female students of Bedford College and 25 male staff of University College, and found that no such relationship existed. Interestingly, while Lee rebelled against the notion of female inferiority, both she and Elderton were convinced of the importance of women's role as wives and mothers. And both were influenced by social Darwinistic arguments concerning the relationship between the quality of motherhood and the future welfare of the race.[67]

In its original nineteenth-century formulation, eugenic concern about the quality of the racial stock focused on the fertility behaviour of middle and upper class women. As early as 1869, Francis Galton, who founded the Eugenics Laboratory (which in 1905 became a Department of University College under the direction of Karl Pearson), recommended a programme of what later became called positive and negative eugenics. Births were to be encouraged among the genetically superior (crudely equated with the higher social classes), and reproduction prevented among the genetically inferior (the working class). The major problem identified by eugenicists during the late nineteenth- and early twentieth-centuries was that the birth rate of the middle class—the eugenically fit—was falling much faster than that of the working class.[68]

In the mid-1880s, Mr Lawson Tait, who as police surgeon in Birmingham during the 1890s exhibited a profoundly misogynist attitude in his treatment of rape victims, commented that 'to leave only the inferior women to perpetuate the species will do more to deteriorate the human race than all the individual victories at Girton will do to benefit it'.[69] Headmistresses and university teachers were anxious to show that their students proved as fertile as the average woman. Mrs Henry Sidgwick conducted one such survey of women students at Oxford and Cambridge, published in 1890, and Dr Agnes Saville and Dr Major Greenwood another for the National Birth Rate Commission (a lay body composed chiefly of clergy, peers and doctors) in 1914. Both concluded that the families of educated women were no smaller than the average. The records of female social workers trained in early twentieth-century Birmingham, however, showed that only 22 per cent of educated women had married and that their average age at marriage was 34 years, some nine years older than the norm.[70] The low percentage marrying and the higher age at marriage probably reflected the fact that such women would have had to give up their careers on marriage.

The call to marriage and motherhood became more insistent during the 1890s, in response to the phenomenon of the 'new woman'. Mrs Lynn Linton, the ubiquitous writer on etiquette, roundly condemned such women for smoking in public, or after dinner with the men, and for repudiating motherhood.[71] Attacks on middle class women for 'shirking' their 'racial duty' were common well into the twentieth century. Grant Allen, writer and biologist, who also stressed the importance of women's sexual emancipation in a novel, *The Woman Who Did* (1895), took up a similar cry: 'A woman ought to be ashamed to say she has no desire to become a wife and mother'. In his view such behaviour showed a total lack of healthy instincts. Havelock Ellis, who deplored the tendency of earlier Victorian scientific research to belittle women's intellectual capacities, nevertheless believed that there were essential advantages to women remaining in their 'proper sphere'. Ellis believed that the women's movement had taken a wrong turn in demanding equality with men in the public sphere and should rather have worked for the elevation of motherhood. As Jeffrey Weeks has pointed out, for Ellis and his fellow socialist Edward Carpenter, sexual equality was above all an ethical concern, involving equal recognition for the work women did as wives and mothers.[72] Many feminists also saw the struggle for the vote in moral terms, but while they were prepared to use maternalist arguments in support of their campaign, they paid little attention to the individual needs of mothers.

In 1889 two biologists, Patrick Geddes and J. Arthur Thompson, published a treatise which significantly modified previous ideas on the origins of sexual difference. They derived a theory which preserved the immutability of separate spheres, but stressed the complementarity of sex roles and cooperation between men and women. The emphasis was no longer placed on male domination, but rather on women's equal but different attributes. Psychological and cultural differences were still thought to be grounded in biology; indeed, Geddes and Thompson believed sex differences to be physiologically based, which held out even less possibility for change than did Spencer's explanation based on evolution. However, the importance of such womanly qualities as nurturance and domesticity to society as a whole was now given full recognition, and Geddes and Thompson wrote fulsomely of the possibilities of civic or social motherhood, lauding woman 'as eupsychic inspirer and eugenic mother, as instructive synthesist, as educationalist, as orderly home planner and citizen, and by her guidance of consumption, directing industry and skill, ennobling utility into art'.[73] Their work was still circulating in the 1940s when Simone de Beauvoir criticised it in *The Second Sex* (1949).

Like other writers at the turn of the century, Geddes and Thompson stressed the importance of women receiving an education that would fit them for motherhood, and of their choosing eugenically sound mates in order to 'beget supermen, of either sex, of course'.[74] Geddes, Thompson and Ellis used the work of the Swedish feminist, Ellen Key in support of their ideas. In 1912, Key wrote of the women's movement as ideally winning back 'the wife to the husband, the mother to the children, and thereby the home to all'. She argued strongly that nineteenth-century feminism had neglected women's need for love and a family life (although this was by no means wholly the case) and that sexual equality did not necessarily mean 'sameness'. Because Key believed that motherhood brought women their greatest fulfilment, her work was widely quoted with approval, although her defence of 'bachelor motherhood' for the unfortunate 'surplus' women achieved a notoriety similar to Grant Allen's apparent advocacy of 'free love' in *The Woman Who Did*.[75]

Early twentieth-century male and female doctors used eugenic concern about the quality and quantity of the race to argue that the welfare of future generations depended on girls being protected from rigorous examination schedules and receiving adequate training in house and mothercraft. More emphasis on domestic subjects in the curriculum of secondary school girls was now recommended on the grounds that 'every girl should be looked upon as a potential wife and mother',[76] just as the Board of Education promoted the teaching of housewifery, laundry and cookery to working class girls. The response by headmistresses of middle class girls' schools parallelled nineteenth-century divisions over the appropriate curriculum for girls. Sara Burstall, the headmistress of Manchester High School, argued in 1907 that mathematics had a 'hardening influence' on femininity. But only a few schools completely integrated the teaching of domestic subjects and science. At Haberdasher's Aske's in London, the girls performed experiments on meat and eggs before cooking them.[77] Further education in domestic science was given at the Women's Department of King's College, which opened in 1909. One feminist writer vehemently condemned the idea of 'young women going to university to learn how to clean', while Rebecca West tersely dismissed all housework as 'rat poison' which took the 'intelligence of rabbits' to learn.[78]

Differentiation between the education of girls and boys continued to be discussed throughout the period. While the 1923 Report to the Board of Education by the Consultative Committee on differentiating the curriculum for boys and girls in secondary schools was not convinced as to 'clear and ascertained differences between the sexes on which education policy may be readily based', it stressed the danger of 'over pressure' in the education of girls. It recommended that the pace of girls' education be slowed, that physical education reflect the need of girls for 'smoothness and expressiveness' and of boys for 'strength and energy', and that allowance be made for the effect of menstruation, which condemned many girls 'to a recurring and temporary diminution of general mental efficiency'.[79] During the 1920s the discovery of hormones led to a new variant in the theory of sexual difference based on emotional instability. Arabella Keneally, a strong anti-feminist and populariser of medical views on women (especially those of Geddes and Thompson), believed that higher education for women induced hormonal imbalance.[80] As late as 1948, John Newsom, in what R. A. Butler (the sponsor of the 1944 Education Act), described as 'wise and humorous recommendations for girls' schools', favoured as separate a curriculum for girls—grounded in domestic subjects—as any advocated by early twentieth-century eugenicists. By the 1940s, government reports purported to consider the needs of the individual child, but as Ann Marie Wolpe has pointed out, prior assumptions were made as to the 'natural' interests of girls and boys and the destiny of girls as wives and mothers; indeed, Miriam David has suggested that the 1940s' curriculum was more differentiated than that of the 1930s.[81] It seems that femininity had always to be 'cultivated, achieved and preserved, while masculinity could be left to look after itself'.[82]

Adult women were urged by doctors such as Caleb W. Saleeby (whose writing Rebecca West described as 'fluffy yet resistant') to take more interest in mothercraft. Elizabeth Sloane Chesser, a doctor who wrote many popular manuals on mothercraft, told her readers that motherhood combined the twin ideals of personal vocation and racial and national progress.[83] Above all, women who left infant-feeding to the care of a nurse were condemned for their selfishness. During the inter-war years attention shifted from the physical development of both infant and potential mother to the psychological needs of the child, whose satisfaction immediately became part of the prescribed duties of mothers. John Bowlby's theory of maternal deprivation, developed during World War II from the almost exclusive study of children completely separated from their families, proved additionally effective in persuading women to stay at home with their young children.[84]

As Freudian ideas entered the popular discourse (which happened but slowly in Britain), they strengthened the view that biology was destiny and that women who did not find satisfaction in motherhood were in some way abnormal. The crude use made of Freud was exemplified by Leo Abse's condemnation of women politicians as 'aberrant':

> And since anatomy is destiny, is Freud correct in his deductive assertion that the discovery that she is 'castrated' is a turning point in a girl's growth? Are many of our

women politicians the little girls who refused to recognise the unwelcome fact that they lacked a penis and, defiantly rebellious, exaggerated their masculinity. . . ?[85]

The tone and innuendo are strikingly similar to that of Sir Almroth Wright, who opposed women's suffrage in 1913 and who wrote within an entirely different scientific discourse.

During the early twentieth century and increasingly during the inter-war years the ideology of motherhood was reinforced legislatively by the marriage bar, which was applied chiefly to professional women and which served firmly to delineate the world of married women from that of men at a time when it was becoming widely acceptable for single middle class girls and women to go out to work. In teaching, for example, married women were charged with being less efficient than men because of their higher absentee rates caused by pregnancy and by their need to stay at home to look after sick children, the fundamental assumption being that marriage and motherhood were incompatible with a career. The TUC ignored this assumption when it denied that the marriage bar was a sex issue, insisting that it was an employment question, caused entirely by the pressures arising from male unemployment.[86] The 1912 Royal Commission on the Civil Service clearly stated that the responsibilities of married life were incompatible with 'the devotion of a woman's wholetime and unimpaired energy to the public service'.[87] This supposition made the marriage bar popular in the press, and accounted for the weakness of an occupational group such as married women teachers, whose position could not be accounted for in terms of lower levels of skill or poor unionisation. In the course of a debate on a Bill to remove the marriage bar, introduced in 1927, MPs expressed feelings of revulsion at the 'travesty of nature' presented by the image of a working mother and in the last instance a father at home looking after the baby,[88] but the same degree of indignation was never aroused by the work of married women of a lower social class. Marriage bars were not formally dropped until the end of World War II. Even during the war-time emergency itself, women with children under fourteen were never conscripted, and evidence from the Ministry of Labour files suggests that interviewing panels behaved with greater leniency towards those married women who had never worked than towards those (predominantly working class) women who had.[89]

Feminists campaigned against the marriage bar on the grounds that marriage *per se* was not incompatible with work. The 1927 Bill was sponsored by the National Union of Societies for Equal Citizenship (NUSEC), the main organised feminist group of the inter-war years.[90] However, mainstream feminists continued to believe that paid employment *was* incompatible with motherhood. What was new in the feminism of the inter-war years was the emphasis on the needs of mothers as individuals, rather than on social maternalism. In many respects it seemed that feminist aims regarding women's rights in the public sphere had been achieved. Women had the vote, and education and employment opportunities had increased significantly for single women. Thus 'new feminism' as Eleanor Rathbone, President of the NUSEC called it, made a deliberate attempt to promote reforms to improve women's position in the home.

The NUSEC actively campaigned for family allowances and free access to birth control information through local authority clinics: measures designed to further women's economic and sexual autonomy. New feminism stressed the importance of women's role in the home, not to argue the case of female uniqueness and social maternalism, but rather in order to demand reforms that would give the individual mother control over her 'conditions of work' and 'her product'. The only campaign undertaken by mainstream feminists in the late nineteenth century to improve the position of wives was in support of the Married Women's Property Acts, which aided only middle class women. In pursuing the campaign for family allowances (initially intended to provide the mother with a wage as well as allowances for children), mainstream feminists of the inter-war years were picking up one of the major demands of labour women's groups prior to World War I and consciously taking on board social issues of importance to working class women. Indeed, Eleanor Rathbone condemned what she viewed as the selfishness of middle class women who, having got 'all they wanted for themselves out of the women's movement when it gave them the vote, the right to stand for Parliament and the local authorities, and to enter the learned professions', then sat back. Nineteenth-century feminists had adhered too strongly to liberal individualism, and were too suspicious of experts and the state to make demands for an increase in the social wage. For example, Miss Buss, the founder of the North London Collegiate School for girls, deplored women's economic dependency on brothers or a father, but saw no problem in a wife's dependency on her husband.[91] Similarly, while Clara Collet felt that all women should have the means to earn their own living, she did not anticipate that married women would use it.[92] Millicent Fawcett vehemently objected to family allowances becoming a feminist plank and clung to the typically nineteenth-century belief that allowances 'would destroy the fabric of family life by wiping out the responsibility of parents for the maintenance of their children'. (It is interesting to compare Fawcett's position to that of Ramsay MacDonald, whose adherence to patriarchal views within the family surpassed his faith in collectivism in the matter of family allowances; he declared that under socialism the mother and children's right to maintenance would be honoured by the male breadwinner, not the state.[93]) Mainstream nineteenth-century feminism fought for, and in large measure achieved, freedom from legal constraint, but this did nothing to rectify the structural inequalities suffered by women.

The attention new feminists paid to women's needs as mothers represented a shift of emphasis and by no means implied a rejection of the equal rights philosophy. Vera Brittain was very much in sympathy with new feminism and together with Eva Hubback set up fee-paying baby clubs for middle class mothers during the late 1920s, because she recognised the anxieties of women struggling to follow the impossible infant-feeding and training schedules advocated by specialists.[94] But she was also active in the Six Point Group, which continued the traditional campaign for a 'fair field and no favour' for women entering the public sphere. The new priority given to the welfare of individual mothers led to major policy changes, for instance, in the matter of protective legislation. Nineteenth-century feminists had viewed this as an impediment to women's employment and as an extension of a legal framework that denied adult women the freedom to contract.[95] Many feminists, including Millicent Fawcett, who continued to hold this view, left the NUSEC in 1926. As Elizabeth Abbott explained: 'New feminism reads a dictionary definition, equality—sameness; men and women are not the same and therefore are not equal'. In reply, Rathbone argued that such feminists had overlooked the fact that 'some aspects of our whole social fabric [are] man-made through generations to suit masculine interests and glorify masculine standards'. Abbott became one of the founding members of the Open Door Council in 1926, dedicated to securing that 'a woman shall be free to work and be protected as a worker on the same terms as a man. . . and to secure for a woman, irrespective of marriage or childbirth, the right at all times to decide whether or not she shall engage in paid work'.[96]

The position of Rathbone and the NUSEC was potentially more radical than pre-War feminists because they were grappling with two new issues, first, the need to improve women's economic position in the family (earlier feminists had suggested celibacy as the only alternative to 'marriage as a trade'), and second, the necessity to get away from defining equality for women on men's terms. However, after 1918 feminist arguments became less and less distinct. In part this was because feminist energy was increasingly channelled into anti-war and anti-fascist activity. (The Women's World Committee against War and Fascism was formed in 1934.) But more important still was that throughout the period feminists used the same analytical frameworks as anti-feminists.[97] Mainstream nineteenth-century feminists had argued within an individualist framework and had accommodated their ideas to scientific and medical notions of sexual difference. Emily Pfeiffer's case for women's education, for example, was couched in language that would appease social Darwinists. Even a radical writer like Olive Schreiner appealed for women's right to work, since it would in the end prove beneficial for the race, 'parasitical mothers', she argued, produced 'softened sons'.[98] In the years following World War I, Eleanor Rathbone and Eva Hubback shared the general dismay at the decline in the birth rate. (One of the most widely discussed population projections forecast that by the year 2033, the total population of England and Wales would be no larger than that of the County of London in 1934.[99]) Rathbone was happy to use population arguments in her campaign for family allowances and thought it would be an advantage if, through the administration of allowances, the state could put its hand on 'the tiller of maternity'. In the inter-war campaign to improve the position of mothers, feminist arguments were particularly liable to become submerged.

On the whole, feminists throughout the period agreed that women were better suited by nature to home-related tasks than were men. In the nineteenth century, they turned around the idea that women's place was in the home to argue that motherly values should be extended beyond it. Similarly, twentieth-century feminists used the importance attached to motherhood to argue for an economic and sexual independence antithetical to the patriarchal attitudes that lay behind theories of sexual difference and maternalism. It is often hard to discern how far feminist use of essentially anti-feminist arguments reflected their acceptance of them, or how far their use was merely strategic.[100] Even in the recent past, feminists combined support of causes which would today be considered incompatible. For example, Stella Browne, a socialist-feminist of the inter-war period, was also an active eugenicist and supported the idea of compulsory sterilisation. Nevertheless, running through all feminist writing is a fundamental regard for female dignity, development and autonomy. Josephine Butler, who put so much emphasis on the importance of women's domestic virtues, deplored the idea that reproduction alone should be 'the essential aim of [women's] existence', and considered such a position to be contrary to 'the unity of moral law'. Similarly, Eleanor Rathbone demanded reforms that women needed to fulfil the 'potentialities of their own natures'.[101]

Nevertheless, the strength of the separate spheres argument was such that late nineteenth- and early twentieth-century feminists never addressed the fundamental question of sexual divisions; Rathbone made it quite clear that she believed women to be 'the natural custodians of childhood. That at least is part of the traditional role assigned to us by men and one that we have never repudiated'. William Beveridge showed more appreciation of the problems posed by the burden of women's household tasks when he stated that the 'housewife's job, with a large family is frankly impossible and will remain so unless some of what has now to be done separately in every home can be done economically outside the home' (although he never failed to assume that the final responsibility for domestic work rested with women).[102] The few feminists who did consider the problem of women's domestic labour came up with a collectivist solution similar to that of Beveridge.[103] But someone like Vera Brittain was only just beginning to explore the problem of 'how a married woman without being inordinately rich, can have children and yet maintain her intellectual and spiritual independence' in the years following World War I.[104] The small number of married women who pursued an active public life between the wars continued to assume that home and family were part of their natural responsibilities and solved the problem—as women with as diverse political views as Brittain and Violet Markham recognised—through the employment of domestic servants.[105] With the decline of domestic service after World War II, the problem of the sexual division of labour in the home would become a much more acute problem in any reformulation of feminism.

NOTES

1. Patricia Branca, *Silent Sisterhood: Middle Class Women in the Victorian Home* (Croom Helm, 1975), p. 45.
2. Elizabeth Fee, 'The Sexual Politics of Victorian Anthropology', in *Clio's Consciousness Raised*, eds. Lois Banner and Mary Hartman (New York: Harper Torchbooks, 1974), pp. 92 and 101.
3. For a summary of these ideas see J. A. Banks and Olive Banks, *Feminism and Family Planning in Victorian England* (Liverpool: Liverpool University Press, 1964), pp. 58-9. I am indebted to Leonore Davidoff for the final point in the paragraph.
4. Susan Sleeth Mosedale, 'Science Corrupted. Victorian Biologists Consider "The Woman Question"', *Journal of the History of Biology* **11** (Spring 1978), p. 1.
5. Greta Jones, *Social Darwinism and English Thought* (Brighton: Harvester Press, 1980); Rodney Barker, *Politics in Modern Britain* (Longman, 1978); and P. Abrams, *The Origins of British Sociology, 1834-1914* (Chicago: University of Chicago Press, 1968).
6. Quoted in Gregory Anderson, *Victorian Clerks* (Manchester: Manchester University Press, 1976), p. 56.
7. Henry Maudsley, 'Sex in Mind and in Education', *Fortnightly Review* XV, (1874), p. 477.
8. Mosedale, 'Science Corrupted', pp. 6-7; Elizabeth Fee, 'Science and the Woman Problem: Historical Perspective', in *Sex Differences: Social and Biological Perspectives*, ed. M. S. Teitlebaum (Garden City: Anchor, 1976), p. 184; and Brian Eastlea, *Science and Sexual Oppression* (Weidenfield and Nicholson, 1981), pp. 141-2.
9. Carol Dyhouse, 'Social Darwinistic Ideas and the Development of Women's Education in England, 1880-1920', *History of Education* **5** (February 1976), pp. 42-3; and Jill Conway, 'Stereotypes of Femininity in a Theory of Sexual Evolution', in *Suffer and Be Still*, ed. Martha Vicinus (Bloomington: Indiana University Press, 1973), p. 141.
10. Karl Pearson, *The Woman Question* (np, 1885), p. 16.
11. Mosedale, 'Science Corrupted', p. 17; Fee, 'Science and the Woman Problem', and 'Nineteenth Century Craniology: The Study of the Female Skull', *Bulletin of the History of Medicine* **53** (Fall 1979), pp. 415-433; and Janet Sayers, *Biological Politics: Feminist and Anti-Feminist Perspectives* (Tavistock, 1982), p. 86.
12. Quoted in Brian Harrison, *Separate Spheres: the Opposition to Women's Suffrage in Britain* (Croom Helm, 1978), p. 66.
13. Lorna Duffin, 'The Conspicuous Consumptive: Woman as Invalid', in Sara Delamount and Lorna Duffin, *The Nineteenth Century Woman: Her Cultural and*

Physical World (Croom Helm, 1978), p. 35; and Maudsley, 'Sex in Mind', p. 475.

14. Elaine Showalter, 'Victorian Women and Insanity', *Victorian Studies* **23** (Winter 1980), p. 171.
15. Vera Skultans, *Madness and Morals. Ideas on Insanity in the Nineteenth Century* (Routledge & Kegan Paul, 1975), p. 74.
16. Karl Figlio, 'Chlorosis and Chronic Disease in Nineteenth Century Britain: The Social Construction of Somatic Illness in a Capitalist Society', *Social History* **3** (May 1978), pp. 167-197. On the issue of a class differential in diagnosis, see also Duffin, 'The Conspicuous Consumptive', p. 31; and Susan Edwards, *Female Sexuality and the Law* (Oxford; Martin Robertson, 1981), p. 84.
17. Showalter, 'Victorian Women and Insanity', pp. 177-8.
18. Duffin, 'The Conspicuous Consumptive', p. 33; and Jean L'Esperance, 'Doctors and Women in Nineteenth Century Society: Sexuality and Role', in *Health Care and Popular Medicine*, eds. John Woodward and David Richards (Croom Helm, 1977), p. 118.
19. Jacques Donzelot, *The Policing of Families* (Hutchinson, 1977).
20. Frances Power Cobbe, *Life of Frances Power Cobbe*, Vol. I (np. 1894), p. 227.
21. P. A. Ryan, 'The Ideology of Feminism in Britain 1900-1920', unpublished MSc. Diss., University of Wales, 1978, pp. 158-9.
22. Constance Rover, *Love Morals and the Feminists* (Routledge & Kegan Paul, 1970), p. 82; and Judith R. Walkowitz, 'Male Vice and Feminist Virtue: Feminism and the Politics of Prostitution in Nineteenth Century Britain', *History Workshop Journal* **13** (Spring 1982), p. 80.
23. Brian Harrison, 'State Intervention and Moral Reform in Nineteenth Century England', in *Pressure from Without in Early Victorian England*, ed. Patricia Hollis (Arnold, 1974), pp. 289-322.
24. Branca, *Silent Sisterhood*, p. 68.
25. Jane Lewis, *The Politics of Motherhood* (Croom Helm, 1980), pp. 128-9.
26. Sayers, *Biological Politics*, p. 31.
27. Jones, *Social Darwinism*, pp. 143-4.
28. John Stuart Mill, *The Subjection of Women*, 1st edn. 1869 (Cambridge, Mass: MIT Press, 1970), pp. 22-28; and John Charvet, *Feminism* (J. M. Dent, 1982).
29. Susan Moller Okin, *Women in Western Political Thought*, 1st edn. 1979 (Virago, 1980), pp. 227-8.
30. J. E. Butler, *Women's Work and Women's Culture* (MacMillan, 1869), pp. xxv and xxx.
31. The interpretation that follows differs significantly from that offered by Olive Banks, *Faces of Feminism: A Study of Feminism as a Social Movement* (Oxford: Martin Robertson, 1981).
32. Frank K. Prochaska, *Women and Philanthropy in Nineteenth Century England* (Oxford: Clarendon Press, 1980), pp. 7-8.
33. Rosalind Rosenberg, 'In Search of Woman's Nature, 1850-1920', *Feminist Studies* **2** (1974-5), p. 142.
34. Teresa Billington Greig, *The Militant Suffragette Movement* (Frank Palmer, nd), p. 159.
35. Emily Pfeiffer, *Women and Work* (Trubner and Co., 1888), p. 163.
36. Paul Atkinson, 'Fitness, Feminism and Schooling' and Sara Delamont, 'The Contradictions in Ladies Education', in Delamont and Duffin, *The Nineteenth Cen-*

tury Woman, pp. 105–8 and 134–187; and Carol Dyhouse, *Girls Growing Up in Late Victorian and Edwardian England* (Routledge & Kegan Paul, 1981), p. 71.

37. Ray Strachey, *The Cause*, 1st edn. 1928 (Virago, 1978), p. 135.
38. Anna Davin, '"Mind that you do as you are told": Reading Books for Board School Girls', *Feminist Review* **3** (1979), pp. 89-98; Sheila Fletcher, *Feminists and Bureaucrats* (Cambridge: Cambridge University Press, 1980); Felicity Hunt, 'Revolution or Evolution? Unexpected or Not? Another look at middle class girls' education in the Victorian age', paper given to the Feminist History Group, 4 February 1983; and Gillian Sutherland, 'The Social Location of the Movement for Women's Higher Education in England 1840-1880', Paper given to the George Eliot Centennial Conference, Rutgers University, November 1980.
39. Dyhouse, *Girls Growing Up*, pp. 172-3.
40. Beatrice Webb, 'The Lords and the Sweating System', *Nineteenth Century* CLX (June 1980), pp. 885-905.
41. Anne Summers, 'A Home from Home—Women's Philanthropic Work in the Nineteenth Century', in *Fit Work for Women*, ed. Sandra Burman (Croom Helm, 1979), pp. 33-63.
42. Beatrice Webb's Diary, TS, 9 May 1884, 7 August 1885, 12 August 1885, 6 October 1885, BLPES.
43. Helen Bosanquet, *The Standard of Life* (Macmillan, 1898), p. 155.
44. Tricia Davis, Martin Durham, Catherine Hall, Mary Langan and David Sutton, 'The Public Face of Feminism: Early Twentieth Century Writings on Women's Suffrage', in CCS, *Making Histories, Studies in History-Writing and Politics* (Hutchinson, 1982), p. 312.
45. Nancy Boyd, *Josephine Butler, Octavia Hill and Florence Nightingale* (Macmillan, 1982), pp. 64, 68, and 218.
46. E. L. Pugh, 'Florence Nightingale and John Stuart Mill Debate Women's Rights', *Journal of British Studies* XXI (Spring 1982), p. 120.
47. Marianne Farningham, *A Working Woman's Life* (James Clarke, 1907), p. 141.
48. PP., 'Survey of Relief to Widows and Children', Cmd. 744, 1920, XXXVII, 129, p. 9; and E. M. Ross, 'Women and Poor Law Administration 1857-1909', unpublished M.A. Diss., LSE, 1956, p. 212.
49. R. G. Walton, *Women in Social Work* (Routledge & Kegan Paul, 1975), pp. 30–31; and Ross, 'Women and Poor Law Administration', p. 225.
50. Papers of the Women's Local Government Society, Box 92, Fawcett Library, City of London Polytechnic.
51. Patricia Hollis, 'Women in Local Government 1865-1914', unpublished paper, 1982. This paper is part of a larger study to be published by the Oxford University Press.
52. Farningham, *A Working Woman's Life*, pp. 96–8; and Margaret Wynne Nevinson, *Life's Fitful Fever* (A & C Black, 1926), p. 169.
53. Mary Stocks, *My Commonplace Book* (Peter Davies, 1970), p. 58; and V. R. Markham, *Return Passage* (Oxford: Oxford University Press, 1953), p. 63.
54. Ross, 'Women and Poor Law Administration', p. 225; and Margaret Llewellyn Davies ed., *Life as We Have Known It*, 1st edn. 1931 (Virago, 1977), pp. 130–4.
55. Mrs. Henry Fawcett, *Home and Politics* (Women's Printing Society, 1894), p. 3.
56. Lee Holcombe, *Wives and Property. Reform of the Married Women's Property Law in*

Nineteenth Century England (Toronto: University of Toronto Press, 1983), p. 212; and Andrew Rosen, *Rise Up, Women!* (Routledge & Kegan Paul, 1974), pp. 10 and 17.

57. Quoted in Harrison, *Separate Spheres*, p. 116. (The 'Appeal' was published in *Nineteenth Century*, June 1889, p. 781.)

58. A. V. Dicey, *Letters to a Friend on Votes for Women* (John Murray, 1909), p. 75; Francis Latham, *Thirty Reasons Why the Enfranchisement of Women is Undesirable* (Simpkin, Marshall, Hamilton, Kent and Co., 1875).

59. Markham, *Return Passage*, p. 103; Harold Owen, *Women Adrift: The Menace of Suffragism* (Stanley Paul and Co., 1912), p. 247; Sir Almroth E. Wright, *The Unexpurgated Case Against Women's Suffrage* (Constable, 1913), p. 71; Rosen, *Rise Up, Women!*, pp. 139–40; and Belfort Bax, *The Fraud of Feminism* (Grant Richards, 1913), p. 142.

60. Harrison, *Separate Spheres*, p. 84; and Beatrice Webb's Diary, TS, 29 June 1889.

61. Albie Sachs, 'The Myth of Male Protectiveness and the Legal Subordination of Women: An Historical Analysis', in *Women Sexuality and Social Control*, eds. Carol and Barry Smart (Routledge & Kegan Paul, 1974), p. 34.

62. Ryan, 'The Ideology of Feminism', p. 236.

63. Martin Pugh, 'Politicians and the Women's Vote, 1914–18', *History* **59** (1974), p. 372.

64. Havelock Ellis, *The Task of Social Hygiene* (Constable, 1912), p. 46.

65. Michael Freeden, *The New Liberalism: An Ideology of Social Reform* (Oxford: Clarendon, 1978); and Stefan Collini, *Liberalism and Sociology: L. T. Hobhouse and Political Argument in England 1880-1914* (Cambridge: Cambridge University Press, 1979).

66. Jones, *Social Darwinism*, p. 180; Sayers, *Biological Politics*, p. 38; Fee, 'Science and the Woman Problem', pp. 206–220.

67. Rosaleen Love, '"Alice in Eugenics Land": Feminism and Eugenics in the Scientific Careers of Alice Lee and Ethel Elderton', *Annals of Science* **36** (1979), pp. 145–158.

68. Francis Galton, *Hereditary Genius*, 1st edn. 1869 (MacMillan, 1914); on eugenics see Lyndsay Andrew Farrall, 'The Origins and Growth of the English Eugenics Movement, 1865-1925', unpublished PhD. Diss., Indiana University, 1970; G. R. Searle, *Eugenics and Politics in Britain 1900-14* (Leyden: Noordhoft Internat. Pub., 1976); Charles Webster ed., *Biology and Medicine* (Cambridge: Cambridge University Press, 1981), pp. 1-13; 212-288.

69. Sayers, *Biological Politics*, pp. 16–17.

70. Banks and Banks, *Feminism and Family Planning*, p. 105; Dyhouse, *Girls Growing Up*, p. 157; and Walton, *Women in Social Work*, p. 189.

71. Rover, *Love, Morals and the Feminists*, p. 135.

72. Grant Allan, 'Plain Words on the Woman Question', *Fortnightly Review* CCLXXIV (October 1889), p. 452; Sheila Rowbotham and Jeffrey Weeks, *Socialism and the New Life: The Personal and Sexual Politics of Edward Carpenter and Havelock Ellis* (Pluto, 1977), pp. 171-3.

73. Patrick Geddes and J. Arthur Thompson, *Sex* (Williams and Norgate, 1914), p. 244. On Geddes and Thompson generally see, Conway, 'Stereotypes of Femininity'; and Flavia Alaya, 'Victorian Science and the "Genius" of Woman', *Journal of the History of Ideas* **38** (April-June, 1977), pp. 261-280.

74. Geddes and Thompson, *Sex*, p. 236.
75. Ellen Key, *The Woman Movement* (G. P. Putnams, 1912), pp. 32 and 171.
76. Mary Scharlieb, *Womanhood and Race Regeneration* (Cassell, 1912), p. 19.
77. Carol Dyhouse, 'Good Wives and Little Mothers: Social Anxieties and the Schoolgirls' Curriculum, 1890-1920', *Oxford Review of Education* 3 (1977), p. 25.
78. Lewis, *Politics of Motherhood*, pp. 93-4; and Jane Marcus ed., *The Young Rebecca: Writings of Rebecca West 1911-17* (Virago, 1983), pp. 38-9.
79. Board of Education, *Report of the Consultative Committee on the Differentiation of the Curriculum for Boys and Girls Respectively in Secondary Schools* (HMSO, 1923), pp. xiii, 74 and 86.
80. Fee, 'Science and the Woman Problem', p. 218; Dyhouse, 'Social Darwinistic Ideas', p. 45; Arabella Kennealy, *Feminism and Sex Extinction* (T. Fisher Unwin, 1920).
81. Miriam E. David, *The State, the Family and Education* (Routledge & Kegan Paul, 1980), p. 197.
82. Pauline Marks, 'Femininity in the Classroom: An Account of Changing Attitudes', in *The Rights and Wrongs of Women*, eds. Juliet Mitchell and Ann Oakley (Harmondsworth: Penguin, 1976), p. 183.
83. Elizabeth Sloane Chesser, *Woman, Marriage and Motherhood* (Cassell, 1913)
84. Susan Isaacs, *The Nursery Years* (Routledge & Kegan Paul, 1929), and *The First Two Years* (University of London Institute of Education and the Home and School Council of Great Britain, 1937); on Bowlby: Denise Riley, 'War in the Nursery', *Feminist Review* No. 2 (1979), pp. 82-108; and Simon Yudkin and Anthea Holme, *Working Mothers and their Children* (Michael Joseph, 1963), pp. 83-5.
85. Leo Abse, *Private Member* (Macdonald, 1973), p. 175.
86. TUC, *The Employment of Married Women* (TUC, 1922).
87. Hilda Martindale, *Women Servants of the State, 1870-1938* (Allen and Unwin, 1938), pp. 147 and 149.
88. House of Commons Debates, 1927, 205, c. 1175.
89. Margaret Allen, 'Women's Place and World War II', unpublished M.A. Diss., University of Essex, 1979, p. 49; see also, 'The Domestic Ideal and the Mobilisation of Woman Power in World War Two', *Women's Studies International Forum* **6** (1983).
90. On NUSEC, Eleanor Rathbone and feminism in the inter-war period, see Jane Lewis, 'Beyond Suffrage: English Feminism in the 1920s', *The Maryland Historian* VI (Spring, 1975), pp. 1-17.
91. Dyhouse, *Girls Growing Up*, p. 145.
92. Clara Collet, *Educated Working Women* (P. S. King, 1902), pp. 122 and 143.
93. Hilary Land, 'The Family Wage', *Feminist Review* No. 6 (1980), p. 75.
94. Lewis, *Politics of Motherhood*, p. 102.
95. Josephine Butler *et. al.*, *Legislative Restrictions on the Industry of Women from the Woman's Point of View* (np, 1872), p. 7.
96. Open Door Council, *Report of a Conference held in Berlin, 1929* (ODC, 1929), p. 1.
97. Ruth First and Ann Scott, *Olive Schreiner: A Biography* (André Deutsch, 1980), p. 284, make a similar point.
98. Olive Schreiner, *Woman and Labour*, 1st edn. 1911 (Virago, 1978), p. 109.
99. Enid Charles, *The Twilight of Parenthood* (Watts and Co., 1934).

100. This issue is discussed by Delamont and Duffin, *The Nineteenth Century Woman*, p. 127; and First and Scott, *Olive Schreiner*, p. 284.
101. Butler *et. al.*, *Legislative Restrictions*, p. 18; and Eleanor Rathbone, *Milestones: Presidential Addresses at the Annual Council Meetings of the NUSEC* (NUSEC, 1929), p. 28.
102. William Beveridge, *Voluntary Action* (Allen and Unwin, 1948), p. 264. I owe this point to discussions with Hilary Land.
103. C. P. Gilman, *Women and Economics*. 1st edn. 1896 (New York: Harper Torchbooks, 1966); leaders of the Women's Labour League also proposed communal facilities for cooking and washing etc., see Caroline Rowan, 'Women in the Labour Party, 1906–20', *Feminist Review* No. 12 (1982), pp. 83–4.
104. Tricia Davis *et. al.*, 'The Public Face of Feminism', p. 323.
105. See Vera Brittain's comments through her heroine Ruth Alleyndene in her novel *Honourable Estate* (MacMillan, 1936), p. 513; Markham, *Return Passage*, p. 32.

Homes and Husbands

The home was the centre of the middle class woman's world and she bore sole responsibility for its management. The interests and concerns of middle class husbands and wives were on the whole profoundly different. In the Victorian country gentleman's house, husbands, wives, servants and guests were spatially segregated. The breakfast- or morning-room served as the ladies' sitting-room and the drawing-room was also a female room where ladies received calls and took tea, while the library, study and billiard-room were all male territory.[1] Not only were the worlds of Victorian husband and wife separate, they were also profoundly unequal, for the majority of middle class wives were financially dependent on their husbands and not infrequently subject to their husband's will. Victorian and Edwardian fathers were known to go to some lengths to ensure that their daughters did not cross the prescribed boundaries between public and private spheres. Mr Jex Blake, for example, did not mind his daughter Sophia (a pioneer of medical education for women) accepting a job to teach mathematics at Queen's College until he discovered that she was to be paid, whereupon he offered to increase her allowance by the amount she would have earned if she refused the salary.[2] Similar patriarchal behaviour was often exhibited by Victorian and Edwardian husbands, although this is not to say that marriages necessarily lacked affection; patriarchal behaviour is incompatible with autonomy, but not with love. The domination of the Victorian husband was reflected in law (especially in property law) and in emotional and sexual relations. While Victorian women were supposed to be passive and pure, Victorian men were excused the odd moral lapse on the grounds that it was a natural result of their virility. But by the mid-twentieth century, husband/wife relationships had changed profoundly both in law and in practice.

THE WORK OF THE MIDDLE CLASS WIFE AND MOTHER

Housekeeping

The vast majority of middle class Victorian women led a generally isolated and limited existence within a tightly knit family circle. Indeed, both popular and 'highbrow' literature often made it hard to visualise the woman as having an identity separate from her home. As early as 1875, Dr Andrew Wynter was commenting on the problem of alcoholism among housebound wives. He speculated that the railway was in part to blame, for 'whilst our residences were in town, they [women] always had that intensely feminine refreshment, shopping, to solve their ennui',[3] but when the workplace became separate from the home during the early part of the century, wives and daughters began to experience the isolation of suburban life. The problem may well have become more widespread among middle class women by the end of the inter-war period, as more of them experienced the profound contrast between the life of a 'working girl' and that of a suburban housewife.

It is difficult to build an accurate picture of what middle class women did in their homes. The image of the perfect Victorian lady, to all intents and purposes decorative and idle, has been fractured by Branca's consideration of the attention to household budgeting and routine demanded of the large numbers of middle class wives responsible for making ends meet on between £100 and £300 a year.[4] In such circumstances the sewing machine might have been as important to the middle class housewife as to the working class homeworker. Ideally the middle class wife concerned herself with the moral training of her children and with the 'accomplishments' that both rendered her a person of culture and refinement and signalled her husband's standing in the community. Such wives provided agreeable 'society' to their husbands, but not necessarily companionship. Mrs Lynn Lynton complained throughout the 1880s and 1890s that wives would let housework go undone rather than do it themselves. While those with a strong sense of duty and those on small budgets were undoubtedly ready to attend personally to domestic details, much was sacrificed, even in less well-off households, to provide the domestic help necessary to achieve a certain degree of gentility. Gwen Raverat, whose American mother raised her to value independence in a manner unusual for the 1880s and 1890s, recalled that it still did not occur to her when first married that 'I could possibly be the cook myself or that I could care of my baby alone, though we were not at all well off at that time'.[5]

The Victorian home symbolised stability, peace and order. The cult of domesticity stressed the sanctity of the home as a refuge from the rapid economic, political and social change outside and from the competitive values of the market-place. Whether actively engaged on household tasks, confined to the ladylike pursuits of needlework and piano, or pressed by a sense of duty to charitable endeavours, the middle class wife was responsible for the machinery that ensured the smooth running of the household. As Deborah Gorham has remarked, women also had to find ways to make good any discrepancy between the family's material wealth and the social status to which it aspired. This was particularly important in respect to the 'new rich'.[6] The wives and daughters of old established families zealously guarded the boundaries between different sources of wealth. The *Lady's Companion* in 1900 commented on the elaborate rituals of 'calling' and 'card leaving' thus:

> Society men will fraternise with the millionaire and ignore his misplaced 'h's' and the absence of good breeding while they drink his wine, but the wives and daughters of those men will not visit his wives and daughters, nor receive them in their own houses if they lack refinement and culture.[7]

The middle class woman's role as the guardian of gentility might be compared to that of the wife of the labour aristocrat, responsible for protecting the family's respectability. Many families attempted to carry on the social rituals of visiting and holding 'At Homes' through the 1920s, despite the increased cost of domestic servants and the general decline in formal social life of this kind. Even Beatrice Webb, who deplored the social snobbery that she observed developing in her sister Kate after her marriage, nevertheless felt it necessary to create a London club for the wives of Labour Party MPs, although she never succeeded in making them either socially acceptable or powerful in the manner achieved by a Margot Asquith.[8] Petty snobberies, particularly in regard to whom children were allowed to mix with, were jealously guarded by middle class wives long after 'gentility' had ceased to be common currency.[9]

As far as budgets permitted, careful ritual was also a part of the internal routine of the middle class household. Many articulate Victorian women, feminist and non-feminist alike, wrote in diaries and novels of feeling stifled by 'gentility' and 'ladyhood'. To Octavia Hill, a pillar of the Charity Organisation Society and a pioneer housing manager, the word 'lady' conjured up all the things she despised and hated: 'first and most universally it suggests want of perseverance and bending small obstacles, a continual "I would if..."'. Florence Nightingale commented on the fate of middle class wives and daughters constantly condemned to doing 'a bit of this and a bit of that'. In her experience many would willingly have broken a leg for the peace and quiet that would have resulted. Any serious outside interest was incompatible with the rituals of 'calling' and what the novelist Elizabeth Robins referred to as the 'sacred rite' of dinner.[10] Only with hindsight is it possible to see that the rituals condemned by articulate women as 'meaningless femininity' were in fact not without purpose in terms of social gatekeeping.

H. M. Swanwick, an active suffragist, recalled what going to Girton represented in this context: 'To have a study of my own and to be told that, if I chose to put "Engaged" on the door, no one would so much as knock was itself so great a privilege as to hinder me from sleep'. As Nightingale perceived, the normal expectation was that middle class women would organise their lives around those of their husbands and families.[11] The image of Mrs Gladstone is typical: 'shaking her husband free of his overcoat as he mounted another platform, two more sentences and he is fairly launched upon a sea of passion, regardless of Mrs G who sits behind, placidly folding her husband's overcoat'. Such was many women's ignorance of the world beyond the home that leading female anti-suffragists found themselves quite unable to organise meetings in support of their cause; one titled lady could not differentiate between minutes and agenda.[12]

Women's household responsibilities were nevertheless substantial. According to Mrs Eliza Warren, author of the popular manual *How I Managed my House on Two Hundred Pounds a Year*, the days of the wife at the lower end of the middle class earnings' hierarchy were filled with housework, washing, cooking, quarrels with the maid, crying children and financial problems.[13] This bears close resemblance to the anguished cries of the middle class (male) editorial correspondents during the inter-war period: 'My wife goes "sticking"—That saves the expense of firewood. Our holidays are generally imaginary. That saves too... Also my wife murders her eyes with sewing, sewing, sewing'.[14] At the other end of the middle class spectrum, Violet Markham discovered how time-consuming the supervision of a large household (where expenditures totalled £2,500-£3,000 per year) could be when she took over the running of her family home for seven years on the death of her mother in 1912. Her mother had imposed a strict routine, with carefully detailed and timed descriptions of the daily and weekly work for each of the nine servants, and had kept minute accounts. When writing about the public duties she undertook during the inter-war years, Markham had no doubt that some domestic help was essential, but felt that the supervision of the staff in her family home had proved itself to be a full-time job.[15]

It is possible that the modern suburban house of the inter-war years, better equipped with labour-saving devices, with either a resident servant or a daily help, and a smaller number of children, provided middle class women with more leisure than either the large household staffs of the Victorian period or the usually servantless home of the post-World War II years,[16] but there are two caveats to this argument. First, there are signs that relations between the mistress and her live-in maid substantially deteriorated during this period, creating considerable tensions. E. M. Delafield provided a portrait of a woman 'ruled by her servants':

> Gladys was twenty-six and Laura thirty-four. Gladys was the servant of Laura, paid to work for her. She had been at Applecourt only six months, and it was highly improbable that she would remain for another six. Nevertheless, it was Gladys who, in their daily interviews, was entirely at her ease and Laura who was nervous.

Virginia Woolf also confided to her diary for 1930 her sense of liberation at having decided to do without servants.[17] The essential problem was that the distancing mechanisms which made it possible for two social classes to live under the same roof were beginning to break down during the inter-war years. Many working class girls were still schooled in obedience and domestic tasks by their mothers and accepted the inevitability of a job as a domestic servant, but an increasing number rejected the cap and apron as 'the badge of servitude', and maintenance of the strict segregation of servant from employer was difficult in the relatively small middle class villas of the period.[18] An Oxford woman graduate who took a series of jobs as a domestic during the 1930s, so as to become better acquainted with the 'servant problem', concluded that the gulf between classes was such that friendly, informal cooperation between mistress and maid was impossible. She considered that the only solution was for the mistress either to employ a middle class girl as a live-in help, or to engage a working class girl on strictly business terms and give her enough freedom to build a life of her own outside.[19]

Secondly a very high standard of housekeeping was expected during the inter-war years. This was reflected by the winning entries in the *Our Homes and Gardens* competition to provide '... an account of how they run, or would run, a servantless house for a middle class family'. The winner considered herself lucky to live in a house built in 1912 so that there was no hearth-stoning to do at the entrance; she also owned a vacuum cleaner, cinder sifter and other appliances. But her gas stove still required a thin coating of oil (a labour-saving alternative to black lead), and she felt that it was necessary to mop daily and dust pictures and skirtings, electric light fixtures and cupboard tops thoroughly once a week. *Good Housekeeping* called housewives 'The craft workers of today', and the editor was particularly pleased to find that no fewer than one half of the magazine's respondents made rather than bought their underwear.[20] Such elaborate household routines and tasks helped fill the day of the ordinary middle class housewife, who often had few outside interests beyond a trip to the library (usually to Boot's or W. H. Smith's—which demanded a weekly subscription—rather than to the public library). Household manuals of the inter-war years stressed the importance of housewives examining the methods they employed and planning their work. Ruth Binnie and Julia Boxall advised housewives to apply the principles of scientific management used by industry, including time and motion studies, to increase their efficiency.[21]

The encouragement given to middle class wives during the inter-war years to devote more time to both housewifery and child care marked a departure from the ambivalent nineteenth-century attitudes regarding the degree of personal involvement in domestic tasks compatible with cultured, ladylike behaviour. The changes brought new stresses, however, particularly in respect to the higher standard of child care that was demanded. Child psychologists, active in the new child study movement, and infant feeding experts both emphasised the importance of elaborate routines and schedules to build the child's character. For one woman, the conscientious attempt to follow the instructions of the child care expert of the inter-war years, Sir Frederick Truby King, regarding feeding schedules, resulted in 'a month of untold agony' for both her and her baby daughter.[22] The isolation of many middle class women made such anxieties difficult to bear. Indeed, during the 1930s evidence began to suggest that depression or 'suburban neurosis' among suburban women (including working class women on the new council estates) might be as prevalent as neurasthenia and hysteria had been in the nineteenth century.[23].

Childbirth, Contraception and Health Status

The vast majority of women no matter what their material circumstances, were, in the nineteenth century at least, condemned to frequent childbirth. Middle class couples began to limit their families in the 1860s, but whether at the behest of husband or wife is a matter for debate. Patricia Branca maintains that middle class women were asserting control over their lives both by seeking the assistance of doctors and by deciding to use birth control, but just as it is impossible to separate women's increasing resort to doctors from the attitudes and ambitions of the medical profession, so it is impossible to wrench women free from their economic and sexual dependency when considering birth control. J. A. Banks has argued strongly that the lead in fertility control was taken by men in professional occupations, who were concerned not about the burden of child*bearing* but about the cost of child*rearing*.[24] Moreover, it is unlikely that the middle class woman would have been able to procure birth control literature of her own volition, as all aspects of sexuality were taboo topics for the late nineteenth- and early twentieth-century middle class woman. (Not even feminists made access to birth control information an issue before World War I.) The situation began to change during the inter-war years, when Marie Stopes' flowery prose and emphasis on 'married love' made the idea of sexual pleasure as well as birth control more acceptable. But during the 1930s the *Lady's Companion* was still routinely refusing to give readers any advice on sexual problems, despite its declaration that 'marriage is the one metier of life and most of us aim at it. Not with the idea of having a home of our own, or of having a companion, but simply for the one truth for which marriage stands'.[25]

Nor was the middle class woman's ready access to a physician likely to be of use in the search for birth control information. Many doctors believed, well into the inter-war period, that birth control led to serious illness. C. H. F. Routh's 1879 list of diseases that might result from the use of contraception included galloping cancer, sterility, mania leading to suicide and, last but not least, nymphomania.[26] Even during the 1920s those few family doctors who would talk to patients about birth control preferred to talk to the husband. It was also unlikely that the middle class wife would be able to consistently employ any method of artificial contraception without her husband's knowledge and consent. Thus, as in the case of the working class wife, fertility control amongst the middle class undoubtedly required at least the cooperation of the husband.

Childbirth was as painful and dangerous for middle class as for working class women, and must have provided wives with a strong incentive to try and limit their families. Queen Victoria could not have been alone in her famous wish not be the 'maman d'une nombreuse famille'. As late as 1932, only 60 per cent of maternity patients at London's Royal Free Hospital received some form of pain relief. During the nineteenth century, middle class mothers generally gained no more protection against septic infection from the attendance of doctors than working class women did from midwives, and during the early twentieth century the private nursing homes favoured by the middle class tended to have the worst mortality records of all. In 1931 the maternal mortality rate in middle class Chelsea was 5.4 per 1000, while in working class Hackney it was 3.2.[27]

Carol Smith Rosenberg has suggested that the tensions produced by the effort to achieve a style of life congruent with ideas of gentility, while at the same time running a household and undergoing frequent childbirth, may explain the large numbers of nineteenth century women diagnosed as hysterics. She suggests that hysteria became a form of escape for middle class women: in adopting the sick role they were able to abrogate their domestic responsibilities, moreover, because doctors declared their condition to be the natural result of female physiological weakness, their behaviour was socially acceptable.[28] It is possible then that the expectation of female ill-health became a self-fulfilling prophecy. The high incidence of female invalidism in the nineteenth century is certainly striking. Emily Davies remarked: 'It is a rare thing to meet with a lady of any age who does not suffer from headaches, languor, hysteria, or some ailment showing want of stamina'.[29] She attributed the problem to the dullness of ladies' lives, but this would not account for the frequent illnesses of Josephine Butler, Octavia Hill, or Olive Schreiner. For some women—Florence Nightingale was one—illness was undoubtedly used as an excuse not to be disturbed. But a large proportion of the physical and mental distress experienced by women probably arose from a conflict between their role prescriptions and the realities of their lives, or from boredom, or from the many disabling illnesses caused by pregnancy and parturition. Whatever the precise cause of invalidism among nineteenth-century middle class women, there is less reference to the 'ailing woman on the sofa' in twentieth-century literature. This may have been a function of middle class women's increased access to medical care, which must have paid dividends as medical knowledge advanced. But it also reflected the dramatic change in lifestyle which middle class women experienced and which had no parallel among their working class counterparts.

During the Victorian period even girls and young women seemed to suffer disproportionately from ill-health. The scanty statistics pertaining to the mortality experience of middle class girls indicate that it was unfavourable compared to that of boys in the mid-nineteenth century, with tuberculosis regularly striking more females than males until the 1880s,[30] a reflection at least in part, of their lifestyle. Subjected to tight-lacing, confined indoors, lacking fresh air or exercise, and, even in prosperous families, often given less food than their brothers, girls and young women certainly led less healthy lives than the men in their families. While Edward Shorter maintains that only 5 per cent of women used tight-lacing and that the practice was in any case innocuous, Mel Davies has suggested that it led to such health problems as distortion of the uterus and amenorrhea. (These in turn may have led either to sexual abstinence or a decreased likelihood of conception, which may help to explain the declining birth rate.) Towards the end of the nineteenth century the ratio of waistline to body height began to show a steady increase and more active leisure pursuits started to become possible for middle class girls and women.[31] In this connection many autobiographies mention the bicycling craze of the mid- and late 1890s. Ray Strachey refers to the bicycle as providing both 'the exquisite pleasure of rapid motion' and the not inconsiderable advantage of permitting women to go as far as six or seven miles from home quite unaccompanied. At the new girls' schools more attention was paid to exercise, Most introduced Swedish drill, while some permitted team games. Winifred Peck, who attended Wycombe Abbey, remembered her hockey dress of short tunic, baggy bloomers and tam o'shanter, which to her represented the long overdue 'freedom and glory' to 'scamper' about 'on an equality' with her brothers.[32]

HUSBANDS AND WIVES

The Legal Framework

In the nineteenth century married women had no legal personality and hence no capacity to enter into contracts in the market-place. The legal doctrine of *couveture*, which stated that husband and wife were as one and that one was the husband, was described clearly in Sir William Blackstone's famous eighteenth-century *Commentaries on the Laws of England*: 'The very being or legal existence of the wife is suspended during the marriage or at least incorporated and consolidated into that of the husband under whose wing, protection and cover she performs everything'.[33] Until 1925 a husband was held responsible for any criminal act committed by his wife in his presence. *Couveture* was popularly regarded by lawyers as providing women with a favoured and protected status. But the doctrine was also the result of married women's total economic dependency, which made the denial of autonomy logical. In respect to voting, for example, women's interests were considered to be the same as those of their husbands. Thus while the nineteenth-century liberal political tradition talked of individuals as the basic units of the political system, it in fact referred only to the voting rights exercised by male heads of families.[34]

The doctrine of *couveture* continued to be defended well into the twentieth century. During the course of the Parliamentary debate over the 1925 Guardianship of Infants Act, which gave women equal guardianship rights over their children, one MP declared:

> The English law, both Common law and Equity, says if two people live together, as you cannot run a home by a committee of two, one of them must have the deciding voice, and I think with wisdom it gives the husband a deciding voice. He has more

experience of the world. In nine cases out of ten he makes the money which keeps the home going, and as he pays he certainly ought to have a commanding voice in the decisions which are come to.[35]

Nevertheless, by the late 1930s women had achieved full rights over their property, legal personality (although aspects of women's legal subordination to their husbands remained), and political citizenship. Moreover, the basis of what was popularly considered ideal marriage had changed profoundly from patriarchy to companionship.

In return for her husband's protection and maintenance, the Victorian wife was bound to provide him with household and sexual services and the pleasure of her society. These obligations were legally designated the husband's right to his wife's *consortium* and meant in effect that the wife was physically tied to the home and that her energies and time were at her husband's disposal. A husband could sue anyone who deprived him of his wife's *consortium*; an 1861 case decided that it was possible to estimate the monetary value of a wife's services and thus to decide the amount of damages due the husband. The husband's right to forcibly detain his wife in order to exact services from her was not called into question until the Jackson case of 1891.[36] Mrs Jackson had gone to live with relatives during the absence of her husband in New Zealand, and refused to rejoin her husband on his return. Mr Jackson proceeded to abduct his wife outside the church one Sunday morning. His lawyers quoted the ancient dicta that the husband had a right to imprison and beat his wife 'but not in a violent or cruel manner', which the Appeal Judge, Lord Halsbury, deplored, commenting that such ideas were 'tainted' with the idea of 'the absolute dominion of the husband over the wife' and were marked 'by the absence of a due sense of delicacy and respect due to a wife whom the husband has sworn to cherish and respect'. Perceiving that Jackson's defence was out of tune with most late Victorian middle class expectations regarding marital relations, the court ruled that he was not entitled to keep his wife in confinement in order to enforce the restitution of conjugal rights, although this did nothing to change the fact that a husband could not be guilty of rape within marriage. Press and popular opinion was by no means unanimous in supporting the decision: *The Times* declared that 'one fine morning last month marriage in England was suddenly abolished', and Mrs Jackson was booed and jostled on her return to her relatives.[37]

Wives had little redress if husbands refused to fulfil their side of the marriage bargain. A husband's withdrawal of maintenance and protection did not provide grounds for divorce (under the heading of desertion) until 1937. A husband could remove himself and the children of the marriage, being their sole guardian in law until the Act of 1925. If he made no financial provision for his wife in his absence her only recourse was to 'pledge his credit', which was legally permissible as long as she confined her expenses to a level compatible with her husband's accustomed style and social status. In doing this, the wife was held to be acting as his agent and was not liable for the debts she incurred. The husband could always put a stop to his wife's agency, and even when he did not do so, the wife's position was by no means without difficulty. In a 1906 court case it was held that a trader could not plead hardship if a woman pledged her husband's credit while she was in fact acting on her own behalf, because traders did not have to give women credit at all. There was no requirement that

> she should communicate to the person with whom she is dealing the fact that she is her husband's agent, or state that she is not acting on her own behalf, or declare that she is married and cohabiting with her husband, or confess that she has not a sixpence in the world which she can really call her own. It can hardly be expected that such domestic confidences should be whispered across the counter or imparted to some forewoman in the comparative privacy of an inner apartment.[38]

While the courts thus proved to be more sensible to the delicate position of the middle class woman than they were in respect to the working class wife's dealings with the 'scotch hawker',[39] the ruling meant that retailers ran considerable risk in extending women credit. This, together with the humiliation the woman risked on her side if questioned about her circumstances, made the right to pledge a husband's credit (not abolished until 1970) a doubtful security.

The doctrine of *couveture* also determined that on marriage women lost control of whatever property they might have to their husbands. Under common law all the wife's personal property in the form of earnings and personal effects belonged to her husband and she was unable to dispose of any freehold or copyhold land she possessed without her husband's consent. During the 1860s and 1870s feminists campaigned with the support of the National Association for the Promotion of Social Science (NAP/SS) and legal reformers for the Married Women's Property Acts. An 1870 Act gave women control of their earnings and therefore benefited primarily working class women, while a further Act in 1882 gave the married woman control over any wealth she might acquire (for instance by inheritance or gift), though her liability in respect to her property was restricted to a proprietary rather than a personal one. This meant that her ability to sue and contract was confined to her own separate property, and not until 1935 did married women gain the same rights and responsibilities with respect to their property as single women. Millicent Garrett Fawcett claimed that her own support for the Married Women's Property Acts dated from the time her purse was stolen and the thief was charged with 'stealing from the person of Millicent Fawcett a purse containing £1 18s 6d, the property of Henry Fawcett', which she said made her feel as though she had been charged with the theft herself. In keeping with their liberal individualist philosophy, nineteenth-century feminists wanted to achieve a formal equality of rights between men and women in the matter of property ownership. But such a demand would have secured economic independence to only that minority of middle class women who inherited substantial amounts of property in their own right. More positive measures to secure an income for wives by means of 'mothers' endowment' or family allowances, or by giving wives a statutory percentage of the husband's wage, were not suggested until the early twentieth century.

Nor is it clear that the 1882 Married Women's Property Act constituted a milestone in the passing of patriarchal society as has been claimed.[40] Rather, as was perceived by politicians at the time, it represented an extension to the middle class of the advantages of settling 'separate property' on daughters, which rich families had always accomplished—at considerable cost—through the law of equity. Such settlements were of primary benefit to the wife's kin group, and because of the danger that a wife might nevertheless be 'kicked or kissed' out of the property by her husband, the terms of settlement often included a clause requiring 'restraint on anticipation', which allowed her to enjoy whatever income could be derived from the property but which prevented her from exercising full powers of alienation over it. Thus the settlement was designed to protect the family capital from the incursions of both husband and wife. Like the common law, equity deemed women to be in need of protection. The Married Women's Property Acts did not stop the use of equity, and 'restraint on anticipation' continued to be used until it was partially abandoned in 1935 (existing restraints were not abolished until 1949), by which time changes in the nature of wealth had rendered it increasingly archaic. Nevertheless, one extensive commentary on the 1935 Act condemned its abolition, believing that it resulted from 'some fanciful notions that all distinctions between men's property and women's property ought to be abolished'.[41]

The Married Women's Property Acts were thus justified as an extension and perpetuation of an ancient right and served to remove the discrepancy between the provision the upper and middle classes were able to make for their daughters. Any idea that the Acts constituted a revolutionary change in family life and the law was refuted, and proponents of the legislation went to some lengths to deny that it would in any way upset the balance of relations between husband and wife. The NAPSS always spoke in favour of the idea that the husband made the final decisions. In debates about married women's property during the 1870s, politicians showed themselves to be concerned above all about the authority of the husband. Conservative MPs in particular refused to contemplate going beyond the 1870 Act; as Priscilla Bright McLaren observed in 1880, husbands could not bear the thought of wives having property and therefore power.[42] The Married Women's Property Bill introduced in 1870 by Russell Gurney would have given married women the legal status of single women, but it was radically altered during its passage through the House of Lords. Beneath the opposition to increasing women's economic independence lurked the fear that it might lead to greater sexual freedom. Lord Penzance hinted at this in his speech against the 1870 Bill: 'A husband who expected his wife to keep his home and attend to the children might find her opening a Berlin wool shop with her cousin John as partner'.[43]

Feminists continued to promote the principle of separate property as a means of achieving equal property rights, but separate property did little to correct the imbalance caused by men's superior earning power, which allowed them to accumulate more property in the first place. The NAPSS recognised the conflict between the doctrine of separate property and the reality of married women's economic dependence, and was careful to stress that 'we think nothing should be done to weaken in the public mind the conviction that a husband is bound to labour for the support of his wife'. After all, 'the husband from his sex, from his strength, from the habits of society, has means of earning a livelihood which are not open to the wife'.[44]

Married women's economic dependency became more problematic as a result of liberalisation of the divorce laws in 1937 (when desertion became grounds for divorce) and the increase in home ownership after World War I. Separated women who tried to assert their right to stay in the matrimonial home found that it was usually registered in the husband's name and that they had no claim to it. In addition any savings that wives made by virtue of careful household management were not covered by the Married Women's Property Acts and therefore were the property of their husbands. Thus in 1943 Mrs Blackwell, who took in paying guests to help pay the mortgage and who was always careful to leave her dividend to accumulate at the Cooperative Society shop, lost the £103 she had managed to accumulate to her husband on the breakdown of her marriage. The Appeal Court Judge ruled that she had used her husband's beds for lodgers and that in saving the money she must therefore have been acting as her husband's agent rather than on her own account. One judge added his opinion that if wives were permitted to save out of housekeeping monies they might be tempted to give their husbands tinned rather than roast meat.[45]

The legal problems posed by disputes over matrimonial property and savings led one lawyer, Otto Kahn Freund, to argue throughout the 1950s against the system of separate property. He recognised that when both working class and middle class incomes (of male breadwinners) began to yield a surplus for saving, the concept of equality inherent in separate property became inadequate. Savings and the acquisition of a home and furniture usually depended on both the husband's industry and the (house) wife's thrift; it was therefore unfair that they should belong in law to the husband alone. Kahn Freund believed that the kind of partnership conceived of by Beveridge in his social insurance programme of 1942 provided a better solution: 'The law of social security, like the law of maintenance is more realistic than the law of property, account is being taken in these branches of law of the existence of the household as an economic unit and of the *natural inequalities in the economic functions of husband and wife*' [my italics]. Interestingly, like Beveridge, Kahn

Freund did not foresee any great change in the labour participation rate of women. Not that this invalidated his observation.[46] The problem lay, however, in reaching an assessment of the material worth of the respective contributions of husband and wife. During the 1950s Edith Summerskill opposed any further liberalisation in the divorce law unless adequate economic protection was assured to wives, for in practice the wife's contribution tended to be grossly undervalued. Other feminist critics of Beveridge's proposals also pointed out that the restructuring of the law to take account of married women's economic dependency would serve to reinforce that dependency.[47]

Nineteenth-century feminists had believed that the removal of legal disabilities would be sufficient to ensure sexual equality, but in the absence of any change in the fundamental separation of spheres between men and women, the courts tended to assess women's claims on the basis of their behaviour as wives and mothers. In divorce cases, for example, the question of the wife's guilt in bringing about the breakdown of the marriage was always considered in arriving at maintenance awards and the share of the marital home due the wife. Some members of the legal profession also tended to take an unfavourable view of the wife if she appeared as the petitioner (which increasing numbers did after the major extension of legal aid in 1949), maintaining that having chosen to forfeit the marital bond, a woman must also have forfeited all claims against her husband.[48] As a result of the strengthening ideology of motherhood during the early twentieth century, and the perceived 'naturalness' of the mother-child relationship, women were increasingly given custody of their children. As Carol Smart and Julia Brophy have pointed out, while married women's rights have appeared to increase at the expense of men's, they have in fact also depended on a normative evaluation of their adequacy as wives and mothers.[49]

Sexual Relations

There was often little communication between husbands and wives and as little interest in each other's worlds. Violet Markham's father's diary for the day she was born read: 'Driving. Rosa had a little girl. 31½ brace of grouse and 2 rabbits'. In her novel *Honourable Estate* (1936) Vera Brittain illustrated what she regarded as the old and new types of marriage. Janet and Thomas Rutherston represented the old pattern: Thomas is a domineering, selfish clergyman, who allows his wife no personal freedom and condemns her to frequent childbearing. The son Denis consciously works to create an equal partnership with his wife Ruth, who goes so far as to retain her career as well as her independent spirit after marriage. Thomas Rutherston's crude domination may not have been typical, though the fact that he and his wife had so little in common probably was.[50] The relationship between Katherine Chorley's parents in pre-World War I Manchester was affectionate, but they lived entirely separate lives. Her father expected his wife to stay at home and provide 'comfort and inspiration and cleansing and rest' when he returned each day from his business. Katherine Chorley marvelled that her mother managed to converse with her father about the day's events, so completely separate were their worlds.

The great strength of Victorian women was supposed to be the 'influence' they wielded, but in many cases this can have amounted to little more than highly developed wheedling tactics. Many women must have developed a persona in dealing with their husbands that differed substantially from their true selves. Clara Collet hinted at this when she wrote:

> They [women] have a magnificent power of self-deception, of persuading themselves that they think and believe the things which those they care about think and believe—they are so little encouraged to think for themselves that many a woman, married when but a girl, has later on discovered that she has a character of her own, hitherto unrevealed to herself and unsuspected by her husband.[51]

Most late Victorian middle class women did not receive a good enough education to converse with their husbands as equals. They were usually educated at home, perhaps spending a few years in a private school. Gwen Raverat remembered that in her school the emphasis 'was all on young ladyhood, slightly tinged with Christianity'.[52] In the typically small and homely private school (of which there were an estimated 10,000-15,000 in 1895), girls were taught 'accomplishments' (for example, French and music), in a family atmosphere which fostered dependence. The more fashionable the private school, the more it resembled a closely knit family. Only the new girls' schools taught a range of examinable academic subjects.[53] The socialisation of middle class girls was thus profoundly different from that of their brothers, who would have attended public or private schools as day boys or boarders, as a matter of course. Eric Trudgill has drawn a biting picture of the Victorian middle class wife as 'a mental and moral cripple', both angel of the house and idiot.[54] Men sought women's society but not their companionship, and indeed the more 'womanly' the woman the more bored the husband was likely to become and the more time he was likely to spend away from home, often at his club or in the company of women who were considerably less pure though possibly more interesting. In the early part of the period expectations of marriage were such that most wives would have accepted the remoteness and separateness of married life as normal and even desirable. Where mutual respect rather than male domination was the hallmark of the relationship there is in fact no reason why such 'separate marriages' should not have worked well, or why we should necessarily consider them in some way inferior to the modern ideal of 'togetherness'.

Female Sexuality During the late nineteenth century many husbands and wives must have met in the marriage bed as two separate races, a state of affairs that had changed considerably by the outbreak of World War II. Victorian male and female ideas about sexuality were also markedly different from those of the years following World War I. One influential strand of medical opinion told Victorian women that they had no sexual identity. William Acton believed that 'Love of home, children and domestic duties, are the only passions they [women] feel. As a general rule, a modest woman seldom desires any sexual gratification for herself. She submits to her husband, but only to please him. . .'[55] The denial of sexuality in children was so complete that the rape of a girl child was considered to be of much less importance than the same crime against an adult. Victorian women were revered for their passivity, innocence and purity, even though the fear of the disruptive potential of female sexuality clearly showed in the Parliamentary debates on adultery during the passing of the 1857 Divorce Act, and again during the debates on the Married Women's Property Acts.[56] It was innocence of sexual feeling that was believed to keep women pure; the innocent woman had no knowledge of her body and remained childlike. For many writers, the ideal marriage seemed to consist of a benevolently paternal relationship where the husband's role (and age) approximated to that of a father. Many educated women married men older than themselves, for example, Mary Paly, one of Newnham's first students, married the anti-feminist economist Alfred Marshall. Such women devoted themselves to helping their husbands with their work as well as, in the case of Mrs Marshall, teaching female students 'political economy from a philanthropic woman's point of view'. Edward Benson, the future Archbishop of Canterbury, revealed in his diary at the age of 23 his love for Mary Sidgwick, then 12, who later became his wife.[57] The insistence on women's childlike qualities was double-edged, for implicit within it was the notion that women were less completely evolved and more likely to do wrong. They were therefore considered to be in need of protection, whether in respect to their property or their sexuality. Lombroso and Ferreo's influential theory of female criminality posited that because women were less evolved than men, the unprotected woman-child could easily turn into a prostitute.[58] This association of criminality in woman with deviant sexual behaviour has persisted.

The burden of innocence and purity was vested in young women. The passionate reaction to H. G. Wells' novel *Ann Veronica* (1909), in which the heroine goes to live with a married man, showed the fear of women's sexual freedom. St Loe Strachey wrote of the book: 'The loathing and indignation which the book inspires in us are due to the effect it is likely to have in undermining the sense of continence and self-control in the individual which is essential to a sound and healthy state'.[59] If women lost their innocence, then they became potential seducers. As Susan Edwards has pointed out, the model of female precipitation that has always informed procedural rules and juridicial precedent in cases of rape and prostitution stands in sharp contrast to the way in which statute law assumes women to be passive.[60] Women were not held to be legally capable of committing either rape or homosexual offences until the 1930s. Thus women were counted both less responsible than men—their childlike qualities made it impossible to invest them with any responsibility for voting, for example—and more responsible. As the moral guardians of the home they were considered to bear responsibility for male sexual behaviour and for imparting a high moral standard of behaviour to society as a whole.[61]

It is difficult to establish how far women internalised the ideal of innocence and asexuality. From a rare contemporary survey of American college women during the 1890s, Carl Degler has suggested that women actively enjoyed sex. Patricia Branca has also suggested that Victorian prudery 'served only to control the behaviour of the young during the long period between puberty and marriage [at an average age of 25]', and speculates that there were no barriers to sexual activity within marriage. Moreover, she argues that by the 1870s younger women were exploring their sexuality, wearing stockings approaching flesh colour, dainty boots, narrow waisted gowns and even cosmetics.[62] But this is not sufficient evidence of a firm sense of sexual identity. Many feminists of the period would have felt that such behaviour was only to be expected of women pursuing marriage as a means to financial security.

Women's statements on sexuality reveal a variety of attitudes. Very few women were prepared to discuss publicly the idea of sexual pleasure. The radical early twentieth-century journal the *Freewoman* did so and also included articles on menstruation and lesbianism. At the other end of the spectrum were those who were prepared to admit that they hated the idea of sex. H. M. Swanwick found that her mother's refusal to talk about sexuality made her very shy and she began to find 'the notion of any sex-element in a girl and boy relationship . . . repellent'; similarly, Constance Maynard found the idea of sex frightening and repugnant. Theresa Billington-Grieg was repulsed more by the experience of her mother, who suffered four miscarriages and whom Theresa believed was 'crushed' and 'thwarted' by her father, whose frequent love affairs flaunted 'the invincibility of her moral standards'.[63]

Sexual passions tended to be viewed as both sinful and as having more to do with the animal kingdom than with human society. Herbert Spencer certainly believed the sex instinct to be a 'lower passion' that should be controlled. William Acton, a physician, counselled continence in men, and, of course, the desexualisation of women aided this idea. Nevertheless, male virility could not be denied and within evolutionary thought was believed to be crucial to the progress of race and nation.[64] The early twentieth-century pamphlet *Rovering to Success*, which sold 200,000 copies, instructed Boy Scouts that they could successfully negotiate the 'rutting season' without loss of semen if they bathed their 'racial organ' in cold water daily.[65] Lack of sexual control, like lack of order and stability, was usually associated with working class behaviour. The experiences recorded in a collection such as the Women's Cooperative Guild's letters on maternity only seemed to confirm to many middle class commentators the brutality of working class sex lives.[66]

Yet women did not simply internalise the doctrine of passionlessness. Florence Nightingale declared that neither women's passions, nor their need for intellectual activity, had ever been satisfied, and Beatrice Webb also acknowledged the power of 'physical instinct and craving for satisfaction' after the end of her relationship with Chamberlain.[67] It is almost too easy to see the ideal of duty and service in women like Beatrice Webb as a sublimation of other desires including the sexual.[68] Women were certainly encouraged to think of their role in the family and the wider community as more spiritual than that of men and were expected to act as moral preceptor to their families.[69] Many women—Josephine Butler is an outstanding example—took their spiritual role and duties extremely seriously, but this does not mean that their lives were necessarily devoid of sexual passion. Constance Maynard, for example, did not marry, but while at Girton formed a passionate attachment to Louisa Lumsden, who called Constance 'her wife'. The private world of married and unmarried women of the late nineteenth and early twentieth centuries permitted a wide variety of emotional behaviour between women who were often also deeply religious, religious and emotional passion often merging in such relationships. As Martha Vicinus has commented in the case of Constance Maynard, 'Since she could not give up earthly love, she reinterpreted it as a sign of God's love. She justified her passionate and deeply disturbing love life as a form of spiritual searching. Duty and need were collapsed into one'.[70] Such friendships between women were not regarded as being in any way sinister or 'deviant' until the inter-war years. Parliament attempted to bring lesbianism within the scope of the criminal law for the first time in 1921, and in 1928 Raclyffe Hall's new novel, *The Well of Loneliness*, which defended female emotional and sexual relationships, was judged obscene by the courts. By the 1930s, the often emotionally intense female networks and support systems taken for granted by nineteenth-century women were no longer possible.

Some women openly acknowledged the existence of a female sexual instinct, but only as an impulse to maternity. Dr Elizabeth Blackwell wrote of the

> power of sexual passion in women . . . the compound faculty of sex is as strong in woman as in man. Those who deny sexual feeling to women, or consider it so light a thing as hardly to be taken into account in social arrangements, quite lose sight of this immense spiritual force of attraction, which is distinctly human sexual power.

Like Ellen Key, Blackwell's main theme was that women should not be denied true fulfilment through motherhood: 'The impulse towards maternity is an inexorable but beneficient law of women's nature, and it is a law of sex'.[71]

This theme became more general as increasing importance was attached to motherhood. Dr Elizabeth Chesser believed that 'the longing of every normal woman to find happiness in sex union and to exercise her functions physically and psychically in marriage and motherhood is an ineradicable instinct'.[72] Havelock Ellis firmly rejected Acton's denial of female sexuality, but stressed both that the chief justification of sexual activity was procreation and that in women there existed a biological imperative to motherhood. Ellis still believed that female sexuality was essentially passive and that sexual activity had to be initiated by the male: the woman 'must be kissed into a woman'. Like Ellis, Olive Schreiner, a more radical feminist and one of the 'new women' of the 1890s, recognised women's sexual feelings, but remained suspicious of sensuality, tending to conflate sex for reproduction with sex for pleasure, and sensuality with the portrayal of women as sex objects. Schreiner was not in favour of celibacy, but opposed non-monogamous sex and considered *The Freewoman* positively licentious. Mona Caird also confessed her late nineteenth-century attack on marriage with an attack on sexuality.[73]

Moral Standards As both Ellen Dubois and Linda Gordon have suggested, the difficulty women experience in drawing a boundary between sex as pleasure and sex as danger remains,[74] but whereas today's discussion centres on the issues of rape and pornography, nineteenth-century women—both feminists and non-feminists—were concerned about the double moral standard and prostitution. Articulate nineteenth-century women demanded a higher, single moral standard, based on that of women, as a means to equality for women, a higher standard of home life and social purity. The crusade for a single moral standard attracted a coalition of feminists, philanthropists, religious leaders and social purity campaigners, just as today the anti-pornography campaign attracts people from across the political spectrum. The main targets of the nineteenth-century campaign mounted by middle class women were first, non-reproductive sex, which involved opposition to artificial birth control, and second, non-marital sex, embodying a campaign against prostitution and in favour of an equal divorce law.

As Judith Walkowitz has argued, this meant that feminists ignored the issue of women's sexuality,[75] but the ideological and economic constraints within which they worked need to be understood. Elizabeth Blackwell, who vehemently opposed birth control, wrote: 'The very grave national danger of teaching men to repudiate fatherhood and welcoming women to despise motherhood and shrink from the trouble involved in the bearing and nurturing of children, demands the most serious consideration'.[76] She was in favour of sex education but, like most feminists prior to World War I, feared that birth control would allow men to indulge their greater sensuality. As Linda Gordon and Angus McLaren have pointed out, feminists were in favour of 'voluntary motherhood', meaning in practice the right to abstain, but feared that artificial contraception would give men greater sexual licence.[77] When it is remembered that women were dependent on their husbands for financial and emotional security, their opposition to artificial contraception is more readily understood.

Similarly, neither feminists nor non-feminists were generally in favour of liberalisation of the divorce law. When women campaigned for a single moral standard at the time of the 1913 Royal Commission on Divorce, they demanded 'levelling up' in order to raise men's moral standards; thus Mrs Fawcett opposed any extension of the grounds for divorce other than for permanent separation or wilful desertion.[78] An equal divorce law that involved 'levelling down' was passed in 1923, but no reform of the grounds for divorce was achieved until 1937, when most feminists supported A. P. Herbert's Bill which extended the grounds from simple adultery to desertion, cruelty and insanity. Herbert called his measure a Marriage Bill and by publicising the hypocrisy of carefully staged hotel scenes designed to provide the evidence needed for a divorce on the grounds of adultery, managed to convince public opinion that reform would in fact protect the institution of marriage.[79] When Leo Abse raised the issue of further liberalisation in the 1950s, however, feminist opposition was again substantial. Edith Summerskill and Helena Normanton of the Married Women's Association (which was divided over the issue) opposed the legislation, mainly because they were worried about the financial implications for economically dependent wives.[80] Again, women had material cause to defend the integrity of the family unit.

The largest campaign against non-marital sex was fought during the late nineteenth century on the issue of prostitution. The image of desexualised womanhood inevitably implied the existence of prostitutes. In his *History of European Morals* (1869), W. E. H. Lecky expressed the famous opinion that the prostitute was 'the most efficient guardian of virtue', without whom the 'purity' of happy homes would be polluted. If men wandered it was usually attributed to women's failure to create a satisfying home environment and to the failure of their redemptive powers.[81] The double moral standard was often explicitly articulated in the nineteenth century. The 1871 Royal Commission on the Contagious Diseases Acts stated that 'with one sex the offence [prostitution] is committed as a matter of gain, with the other it is an irregular indulgence of a natural impulse'. The view that on 'social considerations' the adultery of wives would always be a more serious matter than the infidelity of husbands was widely accepted. Josephine Butler was particularly incensed by the case of an unmarried mother in the Butlers' home town of Oxford, who had been imprisoned in Newgate for the murder of her child, while the father had resumed academic life at the University.[82]

To the middle class woman, prostitution represented a threat to the integrity of home life that was undoubtedly compounded by feelings of humiliation at her husband's liaison with a (usually) working class woman. Middle class Victorian men were fascinated by working class female sexuality. The example of the anonymous author of *My Secret Life* avidly exploring a world of accessible servants and prostitutes is well known.[83] Josephine Butler's campaign against the Contagious Diseases Acts was based on the notion that there should be but one, high moral standard for men and women. In common with many social reform issues of the late nineteenth century, the campaigns against the CD Acts and prostitution were pursued as a moral crusade rather than as a social issue. Housing reform was also promoted in part as a means to achieving greater social modesty among the poor, and education was seen as a cure for drunkenness and profligate habits. Similarly, the slippage between social and moral categories in Booth's empirical investigation of late nineteenth-century poverty is well-documented.[84] In respect to Butler's campaign, it is notable that she showed no interest in the means of preventing or curing venereal disease (which the Acts sought to control by the compulsory medical inspection of prostitutes), firmly believed that health would only follow upon self-control and a higher moral standard.

Women's claim to lead a moral crusade was founded on a belief in the 'natural' concern with home and family, and in their greater spirituality and higher morality. Women of Butler's Ladies' National Association (LNA), formed in 1869 to fight for the repeal of the CD Acts, not only believed that prostitution sullied all relationships between men and women, but also saw prostitutes as the victims of male lust and deplored the way in which they were further subjected to forcible examination by male doctors. LNA members often referred to 'the slavery of men's lust' and 'instrumental rape' in their speeches and sympathised with rather than condemned the prostitute.[85] The feminism of the LNA derived from their belief in women's domestic mission and distinguished Butler's campaign against the Acts from that of other 'social purity' groups. Josephine Butler quoted the moving and arresting statement of a Kent prostitute to illustrate women's lack of autonomy:

> It is men, only men, from the first to the last, that we have to do with! To please a man I did wrong at first, than I was flung about, from man to man. Men police lay hands on us. By men we are examined, handled, doctored and messed on with. In the hospital it is a man again who makes prayers and reads the Bible for us. We are up before magistrates who are men, and we never get out of the hands of men.[86]

It is doubtful whether Butler fully understood the way in which the lives of working class women prostitutes were structured. As Walkowitz has pointed out, her sympathy was based primarily on a libertarian defence of individual rights (which was in keeping with the nineteenth-century feminist's general suspicion of state interference) and on a sense of the prostitute as victim. The fact that the middle class repealers did not consign working class women prostitutes to the semi-vicious and criminal residuum, as did social investigators such as Booth, was important, and their support undoubtedly enabled prostitutes to better resist the police. However, the idea of the prostitute as victim entailed a denial of first, the prostitute's social and cultural existence, often as a member of an urban subculture; second, the role that prostitution sometimes played as seasonal employment for poor women; and third, the prostitute's sexuality. Failure to consider the last was particularly evident in the early twentieth-century panics over 'white slavery', when it was clear that in most cases the prostitutes themselves were upset by the conditions (rather than the fact) of the commercial sex they had experienced in continental Europe.[87]

The identification of the prostitute as a victim also logically resulted in a call for their protection. In the campaign against the CD Acts the LNA made a point of appealing to respectable working class men to come to the defence of their wives and daughters. After the repeal of the CD Acts, a Criminal Law Amendment Act was passed in 1885, which while raising the age of consent for girls to sixteen, also gave the police greater summary jurisdiction over brothel-keepers, effectively destroying the brothel as a family concern and forcing more prostitutes into the hands of pimps.[88] The tendency for protection to result effectively in the greater control of women increased during the remainder of the nineteenth and early twentieth centuries. As with the campaign for family allowances, the feminist impulse behind the moral crusade was unable to control the direction of the campaign, which shifted to emphasising the demand for increased state regulation put forward by social purity groups. This does not mean that feminists were altogether opposed to the new focus. Indeed, even the position of Josephine Butler herself is unclear, for while she opposed greater state regulation, she shared the social purity movement's suspicion of sexuality and its emphasis on the need to protect women and girls against male lust, in order to achieve a higher standard of morality in society.[89] Late nineteenth-century social purity campaigners such as Ellice Hopkins continued to use one of the major tactics of the LNA by enlisting the support of working and lower middle class men though the formation of a White Cross League, whose members pledged to treat all women with respect, to protect them from wrong and degradation and to keep themselves pure.[90] A majority of feminists and anti-feminists agreed that the physical expression of sexuality was a lower animal passion that should be controlled in civilised society. To the leading nineteenth-century social purity society, the National Vigilance Association, formed in 1885, pornography and advertisments for abortificaients were all undifferentiated expressions of male lust.

During the early twentieth century attention focused on venereal disease, which was discussed openly for the first time, as a problem affecting the civilian population. Social purity advocates viewed VD as a threat to the stability of the family and the race, transmitted primarily not through the prostitute, but by the 'amateur' who engaged in promiscuous sexual activity.[91]

Many feminists were also concerned about the issue of racial health, and cooperated in the control of young women's morals by joining volunteer police units during World War I. Thus the VD 'panic' of the early twentieth century brought together a coalition of interests opposed to extra-marital sex. Some social purity advocates also continued to oppose prophylaxis in the treatment of VD, preferring to rely solely on a moral education strategy; venereal disease was, after all, the wages of sin and it was the sin, not its results, that required eradication. The sex education favoured by social purity groups, eugenicists and many feminists (including, for example, Elizabeth Blackwell) was extremely repressive and designed above all to instil fear of the consequences of illicit sex, especially in women. During the inter-war years, the British Social Hygiene Council (founded in 1916 as the National Council for Combatting Venereal Disease) produced films with names like 'The End of the Road', 'The Flaw', 'Damaged Goods', 'Marriage Forbidden', and 'The Girl who Doesn't Know'. In 'The End of the Road' all the women except the heroine came to a bad end and all the VD victims were women.[92] During the early twentieth century feminists such as Christabel Pankhurst and Cicely Hamilton openly warned of the dangers of VD, linking their arguments to the need for women to be able to earn a livelihood other than by marriage. Both clearly implied that the risks of innocent women becoming infected by their husbands were so great that women's only safe course was sexual abstinence. Christabel went so far as to allege in 1913 that 75 to 80 per cent of men were infected with VD. After this, the Women's Social and Political Union's campaign for the vote increasingly took on the characteristics of a moral crusade, promising that with the suffrage women could oppose the three evils of sweating, prostitution and white slavery, and sexual attacks on little girls. Christabel insisted that there could be 'no meeting between the spiritual woman of this new day and men, who in thought or conduct with regards to sex matters are their inferiors'.[93] Her puritanism has been both condemned as inimical to women's struggle to develop a sexual identity, and trivialised,[94] but her response must be located in the context of a male-dominated society which consistently denigrated women. The idea of votes for women constantly met with scorn and laughter inside as well as outside Parliament and, despite a powerful ideology of motherhood, pregnant women were made to feel embarrassed and ashamed to the point where many refused to venture outside except under cover of darkness.[95]

Towards Companionship in Marriage The alliance between social purity campaigners and feminists weakened significantly during the inter-war years. Above all, feminists changed their views on non-reproductive sex, campaigning for greater access to birth control and becoming increasingly attracted to the possibility of a greater marital equality whereby sexual pleasure, as well as employment opportunities and interests outside the home, might be more equally distributed. Vera Brittain had no doubt that this was due to the changes wrought by World War I, which in terms of social behaviour were probably more radical for middle class than for working class women. No longer chaperoned and often with some form of military service—usually as nurses— behind them, women were, according to Brittain,

> sophisticated to an extent which was revolutionary compared with the romantic ignorance of 1914. Where we had once spoken with polite evasion of a "certain condition", of a "certain profession", we now unblushingly used the words "pregnant" and "prostitution". Amongst our friends, we discussed sodomy and lesbianism with as little hesitation as we compared the merits of different contraceptives and were theoretically familiar with varieties of homosexuality and VD of which the very existence was unknown to our grandparents.

Alison Nielans, the Secretary of the Association for Moral and Social Hygiene, agreed, noting in addition that 'the old ideals of chastity and self-control were for many lost'.[96] Katherine Chorley also commented at length on the disappearance of sexual taboos during the war, although her parents continued to exercise absolute control over her life until she married in the early 1920s.

During the War it briefly looked as though women were actually being encouraged to shed older moral values, as pleas were made for sympathy and understanding to be extended to 'war babies' and their unmarried mothers. After the war, sex was relocated firmly within marriage. Very few people—Dora Russell was one—had the temerity to call for complete sexual freedom for women. Irene Clephane went so far as to suggest that an affair might give 'new colour to life', but more usual among the population at large was the vague feeling that marital sex might not, after all, be either a sin or something to fear.[97] In the wake of increased anxieties about the implications that small families and a rising divorce rate were having for the stability of the family, more attention was paid to ways of achieving greater companionship between husbands and wives, and, in particular, to sexual compatibility. David Glass's 1934 assessment was typical: 'If the one- or two-child family becomes common, some new relationship or, rather, some new adjustment of the old relationship will be necessary to maintain its integrity'. In his view, the rise in the divorce rate showed that the required adjustment had not been made. During the 1930s radical ideas regarding marriage, such as those of the American, Judge Ben Lindsey, attracted serious comment. Lindsey advocated 'companionate marriage', which he defined as legal marriage with legalised birth control and the right to divorce by mutual consent for childless couples, usually without alimony.[98] The ideas of the sexual reformers who met in Congress during the inter-war period (the first World Congress on Sexual Reform was held in 1921 and the World League for Sexual Reform was established in 1928),[99] and of Freud regarding the centrality of the sex act, became more popular in a diluted form. For example, *Good Housekeeping* commented in 1938:

> Freud, whether right or wrong, did succeed in convincing them [women] that they had sex desires and that these desires were not wicked; that to repress them was as difficult and dangerous to women as to men, and that they need no longer pretend that all they wanted was at most motherhood, when it was quite as natural for them to want loverhood.[100]

Evidence from 200 letters written by middle class women to Marie Stopes between 1918 and 1939 revealed that women still regarded themselves (as did Stopes) as the passive partner, but were on the whole dissatisfied and disappointed by their sex lives. Ellen Holtzman has suggested that the resemblance between Stopes' and her correspondents' vocabulary especially regarding orgasm (which Stopes referred to as 'the wonderful tides'), probably indicates that women's sexual expectations were raised during this period. Ironically, as Jeffrey Weeks has noted, the new emphasis on sexual satisfaction, intended to provide greater marital satisfaction, in fact made the possibility of separation (on grounds of sexual incompatibility) more likely.[101] In this social climate, the concerns of the purity campaigners and the women who supported them, such as Margaret Wynn Nevinson, who dismissed Freud's ideas as 'unclean', appeared ever more anachronistic.[102] In 1927 and 1928 the National Vigilance Association mounted a large campaign against the advertisements for Kotex sanitary towels that had begun to appear in the major daily newspapers and women's magazines. Full-page advertisements featuring a picture of two women with a woman doctor and listing the product's advantages as: 'no laundering [prior to this period sanitary towels were home-made], utter protection and non-detectable and easy to buy anywhere (in plain wrappers)', under such titles as 'Now Science Solves Women's Oldest Problem' and 'A Great Hygienic Handicap your Daughter will be Spared', were condemned as 'blatantly immodest'.[103] Similarly, the arguments of Helena Normanton and Edith Summerskill against further liberalisation of the divorce laws were much more out of step with the drift of public opinion than had been Millicent Fawcett's 1912 stand.

By World War II, both the prescribed roles and the reality of married middle class women's experience had changed, and the changes within marriage were more dramatic than for working class women. Middle class married women were no longer assumed to be passive, weak and 'naturally' inferior, although men remained very much the dominant partners. Within marriage they had greater mobility, more legal freedom and probably increased expectations of sexual pleasure. Nevertheless, the strict separation of spheres was staunchly defended and any change such as reform of the legal position of married women, the vote, or the abolition of the marriage bar, all of which threatened to blur the boundaries between spheres was resisted. In general, women's education remained inferior to men's and they also remained largely excluded from the male world of leisure (particularly male clubs) and public office, as well as paid employment. The problems of the middle class housewife, made known by Betty Friedan during the 1960s, were already extant by the inter-war years.

NOTES

1. Jill Franklin, *The Gentleman's Country House and its Plan, 1835-1914* (Routledge & Kegan Paul, 1981), pp. 39–48.
2. E. Moberly Bell, *Storming the Citadel. The Rise of the Woman Doctor* (Constable, 1953), p. 65.
3. Vera Skultans, *Madness and Morals. Ideas on Insanity in the Nineteenth Century* (Routledge & Kegan Paul, 1975), pp. 235–6.
4. Patricia Branca, *Silent Sisterhood. Middle Class Women in the Victorian Home* (Croom Helm, 1975), pp. 40–45.
5. Gwen Raverat, *Period Piece: A Cambridge Childhood* (Faber, 1952), p. 48. On the ideal role of the middle class wife and mother, see J. A. Banks, *Prosperity and Parenthood* (Routledge & Kegan Paul, 1954); and J. A. Banks and Olive Banks, *Feminism and Family Planning in Victorian England* (Liverpool: Liverpool University Press, 1964).
6. Deborah Gorham, *The Victorian Girl and the Feminine Ideal* (Croom Helm, 1982), p. 8. See also Joan N. Burstyn, *Victorian Education and the Ideal of Womanhood* (Croom Helm, 1980); Eric Trudgill, *Madonnas and Magdalens. The Origins and Development of Victorian Sexual Attitudes* (Heinemann, 1976), pp. 39–47; and, most important, Leonore Davidoff, *The Best Circles* (Croom Helm, 1973).
7. Cynthia L. White, *Women's Magazines 1693-1968* (Michael Joseph, 1970), p. 79.
8. Davidoff, *The Best Circles*, pp. 70 and 88–9.
9. Raphael Samuel, 'The Middle Classes between the Wars, Pts. I and II', *New Socialist* **10** (January/February 1983), pp. 30–6, and (March/April 1983), pp. 28–32.
10. Nancy Boyd, *Josephine Butler, Octavia Hill and Florence Nightingale* (MacMillan, 1982), p. 104; and Elizabeth Robbins, *The Convert*, 1st edn. 1907 (Women's Press, 1980), p. 168.
11. H. M. Swanwick, *I Have Been Young* (Gollancz, 1935), p. 118; Florence Nightingale, 'Cassandra', in *The Cause* by Ray Strachey, 1st edn. 1928 (Virago, 1978), Appendix, pp. 395–418.
12. Brian Harrison, *Separate Spheres: The Opposition to Women's Suffrage in Britain* (Croom Helm, 1978), pp. 69 and 113.
13. Branca, *Silent Sisterhood*, p. 13.
14. R. Lewis and A. Maude, *The English Middle Class* (Phoenix House, 1949), p. 78.
15. Violet R. Markham, *Return Passage* (Oxford: Oxford University Press, 1953), p. 26.
16. Albie Sachs, 'The Myth of Male Protectiveness and the Legal Subordination of

Women: An Historical Analysis', in *Women Sexuality and Social Control*, eds. Carol and Barry Smart (Routledge & Kegan Paul, 1978), p. 39 suggests this.

17. Nicola Beauman, *A Very Great Profession. The Woman's Novel, 1914-39* (Virago, 1983), pp. 96-7 and 108.
18. Jean Rennie, *Every Other Sunday: The Autobiography of a Kitchen Maid* (Arthur Baker, 1955), p. 20; and Pam Taylor, 'Daughters and Mothers—Maids and Mistresses: Domestic Service between the Wars', in *Working Class Culture*, eds. John Clarke, Chas Critcher, and Richard Johnson (Hutchinson, 1979), pp. 121-139.
19. C. Fremlin, *The Seven Chars of Chelsea* (Methuen, 1940, p. 158.
20. Beaumann, *A Very Great Profession*, p. 110; White, *Women's Magazines*, p. 103.
21. R. Binnie and J. E. Boxall, *Housecraft, Principles and Practice* (Pitman and Sons, 1926), pp. 198-203.
22. Christina Hardyment, *Dream Babies. Child Care from Locke to Spock* (Cape, 1983); and John and Elizabeth Newson, 'Cultural Aspects of Childrearing', in *The Integration of a Child into a Social World*, ed. Martin P. M. Richards (Cambridge: Cambridge University Press, 1974), p. 62.
23. Stephen Taylor, 'The Suburban Neurosis', *Lancet*, 26 March 1938, p. 759; see also the comment in one of the major World War II planning reports: PP., 'Report of the Royal Commission on the Distribution of the Industrial Population', Cmd. 6153, 1939–40, IV, 263, p. 49.
24. Branca, *Silent Sisterhood*; and J. A. Banks, *Victorian Values. Secularism and the Size of Families* (Routledge & Kegan Paul, 1981), p. 73.
25. Marie Stopes, *Married Love* (New York: Critic and Guide, 1918); and White, *Women's Magazines*, p. 111.
26. Trudgill, *Madonnas and Magdalens*, p. 69.
27. Jane Lewis, *The Politics of Motherhood* (Croom Helm, 1980), pp. 38, 129, 134.
28. Carol Smith Rosenberg, 'The Hysterical Woman: Sex Roles and Conflict in Nineteenth Century America', *Social Research* **39** (1972), pp. 652-678.
29. A. J. Hammerton, *Emigrant Gentlewomen: Genteel Poverty and Female Emigration, 1830-1914* (Croom Helm, 1979), p. 21.
30. Sheila Ryan Johansson, 'Sex and Death in Victorian England' in *A Widening Sphere*, ed. Martha Vicinus (Bloomington: Indiana University Press, 1978), pp. 163–181.
31. Edward Shorter, *A History of Women's Bodies* (New York: Basic Books, 1982), pp. 28-30; and Mel Davies, 'Corsets and Conception: Fashion and Demographic Trends in the Nineteenth Century', *Comparative Studies in Society and History* 24 (October 1982), pp. 611–41.
32. Strachey, *The Cause*, p. 387; David Rubinstein, 'Cycling in the 1890s', *Victorian Studies* **21** (Autumn 1977), p. 47-71; and Winnifred Peck, *A Little Learning* (Faber, 1952), p. 122.
33. Leonore Davidoff, 'The Employment of Married Women in England 1850–1950', unpublished M.A. Diss., LSE, 1956, p. 70 note 1. The material in this section draws heavily on PP., 'Report of the Committee on One-Parent Families', Cmnd. 5629-I, 1974, XVI, 1113, Appendix 5; R. H. Graveson and F. R. Crane eds., *A Century of Family Law* (Sweet and Maxwell, 1957); Lee Holcombe, *Wives and Property. Reform of the Married Women's Property Law in Nineteenth Century England* (Toronto: University of Toronto Press, 1983); O. R.

McGregor, Louis Blom Cooper and Colin Gibson, *Separate Spouses* (Duckworth, 1970); Albie Sachs and Joan Hoff Wilson, *Sexism and the Law* (Oxford: Martin Robertson, 1978); and Erna Reiss, *The Rights and Duties of Englishwomen* (Manchester: Sherrat and Hughes, 1934).

34. Susan Moller Okin, *Women in Western Political Thought*, 1st edn. 1979 (Virago, 1980), p. 202.
35. Davidoff, 'Employment of Married Women', p. 105 note.
36. The Queen v. Jackson, 1891, 1 QB 671.
37. C. A. Morrison, 'Contract', in *Century of Family Law*, es. Graveson and Crane, p. 116.
38. Pacquin Ltd. v. Beauclerk, 1906, A.C. 148.
39. See above, p. 52.
40. For example by Lee Holcombe, 'Victorian Wives and Property', in *A Widening Sphere*, ed. Martha Vicinus (Bloomington: Indiana University Press, 1977), p. 4.
41. Sir Arthur Underhill, *The Law Reform (Married Women and Tortfeasors) Act 1935* (Butterworths, 1936), p. 8.
42. Holcombe, *Wives and Property*, p. 154.
43. House of Lords, Debates, 1970, CCII, col. 604.
44. NAPSS, *The Laws Relating to the Property of Married Women* (NAPSS, 1868), p. 10.
45. Edith Sumerskill, *A Woman's World* (Heinemann, 1967), p. 144.
46. Otto Kahn Freund, 'England', in *Matrimonial Property Law*, ed. W. Friedmann (Stevens, 1955), p. 313; and 'Matrimonial Property—Some Recent Developments', *Modern Law Review* **22** (May 1959), pp. 241-272.
47. Summerskill, *A Woman's World* p. 137; and Elizabeth Abbott and Katherine Bompass, *The Woman Citizen and Social Security* (By the Author, 1943).
48. J. L. Burton, 'The Enforcement of Financial Provisions', in *Century of Family Law* eds. Graveson and Crane, p. 359.
49. Julia Brophy and Carol Smart, 'From Disregard to Disrepute: the Position of Women in Family Law', *Feminist Review* No. 9 (1981), pp. 1-16.
50. Markham, *Return Passage*, p. 2; on Vera Brittain see M. Mellown, 'Vera Brittain: Feminist in a New Age', in *Feminist Theorists*, ed. Dale Spender (Women's Press, 1983), p. 319; Katherine Chorley, *Manchester Made Them* (Faber, 1950), pp. 268 and 21.
51. Clara Collet, *Educated Working Women* (P. S. King, 1902), p. 24.
52. Raverat, *Period Piece*, p. 70.
73. Carol Dyhouse, *Girls Growing Up in Late Victorian and Edwardian England* (Routledge & Kegan Paul, 1981), pp. 46-50; and J. S. Pedersen, 'Schoolmistress and Headmistress: Elites and Education in Nineteenth Century England', *Journal of British Studies* **15** (November 1975), pp. 142-5.
54. Trudgill, *Madonnas and Magdalens*, p. 66.
55. Trudgill, *Madonnas and Magdalens*, p. 56; and Jeffrey Weeks, *Sex Politics and Society. The Regulation of Sexuality since 1800* (Longman, 1981), p. 41.
56. Mary Lyndon Stanley, '"One Must Ride Behind": Married Women's Rights and the Divorce Act of 1857', *Victorian Studies* **25** (Spring 1982), pp. 355-376; and see above p. 123.
57. Peter T. Cominos, 'Innocent Femina Sensualis in Unconscious Conflict' in *Suffer and be Still*, ed. Martha Vicinus (Bloomington: Indiana University Press, 1975), p. 169; J. A. Banks, *Victorian Values. Secularism and the Size of Families*

(Routledge & Kegan Paul, 1981), p. 89; Dyhouse, *Girls Growing Up*, pp. 34 and 77; Trudgill, *Madonnas and Magdalens*, 98; and Edward J. Bristow, *Vice and Vigilance, Purity Movements in Britain since 1700* (Dublin: Gill and Macmillan, 1977), p. 101.

58. Carol Smart, *Women Crime and Criminology: A Feminist Critique* (Routledge & Kegan Paul, 1976), pp. 28-53; and Anne Campbell, *Girl Delinquents* (Oxford: Basil Blackwell, 1981), p. 40-1.
59. Bristow, *Vice and Vigilance*, p. 217.
60. Susan Edwards, *Female Sexuality and the Law* (Oxford: Martin Robertson, 1981), p. 49.
61. Lucy Bland, '"Guardians of the Race", or "Vampires upon the Nation's Health?": Female Sexuality and its Regulation in early Twentieth Century Britain', in *The Changing Experience of Women* ed., Elizabeth Whitelegg *et. al.* (Oxford: Martin Robertson, 1982), p. 385.
62. Carl Degler, 'What ought to be and what was: Women's Sexuality in the Nineteenth Century', *American Historical Review* **79** (December, 1974), pp. 1467-1490; Branca, *Silent Sisterhood*, p. 26.
63. Swanwick, *I Have Been Young*, p. 83; Gorham, *The Victorian Girl*, p. 160; and Andrew Rosen, *Rise Up, Women!* (Routledge & Kegan Paul, 1974), p. 44.
64. Peter T. Cominos, 'Late Victorian Sexual Respectability and the Social System', *International Review of Social History* **8** (1963) Pt. I, pp. 18–48, and 'Innocent Femina Sensualis', p. 158; and Brian Eastlea, *Science and Sexual Oppression* (Weidenfeld and Nicholson, 1981), p. 128.
65. Bristow, *Vice and Vigilance*, p. 140.
66. See above, p. 15.
67. Nightingale, 'Cassandra', p. 398; and Barbara Caine, 'Beatrice Webb and the Woman Question', *History Workshop Journal* **14** (Autumn 1982), p. 28.
68. For example, Cominos, 'Late Victorian Sexual Respectability, p. 24.
69. Burstyn, *Victorian Education*, p. 39.
70. Martha Vicinus, 'One Life to Stand Beside Me: Emotional Conflicts in First Generation College Women', *Feminist Studies* **8** (Fall 1982), p. 609; and Jeffrey Weeks, *Coming Out. Homosexual Politics in Britain, from the Nineteenth Century to the Present* (Quartet, 1977), p. 87-111. See also Carol Smith Rosenberg, 'The Female World of Love and Ritual: Relations Between Women in Nineteenth Century America', *Signs: A Journal of Women in Culture and Society* **1** (Autumn 1975), pp. 1-29.
71. Elizabeth Blackwell, *The Human Element in Sex* (J. & A. Churchill, 1884), pp. 44-5 (I am grateful to Margaret Foster for this reference); and Ellen Key, *The Woman Movement* (G. P. Putnams, 1913), pp. 78, 85–6, 170.
72. Quoted by Bland, '"Guardians of the Race"?', p. 376.
73. Sheila Rowbothan and Jeffrey Weeks, *Socialism and the New Life: The Personal and Sexual Politics of Edward Carpenter and Havelock Ellis* (Pluto, 1977), pp. 168–171; Ruth First and Ann Scott, *Olive Schreiner: A Biography* (André Deutsch, 1980), pp. 290-2; and Mona Caird, *The Morality of Marriage and Other Essays on the Status and Destiny of Women* (George Redway, 1897).
74. Linda Gordon and Ellen Dubois, 'Seeking Ecstasy on the Battlefield: Danger and Pleasure in Nineteenth Century Feminist Sexual Thought', *Feminist Review* No. 13 (Spring, 1983), pp. 42-54.

75. Judith R. Walkowitz, 'Male Vice and Feminist Virtue: Feminism and the Politics of Prostitution in Nineteenth Century Britain', *History Workshop Journal* **13** (Spring 1982), pp. 79-93.
76. Banks and Banks, *Feminism and Family Planning*, p. 93.
77. Linda Gordon, *Woman's Body, Woman's Right*, 1st edn. 1974 (Harmondsworth: Penguin, 1977); and Angus McLaren, *Birth Control in Nineteenth Century England* (Croom Helm, 1978).
78. PP., 'Minutes of Evidence taken before the Royal Commission on Divorce and Matrimonial Causes', Cd. 6480, 1912-13, XIX, 1, Q 21732.
79. A. P. Herbert, *Holy Deadlock* (Methuen, 1934).
80. Papers of the Married Women's Association, Box 233, Fawcett Library, City of London Polytechnic.
81. Leonore Davidoff, Jean L'Esperance and Howard Newby, 'Landscape with Figures: Home and Community in English Society', in *The Rights and Wrongs of Women*, eds. Juliet Mitchell and Ann Oakley (Harmondsworth: Penguin, 1976), p. 155; and Gorham, *The Victorian Girl*, pp. 42-5.
82. Constance Rover, *Love Morals and the Feminists* (Routledge & Kegan Paul, 1970), p. 75; and Boyd, *Josephine Butler*, p. 32.
83. Brian Harrison, 'Underneath the Victorians', *Victorian Studies* X (March, 1967), pp. 239-62; see also Leonore Davidoff, 'Class and Gender in Victorian England: The Diaries of Arthur J. Munby and Hannah Culwick', *Feminist Studies* **5** (Spring, 1979), pp. 87-141.
84. E. P. Hennock, 'Poverty and Social Theory in England: the Experience of the 1880s', *Social History* **1** (January 1976), pp. 67-92.
85. Walkowitz, 'Male Vice and Feminist Virtue', p. 80.
86. Quoted in J. Unglow, 'Josephine Butler: from Sympathy to Theory', in *Feminist Theorists*, ed. Spender, p. 155.
87. Walkowitz, 'Male Vice and Feminist Virtue', pp. 81-3; see also Deborah Gorham, 'The Maiden Tribute of Modern Babylon Re-Examined: Child Prostitution and the Idea of Childhood in Late Victorian England', *Victorian Studies* **21** (Spring, 1978), pp. 353-79.
88. Judith R. Walkowitz, *Prostitution and Victorian Society* (Cambridge: Cambridge University Press, 1980), pp. 211 and 247.
89. Eugene C. Black, 'Feminists, Liberalism and Morality', Fawcett Library Papers No. 2 (1981), p. 37, note 37, has challenged Walkowitz's view that Butler was opposed to the new direction.
90. Bristow, *Vice and Vigilance*, pp. 100-104.
91. Lucy Bland, 'Cleansing the Portals of Life: the VD Panic of Early Twentieth Century Britain', in *Crisis of Hegemony: Aspects of the British State 1880-1920*, ed. CCCS State Group (Hutchinson, 1984).
92. Bland, '"Guardians of the Race"?', p. 385.
93. Christabel Pankhurst, *The Great Scourge and How to End It* (E. Pankhurst, 1913), pp. vi and 98; on the WSPU's campaign see Rosen, *Rise Up, Women!*, p. 185.
94. David Mitchell, *Queen Christabel* (McDonald and Jones, 1977) is an example of the latter. For a radical reassessment and defence of Christabel Pankhurst, see Elizabeth Sarah, 'Christabel Pankhurst: Reclaiming her Power', in *Feminist Theorists*, ed. Spender, pp. 256-284.
95. See for example the moving confirmation of this in Innes Pearse and Lucy

Crocker, *The Peckham Experiment* (Allen and Unwin, 1943), p. 152.

96. P. A. Ryan, 'The Ideology of Feminism in Britain, 1900–20', unpublished MSc. Diss., University of Wales, 1978, pp. 202–4; Chorley, *Manchester Made Them*, pp. 261-267.
97. Dora Russell, *The Tamarisk Tree* (Virago, 1977); and Irene Clephane, *Towards Sex Freedom* (John Lane, 1935), p. 222.
98. David V. Glass, 'Divorce in England and Wales', *Sociological Review* **26** (July 1934), p. 308; and Judge Ben Lindsey and W. Evans, *The Companionate Marriage* (Bentanos, 1928).
99. Weeks, *Sex, Politics and Society*, p. 184.
100. White, *Women's Magazines*, pp. 107–8.
101. Ellen M. Holtzman, 'The Pursuit of Married Love: Women's Attitudes towards Sexuality and Marriage in Great Britain, 1918–39', *Journal of Social History* **16** (Winter 1982), pp. 39-51; and Weeks, *Sex, Politics and Society*, p. 215.
102. Margaret Wynne Nevinson, *Life's Fitful Fever* (A. & C. Black, 1926), p. 1.
103. NVA Papers, Box 115, Fawcett Library, City of London Polytechnic.

II EMPLOYMENT

4 Patterns of Employment

Industrialisation brought with it the separation of the home and the workplace, even though the separation was far from complete even at the end of the nineteenth century, when goods as various as sweets, cutlery, chains and clothing were still produced in household kitchens and backyard workshops.[1] Nevertheless, the large scale removal of paid employment from the home (including retail businesses, which in the early nineteenth century employed wives and daughters) was accompanied by a redefinition of work which involved women in an extremely prolonged, complicated and often painful period of adjustment.

The separation of home and workplace resulted in heightened tension between women's reproductive and productive roles and in increasing debate over which activities adult women were suited for and which, if any, form of paid employment was suitable for women. Towards the end of the nineteenth century the ideal of the family wage and the concept of the wife engaged in unpaid domestic work in the home became increasingly widespread. Women writers reflecting on the female work experience during the early twentieth century accurately perceived the nature of the changes wrought by nineteenth-century industrial capitalism, although they came to very different conclusions as to their merit. Ivy Pinchbeck viewed the emergence of the family wage, and what she regarded as the increasing specialisation of male and female roles into breadwinner and housewife, as a progressive development bringing women more leisure and greater comfort, despite the loss of whatever financial independence they might have enjoyed as their husbands' economic partners. She considered that single women on the other hand had increased their economic independence through wage earning in a way that would not have been possible had they still been employed as part of the family work unit. This view, repeated more recently by Edward Shorter, seriously underestimates the extent to which unmarried daughters continued to contribute their wages to the family coffers.[2] Olive Schreiner, writing some fifteen years before Pinchbeck, also perceived that industrialisation had meant that fewer married women were employed in productive labour, but, contrary to Pinchbeck, she considered this to be a negative development, believing that it denied women the possibility of full self-development. Schreiner was thinking primarily of middle class women, but as Mabel Atkinson pointed out, working class women married to poor husbands unable to earn a family wage had no choice other than to add to their domestic duties the burden of usually unfulfilling labour outside. For them, mechanisation had created rather than destroyed jobs. The solution Mabel Atkinson proposed was that favoured generally by the Fabian Women's Group to which she belonged: the payment of an individual wage to all, which would ensure that married women could stay at home and yet be paid for their domestic work.[3] Irrespective of the merits or practicability of the call for the 'endowment of motherhood', the perception that the separation of home and workplace had resulted in a redefinition of work that excluded women's domestic labour was an important one.

It was not until 1881 that the Census excluded women's household chores from the category of productive work, it being argued that many women would otherwise be counted twice, once as housewives and again as engaged in a specific occupation. Thus in 1881, for the first time, housewives were classified as 'unoccupied', although uncertainty as to the proper classification of wives' and daughters' domestic work persisted until after the 1891 Census. In 1911, enumerators were firmly instructed that no entry was to be made for wives or daughters wholly engaged in domestic labour at home. As Catherine Hakim has pointed out, once women engaged in domestic labour were defined as 'unoccupied', the female activity rate was cut by almost half. Between 1851 and 1871 there was little difference between the economic activity rates for men and women over twenty, both being about 98 per cent of the total age group. When household work was excluded, however, the rate for women dropped to 42 per cent.[4]

The range of opportunities during the nineteenth century for women's employment outside the home was confined largely to textile manufacture and domestic service; it was only with the shifts in the structure of occupations during the last quarter of the century that the number of primarily single-women workers increased. Not until 1971 did the economic activity rate for women (excluding those in unpaid domestic work) again reach the level recorded in the 1861 Census.[5]

It should not therefore be altogether surprising that the proportion of the female labour force remained remarkably constant at about 29 per cent for each census during the early twentieth century[6] (Table 4). The 1951 Census recorded the beginnings of what was to develop into a steady increase thereafter. The overall female participation rate[7] (excluding those in unpaid domestic work) actually declined from 1871 to 1901, increased 1911, declined 1921 and then rose to 1951 (Table 5). While 1871 is not a good base for such a comparison because the census registered as occupied those who had retired, it nevertheless appears that a greater percentage of women worked outside the home at the beginning of the last quarter of the nineteenth century than in the mid-twentieth (always remembering that the census failed to record much of the casual work performed by married women, in particular). Thus the enormous increase in female employment during World War I had little long-term effect, contrary to the hopes expressed by feminists in 1918. By 1918, of the 1,350,000 women who had entered the war industries, not more

Table 4: Participation rates,[a] Males and females, England and Wales, 1901–1951

Year	*Males*	*Females*	*Women as % of labour force*
1901[b]	837	316	29.1
1911[b]	838	325	29.7
1921[c]	871	323	29.5
1931[d]	905	342	29.7
1951[e]	875	349	30.8

a. Number per 1000 in each category in the labour force
b. Persons aged 10 or over
c. Persons aged 12 or over
d. Persons aged 14 or over
e. Persons aged 15 or over. There is no Census information for 1941.

Source: C. Hakim, *Occupational Segregation*, Research Paper No. 9, Table 13, (London: Dept. of Employment, 1979), p. 25.

Table 5: Age specific participation rates,[a] females, England and Wales, 1871–1951

<table>
<tr><th>Year</th><th>≥ 15</th><th>≥10</th><th>10–14</th><th>15–19</th><th>20–24</th><th>25–34</th><th>35–44</th><th>45–54</th><th>55–64</th><th>65–74</th><th>75+</th></tr>
<tr><td>1871[b]</td><td>416</td><td>387</td><td>205</td><td>763</td><td>584</td><td>355</td><td>298</td><td>296</td><td>310</td><td>294</td><td>231</td></tr>
<tr><td>1881</td><td>372</td><td></td><td></td><td>681</td><td>560</td><td colspan="2">290</td><td colspan="2">261</td><td colspan="2">183</td></tr>
<tr><td>1891[c]</td><td>381</td><td>350</td><td>163</td><td>686</td><td>578</td><td>330</td><td>251</td><td>254</td><td>244</td><td colspan="2">160</td></tr>
<tr><td>1901</td><td>345</td><td>316</td><td>120</td><td>659</td><td>563</td><td>305</td><td>225</td><td>217</td><td>207</td><td>167</td><td>75</td></tr>
<tr><td>1911</td><td>356[d]</td><td>325</td><td>104</td><td>688</td><td>620</td><td>338</td><td>241</td><td>230</td><td>204</td><td>138</td><td>57</td></tr>
<tr><td></td><td></td><td>14–15</td><td>16–17</td><td>18–20</td><td>21–24</td><td></td><td></td><td></td><td></td><td></td><td></td></tr>
<tr><td>1911</td><td>356[d]</td><td>480</td><td>693</td><td>739[e]</td><td>620[f]</td><td>338</td><td>241</td><td>230</td><td>204</td><td>138</td><td>57</td></tr>
<tr><td>1921</td><td>337[d]</td><td>448</td><td>709</td><td>763[e]</td><td>622[f]</td><td>335</td><td>229</td><td>210</td><td>193</td><td>126</td><td>46</td></tr>
<tr><td>1931</td><td>342[d]</td><td>509</td><td>756</td><td>790</td><td>651</td><td>363</td><td>245</td><td>211</td><td>178</td><td>102</td><td>38</td></tr>
<tr><td>1951[g]</td><td>349</td><td>611[h]</td><td>812</td><td>848</td><td>655</td><td>373</td><td>358</td><td>350</td><td>218</td><td>70</td><td>20</td></tr>
</table>

a. Number per 1000 in each category in the labour force
b. In 1871 all retired persons were classified according to their former occupation and included in the labour force.
c. In 1891 daughters and other female relatives of the 'head of family' not otherwise occupied were included in the labour force in the Domestic Service (Indoor) category.
d. ≥ 14 years
e. 18 + 19 years
f. 20–24 years
g. There is no Census information for 1941
h. 15 years

Source: Derived from Censuses, 1871 to 1911; 1931 Census, *General Report* Table LXVII, (HMSO, 1950), p. 163; and 1951 Census, *Occupational Tables*, Tables 2 to 5 (HMSO, 1956).

than 150,000 could be accounted for by normal population growth,[8] but by 1921 the female participation rate was 2 per cent lower than before the outbreak of war. The retreat of women from the workforce after World War II was also dramatic, and by 1951 women's economic activity rate was almost exactly the same as that for 1931. Nevertheless, between 1923 and 1939 the number of insured female workers increased more rapidly than that of men, and the period between 1939 and 1948 (by which time the movement of women out of industry had come to an end) saw an increase in the number of female workers at the expense of their male counterparts. C. V. Leser calculated that as many as 800,000 women were substituted for male workers between 1939 and 1948.[9]

The pattern of age-specific female participation rates between 1870 and 1950 is more complex (Table 5). Women over 65 years of age experienced a general decline in their involvement in the workforce throughout the period, and the decline in their participation was greater than that of men of the same age (Table 6). Similarly, the participation rates of women under 15 also showed a steady decline, reflecting the full implementation from 1880 of compulsory elementary school education and the progressive raising of the school leaving age from eleven in 1893, to twelve in 1896 and fourteen in 1918. The participation rates of women between 15 and 25 years of age showed a general absolute increase during the period, and after 1881 women aged 20–35 increased their participation in the labour force relative to men of the same

Table 6: Female age specific participation: rates[a] as percentage of male rate, England and Wales, 1871–1951

Year	*< 15*	*20–24*	*25–34*	*35–44*	*45–54*	*55–64*	*65–74*	*75+*
1871	42.7	59.7	35.9	30.3	30.2	31.9	31.3	27.2
1881	39.4	57.7	29.8 (25–44)		27.5 (45–64)		24.9 (65+)	
1891[b]								
1901	36.9	57.8	31.0	23.0	22.6	23.3	24.2	19.2
1911	38.4[c]	63.7	34.3	24.5	23.8	22.7	21.4	18.3
1921	36.8[c]	64.2	34.3	23.4	21.7	21.0	18.2	17.0
1931	37.8[c]	66.9[d]	36.9	24.9	21.8	19.6	18.3	16.7
1951[e]	39.9	69.0[d]	38.1	36.3	35.9	23.8	18.1	15.9

a. Number per 1,000 in each category in the labour force
b. 1891 figures are not comparable with those for other years because in that census daughters and other female relatives of the 'head of family' not otherwise occupied were included in the labour force in the Domestic Service (Indoor) category.
c. < 14 years
d. 21–24 years
e. There is no Census information for 1941.

Source: See Table 5.

age. Thus, while in 1901 a woman aged between 20 and 24 was only 58 per cent as likely as her male counterpart to work, by 1951 this figure had risen to 69 per cent. This was mainly due to the increasing tendency of single women of all ages and classes to work, and to the substantial number of married women (after 1921) who continued to work until the birth of their first child. The pattern of workforce participation for those women aged 35-64 years was not consistent. Table 5 shows that the 1951 figure is greater than that for 1901 for all three age sub-groups, but the pattern is not one of consistent gain; indeed for women aged 45-64, the 1921 and 1931 participation rates are lower than the 1901 figure, probably as a result of women leaving the workforce after the war, but there is a steep rise between 1931 and 1951, in line with the increasing number of women in insured trades observed by Leser.

The level of women's participation in the workforce was by no means evenly distributed geographically. There were large regional variations throughout the period, reflecting on the one hand the opportunities available to women (which were in turn dependent on the scale and technique of production) and, on the other, the wages of men and customs respecting women's labour. The interplay of these factors makes it difficult to generalise about the nature and degree of female employment even in particular occupational categories.[10] For example, in the nineteenth century, women did not usually work in the coalfields of Northumberland and Durham, whereas their employment (chiefly as single women) was quite normal in the coalfields of Wigan, St Helens and West Lancashire.[11] Similarly, while many married and single women were employed in the textile factories of Lancashire and the hosiery works of Leicester during the late nineteenth century, the same was not true of the lace and hosiery factories of Nottingham, where women were employed as outworkers. Yet in all these towns there was a strong tradition of women's work, a large proportion of men who did not earn a family wage, and relatively high rewards for the married woman factory worker. During the inter-war years the growing importance of the 'new industries', particularly light engineering and rayon manufacture, meant that large numbers of women were employed in London and the South-East, as well as in the traditional areas of textile manufacture in the North-West, while in the rest of the North and in Wales the proportion of women employed remained relatively low. This regional variation in terms of the increase in the female labour force persisted after World War II.[12]

MARRIED WOMEN'S PARTICIPATION RATES

Evidence suggests that the number of married women working in the late nineteenth and early twentieth centuries was substantially lower—probably less than half—than it was in the mid-nineteenth century.[13] From 1911, when the census first presented data on married women workers as a group, to 1931, the proportion of married women who worked remained steady at about 10 per cent (Table 7). Moreover, once women left the labour force they tended not to rejoin it. The idea of women entering the labour force once their children were in school or had left home, which has become familiar since 1950, did not apply to the late nineteenth and early twentieth centuries, and indeed, the participation rate of women aged over 45 decreased between 1911 and 1931 (Table 5).

The participation rates of married women aged 18-24, however, increased between 1911 and 1921 and again between 1921 and 1931 (Table 7), while those for married women aged 25-34 also increased after 1921. The participation rate of widowed and divorced women was more than twice that of married women, but less than half that of single women. Moreover, the labour force participation of widowed and divorced women declined through the rest of the period, especially for the older age groups. Barbara Hutchins believed that widows composed a significant proportion of the earners in the joint 1901 Census category of married women and widows (the number of

Table 7: Age specific participation rates,[a] females, by marital status, England and Wales 1911–1951

Year	*≯15*	*14–15*	*16–17*	*18–20*	*21–24*	*25–34*	*35–44*	*45–54*	*55–64*	*65–74*	*75+*
Single Women											
1911	677[b]	480	707	756[c]	777[d]	740	661	589	462	260	94
1921	683[b]	448	710	789[c]	805[d]	763	682	604	490	271	86
1931	719[b]	509	759	830	841	805	728	645	510	254	88
1951[e]	730	(	n.a.	)	912	869	812	750	501	249	45
Married Women											
1911	103[b]	(n.a.	)	137[c]	129[d]	106	106	105	88	57	23
1921	91[b]	(n.a.	)	150[c]	132[d]	99	93	88	76	49	20
1931	104[b]	(n.a.	)	196	193	138	105	88	66	33	12
1951[e]	225	(	n.a.	)	377	252	267	246	221	33	10
Widowed and Divorced											
1911	301[b]	(n.a.	)	500[c]	592[d]	664	623	470	321	170	58
1921	261[b]	(n.a.	)	445[c]	504[d]	468	458	411	294	147	44
1931	216[b]	(n.a.	)	490	599	556	457	360	256	113	35
1951[e]	212	(	n.a.	)	669	679	643	548	480	76	17

a. Number per 1,000 in each category in the labour force
b. ≯14 years
c. 18 + 19 years
d. 20–24 years
e. There is no Census data for 1941.

Source: Derived from 1931 Census, *General Report*, Table LXVII (HMSO, 1950), p. 163; and 1951 Census, *Occupational Tables*, Tables 2 to 5, (HMSO, 1956).

divorcees at that time was negligible). She cited the example of Liverpool, where 14.5 per cent of married and widowed women worked in 1901. The figure for those aged 45–65 years rose to 20 per cent, an increase she believed to be due largely to working widows, the male death rate in Liverpool being very much above the average for England and Wales.[14] The decline in the participation of older widows and divorcees during the period 1921 to 1931 was probably due to the granting of widows' pensions in 1925. The younger age groups exhibited similar changes in participation rates to single females, probably as a result of the increasing numbers of divorced women.

In seeking to explain the increase in the labour force participation of young married women, Ray Strachey suggested that it could be accounted for in large part by high levels of male unemployment, noting that the percentage of married women workers in Oldham, Rochdale and Blackburn had increased by 4.1, 7.2 and 3.0 per cent respectively between 1921 and 1931.[15] However, the major new employers of female labour in the 1930s were the new industries and these tended to be located in the areas of low male unemployment. Undoubtedly it was a combination of supply and demand factors which accounted for the increase in the numbers of married women workers during the inter-war years and the nature and balance of the factors involved would have varied by region and occupation. The substantial increase in the numbers of women employed in insured trades during the 1930s in particular, in areas where the level of male unemployment was not high, indicates a change in attitude on the part of younger married women (and probably their husbands) away from the ideal of the respectable, non-working wife and towards the desirability of wage earning, although more crucial still was the demand for women workers in new unskilled and semi-skilled processes.

In the years immediately following World War I, the exodus of married women from the workplace was rapid, owing to trade-union agreements made at the beginning of the war, and the intense pressure exerted by the press, government committees and trade unionists (male and female) for married women to give up their jobs for the sake of returned men, and the future welfare of the race. Barbara Hutchins correctly predicted in 1917 that 'a crusade under the guise of patriotism for an indiscriminate raising of the birth rate' would follow the war.[16] But with a further decline in the birth rate during the inter-war years and the increased ownership of labour-saving devices by 1949 (79 per cent of households in Britain had a gas supply, 86 per cent had electricity and 68 per cent had both), it is possible that many young wives whose husbands were employed and who, given the rise in real wages during the 1930s, did not need to work for financial reasons, would have welcomed the opportunity to take a job had work been more readily available and had a marriage bar not existed in many occupations. It is nevertheless important to remember that for many married women domestic labour remained arduous. Most homes used electricity only for heating and ironing, only 19 per cent had an electric cooker in 1948, 15 per cent a water heater, 4 per cent a washing machine and 2 per cent a refrigerator. Also, urban women were usually considerably better off in respect to domestic appliances than rural women. In 1942 for example, 82 per cent of Londoners cooked by gas, but only 3 per cent of people in rural Gloucestershire.[17]

Certainly after World War II married women's return to the home was by no means so great as it had been after World War I, with the result that the marital composition of the female labour force began to show a significant change, a trend that was to intensify during the 1960s and 1970s (Table 8). In part this was due to an increase in the proportion of married women and to a fall in the average age at marriage. Taken together with a decline in the numbers of teenage workers following the low birth rate of the inter-war years, and the fact that, unlike the years after World War I, the size of the labour force was maintained and increased,[18] some change in the pattern of female employment was inevitable. Women were actually encouraged to stay in the labour force after World War II. In 1947 an economic survey recorded the fact that the prospective labour force of 18,300,000 men and women fell 'substantially short' of that required to reach national production objectives and the government therefore appealed 'to women who are in the position to do so to enter industry'. The survey emphasised the labour needs of manufacturing industries such as textiles, but there was also a shortfall in service industries and in professional occupations such as teaching. Birmingham infant schools were 600 teachers short in 1948, and during 1948–49 a recruitment target of 6000 women teachers was set, but only 4000 found.[19]

Many women had entered the labour force during World War II, as in the First War, not only for patriotic reasons but because they needed the money. A serviceman's wife's basic weekly allowance amounted to only 24/- plus child benefits on a decreasing scale from 5/- for the first child. In 1940 a report

Table 8: Composition of female labour force by marital status, England and Wales, 1901–1951

Year	*Percentage of working women* *Single*	*Married*	*Widowed or divorced*	*Total %*
1901	78	13[a]	9[a]	100
1911	77	14	9	100
1921	78	14	8	100
1931	77	16	7	100
1951[b]	52	40	8	100

a. Estimate based on data for ever-married women

b. There is no Census data for 1941.

Source: C. Hakim, *Occupational Segregation,* Research paper No. 9, Table 7, (London: Dept. of Employment, 1979), p. 11.

on servicemen's families in Bristol revealed that the average gap between income and expenditure in homes where there were children under five years old, and where the wife was not in paid employment was 15/6d.[20] Whether married women wished to continue their wartime jobs after the conflict had ended depended very much on the kind of work they were doing. A 1943 survey found that as many as three-quarters of professional women wanted to keep their jobs, while women doing monotonous jobs objected to them and presumably had little desire to stay in them after the war.[21] These feelings were undoubtedly exacerbated by the marked reluctance of the government to provide adequate collective assistance for women in the performance of their domestic work, especially in respect to shopping and childcare. Shopping remained an individual responsibility and nursery school provision for the under-fives extended to only about one-quarter of the children of working mothers. The rest had to make their own arrangements.[22] It is, in any case, doubtful as to how far the attitude of married women (especially that of older women) towards work changed as a result of either war. The idea that the respectable wife did not engage in paid employment and that her home and children should come first is unlikely to have been completely swept away by the temporary wartime emergencies. Nella Last, whose children were grown up when World War II broke out, changed her views on husband-wife relationships, on housework and even on the propriety of women wearing trousers, but remained convinced that women with school-age children should not go out to work.[23]

It was changes in demand factors during the immediate post-war period, and in particular the prospect of a labour shortage, that were perhaps the most important in producing a difference in the climate of opinion on the question of married women's work.

What emerged from the wartime experience was, as Penelope Summerfield has convincingly argued, the conviction of policy makers that it was possible for women to combine work, marriage and motherhood without their home responsibilities being seriously undermined. Both government and industry saw the extension of part-time work for women as an ideal means of ensuring that women would be able to fulfil their responsibilities as both workers and as wives and mothers. The Report of the Royal Commission on Population, published in 1949, welcomed the idea of women doing two jobs, and, anticipating the increased demand for married women's labour, agreed that there was 'nothing inherently wrong in the use of mechanical means of contraception'. Similarly, the economic survey of 1947 urged employers to 'adjust the conditions of work to suit, so far as possible, the convenience of women with household responsibilities'.[24] One response to this took the form of the Factories (Evening Employment) Order of 1950, which instigated the early evening 'twilight' shifts worked by housewives. Indeed, Viola Klein calculated that the 1951 Census seriously underestimated the amount of part-time work already being done by married women.[25]

SINGLE WOMEN'S PARTICIPATION RATES

Until World War II the vast majority of the female labour force was single and therefore also mostly young (Table 9). The participation rates for age groups from 15 to 65 increased steadily throughout the period. George Joseph has pointed out that over time the labour force age-pyramids of single women, and to a lesser extent of widowed and divorced women, have increasingly tended to show a pattern similar to that of their respective population age-pyramids.[26] This reflects the widening opportunities for women's work, particularly in teaching, clerical work and retailing; the growing expectation that unmarried women would support themselves; and, especially after World War I, the acute imbalance in the sex ratio that made marriage out of the question for many women. In 1939 one woman in six died unmarried, compared with one man in ten.[27]

The persistent tendency to regard all women as 'normally' economically dependent on a man was bitterly resented by women who remained single, for whom the ageing process brought additional difficulties in respect to their ability to earn a living. In 1931 single women comprised 51 per cent of the female workforce aged over 35, but because their numbers were relatively small, their problems tended to be overlooked. Ladies' maids, for example, had good reason to fear that their mistresses might wish to replace them with a younger servant. Prior to World War I barmaids were reckoned to be unemployable at 35 and shop assistants had great difficulty finding a new job if they were over 30.[28] In 1907 most of the applicants to the Women's Work Committee of the Central Unemployment Body (set up in 1906 to deal with

Table 9: Age profiles of women and women in the labour force aged 15–59, England and Wales, 1901, 1931 and 1951

Year	*Description*	*15–34*	*35–44*	*45–49*	*Total %*[a]
1901	All women	59	20	20[a]	100
	Working women[b]	77	13	11[a]	100
1931	All women	52	21	27	100
	Working women[b]	72	14	14	100
1951	All women	44	24	32	100
	Working women[b]	55	20	25	100

a. Estimates based on data for women aged 55–64 and 65 or over
b. Women who are 'occupied' or 'economically active'

Source: C. Hakim, *Occupational Segregation*, Research Paper No. 9, Table 9, (London: Dept. of Employment, 1979), p.12.

single unemployed women) were widows over 40.[29] A government report on pensions for unmarried women, presented in 1938 admitted that spinsters aged 45-55 found it much harder both to retain and regain work than did a man of similar age,[30] though it is possible that the committee overestimated the age at which women began to experience difficulties. A group of single working women formed the Over Thirty Association in 1935, and it was not until a decade later that its name was changed to the Over Forties Club.[31] The reports received by Violet Markham in her capacity as a member of the Unemployment Assistance Board during the late 1930s commented repeatedly on the plight of older unmarried women, many of whom were said to be poorly nourished and too physically unfit to retrain as domestic servants. Two-thirds of the unemployed insured women workers were over 30 and one-half over 40. Markham agreed that such women had a claim to the 2/- a week extra 'dignity money' paid to men over 55.[32]

For women who remained in work, late middle and old age was still often beset by financial difficulties. In indoor domestic service, (which still employed over one million women—23 per cent of the total female labour force—during the inter-war period), wages increased minimally with age, and very few servants received a pension from their employer after retirement. Many elderly women took on charring jobs; 10,500 of the 72,500 chars recorded in the 1911 Census were unmarried and aged between 45 and 75.[33] The National Spinsters' Association, formed in 1935, believed that 5 per cent of unmarried women aged 55-65 were already in receipt of poor relief. Sickness was an additional hazard; servants still tended to be sent home if they were ill, despite the coverage they received under the 1911 National Health Insurance Act. The sickness rate of insured single women workers was not as high as that of married women, but was in 1931-32 still 25 per cent higher than experts had predicted.[34]

The bitterness felt by many single women workers often expressed itself in terms of resentment towards married women. Ada Nield Chew was undoubtedly not alone when she wrote in 1894 that she considered it 'unjust' that women with husbands in work should be allowed to take the 'means of subsistence from girls who are dependent for a livelihood on their earnings'.[35] Such antagonism was not surprising in a society in which married women enjoyed a higher status than single women, even during the inter-war years. The National Spinsters' Association managed to collect one million signatures for a petition seeking pensions for unmarried women at 55. The Association believed that part of single women's pension contributions were going to support widows (who were able to draw pensions at 55), which it bitterly resented, claiming that their members deserved to be considered 'War Spinsters' and compensated accordingly.[36]

OCCUPATIONAL DISTRIBUTION OF WOMEN WORKERS

Throughout the period women had been concentrated in certain 'women's jobs'. Table 10 shows that four main occupations accounted for 76 per cent of employed women in 1881, and that even in 1951, 77 per cent of women were still confined to six occupations, while in addition there was a substantial concentration of women workers within various occupational subgroups. Women in the 'Professional and Technical' category were mostly teachers and nurses and those in the 'Commercial and Finance' group were mostly shop assistants.

By 1951, a dramatic shift had taken place from the traditional late nineteenth-century areas of women's work, particularly domestic service, the clothing trade and the textile industry, to the clerical and typing sector (Table 10). Agriculture, which had accounted for 12 per cent of women workers earlier in the nineteenth century, had already ceased to be a major employer of women by 1880, although it was still the case in the early twentieth century that the wives of Dorset farm labourers had to perform field labour when

Table 10: Occupational distribution of women, percentages in major occupational groups, England and Wales, 1881–1951

	1881	1891	1901	1911	1921	1931	1941	1951
Personal Service	–	–	42	39	33	35	–	23
Indoor Domestic	36	35	33	27	23	24	–	11
Other	–	–	9	12	10	11	–	12
Clerks, Typists etc.	–	–	1	2	8	10	–	20
Commerce and Finance	–	–	7	9	10	11	–	12
Professional and Technical	5	6	7	8	7	7	–	8
Textile Goods and Dress	18	17	16	14	11	9	–	7
Textile Workers	17	15	14	13	12	10	–	6
Metal Manuf. and Engineering	–	–	1	2	3	2	–	3
Storekeepers, packers etc	–	–	–	–	2	3	–	3
Transport, etc	–	–	–	–	2	3	–	3
Paper, Printing	1	2	2	2	2	2	–	1
Food, Drink, Tobacco	–	–	1	1	2	1	–	1
Leather, Fur	–	–	–	–	3	1	–	1
Agriculture	2	1	1	2	2	1	–	1
Unskilled/unspecified	–	–	–	–	1	3	–	6

Source: E. James, 'Women and Work in Twentieth Century Britain', *Manchester School of Economics and Social Science*, XXX, (Sept. 1962), Figure 2, p. 291.

asked to do so or risk 'giving offence'.[37] (Much of this labour would have been casual and probably went unrecorded by the census.) Increasing numbers of young rural women went into domestic service, where they were better paid, receiving £12–£15 a year rather than the £10 paid to fieldworkers, and were in addition given board and lodging.[38] Domestic service and fieldwork remained the only two options open to the majority of rural women until after World War II, and the migration of rural girls to towns in search of work as servants continued to be considerable during the later nineteenth century. Only a quarter of London servants were London born, and in Lincoln, Reading, Coventry and Bath over three-quarters of the servants came from rural districts, 45–55 per cent being born within a twenty-mile radius, the rest coming from farther afield. As Theresa McBride has pointed out, while many more men than women emigrated overseas, within the British Isles female migration was the more important.[39]

The decline in the numbers of women employed in textiles, clothing and domestic service was, by 1911, substantial, but unlike other European countries such as France, Belgium and Switzerland, where the proportion of women in employment dropped, these women were reabsorbed primarily by the clerical and distributive services and to a lesser extent by the metals, paper, chemicals and food, drink and tobacco trades.[40] The growth in these occupations was sufficient to absorb a particularly large increase in the *numbers* of women working between 1901 and 1911.

The trend away from traditional women's occupations continued during the inter-war years, although domestic service saw a resurgence, largely because it was one of the few sectors experiencing a labour shortage. This was a fact exploited by successive governments in their policies towards unemployed women, which were designed either to force women back into service, or to make them retrain as servants. Despite the increase in the numbers of servants, more implicit and explicit criticisms of the paternalistic and deferential relations which characterised the job were forthcoming during the inter-war years from both servants themselves and those active in the labour movement. More girls entering service sought non-private situations and the average age of those in the occupation became progressively older, reflecting its increasing unpopularity. Recommendations were made by government committees and trade unionists for the use of formal contracts by employers, stipulating hours, days off, holidays and pay.[41] But many mistresses seem to have shared the opinion of the Marchioness of Londonderry, who refused to sign the 1919 government committee report on the 'servant problem' because she objected to any attempt to regulate what she regarded as an essentially private relationship.[42] Between 1939 and 1948 the decline in the number of servants was dramatic, reflecting in part the increased demand for women clerks and typists. The number of women working in the service of local and central government increased almost fourfold during these years.

In respect to inter-war industry, there was some displacement of men by women in areas such as engineering and textiles, although this did not mean that women necessarily took men's jobs, but rather that the sections of the industry employing women expanded, opening up new areas of employment for them. This was especially true of the new light electrical engineering industries: batteries and electric light bulbs, for example, were made by an entirely female labour force. Similarly, the new rayon industry employed 30,300 people in 1936, of whom just over a third were women. Between 1939 and 1948 the numbers of women and men employed in light industry increased substantially, and in heavy industry women also formed a much higher proportion of the workforce by 1948 than they had done in 1939.[43]

But the shift to white-blouse work was the major feature of the change in the occupational distribution of women during the period. While the number of women engaged in such work (mainly teaching, retailing, office work and nursing) increased by 161 per cent between 1881 and 1911, the number working in manufacturing industry and domestic service increased by only 24 per cent.[44] Moreover, the expansion of the non-manual sector was much more rapid for women than for men and to some extent this opened channels of social mobility to working class girls. The pupil-teaching system, for example, provided late nineteenth-century working class girls with the opportunity to enter elementary school teaching, although as the training period was extended during the early twentieth century, lower middle and middle class girls began to enter the occupation in increasing numbers. In 1910 a male bookbinder commented that young working class girls were no longer so eager to enter his trade, traditionally a respectable occupation for women, but rather were set on becoming 'a type-writer or a waitress'.[45]

The movement of women into non-manual occupations did not by any means involve a leap to middle class status. State elementary school teaching in the late nineteenth century would have been considered far too rough an occupation for a middle class girl, while the conditions endured by shop assistants under the living-in system—boarded in often crowded and insanitary conditions above or near their employers' shops—proved too much for many respectable working class girls, let alone their middle class counterparts. As for women office workers, it is important to remember that prior to World War I over 90 per cent of female clerks were employed in commercial and business premises—the inferior end of the office work hierarchy. Between the wars, as the number of women clerks in government offices increased, lower middle class recruitment became more important.[46] On the whole, regardless of their occupation, women workers were found in low status jobs that paid wages barely adequate for the maintenance of a respectable lifestyle.

NOTES

1. Raphael Samuel, 'The Workshop of the World: Steam Power and Hand Technology', *History Workshop Journal* **3** (Spring 1977), pp. 6-72.
2. Ivy Pinchbeck, *Women Workers and the Industrial Revolution 1750-1850* (Routledge & Kegan Paul, 1930); and Edward Shorter, 'Illegitimacy, Sexual Revolution, and Social Change in Modern Europe', *Journal of Interdisciplinary History* **2** (Winter 1972), pp. 237-61.
3. Olive Schreiner, *Women and Labour*, 1st edn. 1911 (Virago, 1978); Mabel Atkinson, *The Economic Foundations of the Women's Movement*, Fabian Tract No. 175 (1914).
4. Catherine Hakim, 'Census Reports as Documentary Evidence: The Census Commentaries 1801-1951', *Sociological Review* **28** (1980), pp. 556-60.
5. Eric Richards, 'Women in the British Economy since about 1700: An Interpretation', *History* **59** (October, 1974), pp. 337-357; and Neal A. Ferguson, 'Women's Work: Employment Opportunities and Economic Roles 1918-1939', *Albion* (Spring 1975), pp. 55-68.
6. The pre-1901 data are problematic. In 1871 the figures are distorted because the retired were registered in the census according to their former occupation, while in 1881 and 1891 the domestic labour of many daughters and other female relatives of male 'heads' of household was included under the category of paid domestic service.
7. The participation (or activity) rate is the number per 1000 women with jobs.
8. A. C. Pigou, *Aspects of British Economic History 1918-25* (Macmillan, 1947), p. 19.
9. C. V. Leser, 'Men and Women in Industry', *Economic Journal* **62** (June 1952), p. 332.
10. Sally Alexander, Anna Davin and Eve Hostettler, 'Labouring Women: A Reply to Eric Hobsbawm', *History Workshop Journal* No. 8 (Autumn 1979), pp. 174-82.
11. Angela V. John, *By the Sweat of Their Brow. Women Workers at Victorian Coal Mines* (Croom Helm, 1980).
12. Leser, 'Men and Women in Industry', pp. 337-8; and Guy Routh, *Occupation and Pay 1906-1960* (Cambridge: Cambridge University Press, 1965), p. 46.
13. Clara Collet, 'The Collection and Utilisation of Official Statistics bearing on the Extent and Effects of the Industrial Employment of Women', *Journal of the Royal Statistical Society* CXI (June 1898), p. 229; and Margaret Hewitt, *Wives and Mothers in Victorian Industry* (Rockliff, 1958), p. 19.
14. B. L. Hutchins, 'Statistics of Women's Life and Employment', *Journal of the Royal Statistical Society* LXXII (June 1909), p. 221.
15. Ray Strachey, 'Current Social Statistics. The Census Occupations of Women', *Political Quarterly* **5** (October/December 1934), p. 557.
16. B. L. Hutchins, *Women in Industry after the War*, Social Reconstruction Pamphlets No III, (1917), p. 8.
17. Caroline Davidson, *A Woman's Work is never Done* (Chatto and Windus, 1982), pp. 38-9 and 68.
18. Edward James, 'Women at Work in Twentieth Century Britain', *Manchester School of Economic and Social Studies* XXX (September 1960), p. 293.
19. PP., 'Economic Survey for 1947', Cmd. 7046, 1946-7, XIX, para. 124; and G.

Partingdon, *Women Teachers in the Twentieth Century* (NFER Pub. Co., 1976), pp. 74–5.

20. Penelope Summerfield, 'Women, Work and Welfare: A Study of Child Care and Shopping in Britain in the Second World War', *Journal of Social History* 17 (December 1983), pp. 249–70; and Vera Douie, *The Lesser Half* (Women's Publicity Planning Association, 1943), p. 45.
21. Sarah Boston, *Women Workers and the Trade Union Movement* (Davis Poynter, 1980), p. 205; and Penelope Summerfield, 'Women Workers in the Second World War. A Study of the Interplay in Official Policy between the Need to Mobilise Women for War and Conventional Expectations about their Roles at Work and at Home in the period 1939-1945', unpublished PhD. Diss., University of Sussex, 1982, pp. 83 and 314.
22. Summerfield, 'Women Work and Welfare'.
23. Richard Broad and Suzie Fleming, *Nella Last's War*, 1st edn. 1981 (Sphere Books, 1983), p. 201.
24. Summerfield, 'Women Workers in the Second World War', p. 336; PP., 'Report of the Royal Commission on Population', Cmd. 7695, 1948-9, XIX, 635, pp. 159-60; and Cmd. 7046, para. 124.
25. Sheila Lewenhak, *Women and Trade Unions* (E. Benn, 1977), p. 266; and Viola Klein, *Working Wives* (Institute of Personnel Management Occasional Papers No. 15, 1960), p. 9.
26. George Joseph, *Women at Work. The British Experience* (Oxford: Philip Allan, 1983), p. 75.
27. James, 'Women at Work in Twentieth Century Britain', p. 284.
28. Pamela Horn, *The Rise and Fall of the Victorian Servant* (New York: St. Martin's Press, 1975), p. 59; Jill Quadagno, *Aging in Early Industrial Society: Work, Family and Social Policy in Nineteenth Century England* (Academic Press, 1982), p. 147; and Lee Holcombe, *Victorian Ladies at Work. Middle Class Working Women in England and Wales, 1850-1914* (Hamden: Archon Books, 1973), p. 116.
29. Elizabeth Abbott, 'The Municipal Employment of Unemployed Women in London', *Journal of Political Economy* **15** (November 1907), pp. 513-530; Jeanette Tawney, 'Women and Unemployment', *Economic Journal* **21** (March 1911), pp. 131-9; Ellen Mappen, 'Women Workers and Unemployment Policy in late Victorian and Edwardian London', unpublished PhD. Diss., Rutgers University, 1977.
30. PP., 'Report of the Committee on Pensions for Unmarried Women', Cmd. 5991, 1938-9, XIV, 235.
31. Douie, *The Lesser Half*, p. 16; and Boston, *Women Workers and the Trade Union Movement*, p. 184.
32. Markham Papers, 7/21, 'Tour of Unemployment Areas 1937', and 7/27, V. Markham to Mr. Reid, 25 January, 1939, BLPES.
33. C. V. Butler, *Domestic Service. An Enquiry by the Women's Industrial Council* (G. Bell, 1916), p. 68.
34. Cmd. 5991, p. 39; and Jane Lewis, *Politics of Motherhood* (Croom Helm, 1980), p. 44.
35. Doris Nield Chew, *Ada Nield Chew: The Life and Writings of a Working Woman* (Virago, 1982), p. 101.
36. Cmd. 5991, p. 45.

37. George Fussell and Kathleen R. Fussell, *The English Countrywoman* (Andrew Melrose, 1953), p. 208.
38. A. Wilson Fox, 'Agricultural Wages in England and Wales during the Last Half Century', *Journal of the Royal Statistical Society* LXVI (June 1903), pp. 298 and 301.
39. Mark Ebury and Brian Preston, *Domestic Service in Late Victorian and Edwardian England, 1871-1914* (Reading: University of Reading, 1976), p. 79; and Theresa McBride, *The Domestic Revolution* (New York: Holmes and Meier 1976), pp. 14 and 37.
40. James, 'Women at Work in Twentieth Century Britain', pp. 291-2.
41. Labour Party, *The Domestic Workers' Charter* (LP, 1931).
42. PP., 'Report of the Women's Advisory Committee of the Ministry of Reconstruction on the Domestic Service Problem', Cmd. 67, 1919, XXIX, 7, p. 31.
43. Leser, 'Men and Women in Industry', p. 330; and A. Plummer, *New British Industries in the Twentieth Century* (Pitman, 1937), pp. 58, 60, 217.
44. Holcombe, *Victorian Ladies at Work*, p. 216.
45. Frances Widdowson, 'Elementary Teacher Training and the Middle Class Girl, c. 1846-1914', unpublished M.A. Diss., University of Essex, 1976, p. 1 [this thesis is now available in a revised form: *Going up into the Next Class. Women and Elementary Teacher Training 1840–1914* (Hutchinson, 1983)]; and Felicity Hunt, 'Women in the Nineteenth Century Bookbinding and Printing Trades, 1790-1914', unpublished M.A. Diss., University of Essex, 1979, p. 81.
46. Theresa Davy, 'Female Shorthand Typists and Typists, 1900–1939', unpublished M.A. Diss., University of Essex, 1980, p. 49.

5 Characteristics of Women's Work

LOW PAY AND SEGREGATION

Employers, trade unions and women workers themselves shared the dual concept of 'a woman's job' and 'a woman's rate', and both were regarded as 'natural' phenomena. In 1901 a male factory inspector wrote to May Tennant, the Chief Woman Inspector of Factories, that the sexual division of labour was, in his opinion, determined by economic factors. Men's greater acumen and adaptability made them better value for money. He concluded that 'women will never become engineers, mechanics, stonemasons, builders, miners and so on. And men are not likely to become operatives, dressmakers, milliners (I know one or two exceptional cases), or launderers'.[1] (In fact the number of men in the laundry trade was about to double with the advent of machine washing.) At the Courtauld silk mill in Essex, men and women workers accepted the established sexual division of labour; in the 1890s the women objected to being required to clean the looms, claiming it to be men's work.[2] Similarly in printing a female worker responded to an employer's request that she varnish books with the words, 'I know my place and I'm not going to take men's work from them'. Professor F. Y. Edgeworth regarded this comment as proof of the existence of 'natural monopolies' of custom regarding male and female work practices. Ramsay McDonald, who wrote the classic book on women in the printing trades, published in 1904, commented that suggestions to the effect that women might undertake tasks commonly performed by men were not only rejected, but treated as though something 'indelicate' had been proposed.[3]

Patterns of sexual segregation were by no means fixed in the same manner throughout the country. Nineteenth-century brickmaking, for example, was a woman's trade in the Black Country where men worked in ironworks and coalpits, but in Lancashire, where women worked in cotton and where openings for men were scarce, it was a male preserve.[4] While the pattern of sexual segregation varied, it was rare not to see a clear dividing line between women's and men's jobs within occupations, and between women's and men's processes. In so far as the census categories permit, Catherine Hakim has constructed a measure of horizontal segregation which captures the way in which men and women tend to work in separate occupations. The proportion of all occupations in which women were at least as well represented as men in the labour force has remained virtually constant at about 25 per cent of the total since 1901. Similarly, occupations with rather more men than expected have remained fairly constant at about 75 per cent. The proportion of 'feminised' occupations in which women were 70 per cent or more of the workforce rose slightly.

Women also experience vertical segregation at work, finding themselves working in lower grade occupations than men. Hakim shows that the trend towards vertical segregation increased between 1911 and 1951. As non-manual women became increasingly concentrated in clerical and sales jobs, the proportion in managerial and administrative or lower professional and technical occupations declined. In manual work the trend has also been towards greater segregation, with women becoming increasingly over-represented in unskilled work and men in skilled jobs. As Hakim points out, these changes have far outweighed the gradual but small improvements in women's share of the higher professions, employers' and proprietors' categories.[5]

Women's jobs commanded a women's rate, even where women were engaged on exactly the same processes as men, they still usually received lower pay. During the 1890s, Sidney Webb was puzzled by the example of women compositors who received 5½d for setting '1000 ens' of work, while the men received 8½d.[6] Weaving was one of the very few occupations in which men and women performed the same task for the same rate of pay. The Secretary of the Cotton Spinners' and Manufacturers' Association attempted to explain this to the 1919 War Cabinet Committee on Women in Industry in the following terms: 'Weaving is not a man's job. It is exceptionally light work and they are always under cover and under good conditions'.[7] The idea of a notional women's rate dominated the debates over equal pay which began in the late nineteenth century and continued through World War II. In 1909 the Trade Board for the tailoring industry set an hourly rate of 3¼d for women and 6d for men. During World War II the government automatically built a male/female differential into its scale of compensation for civilian injuries, which a Treasury spokesman justified to the Select Committee appointed to look into the issue in the following way:

> The principle of sex differentiation, whether it is right or wrong, is at present a matter of government policy and it runs right through a large part of the social structure—it appears in all the social services, with the exception of old age pensions.[8]

The comment was accurate, and while there were considerable variations, a male/female differential existed in almost all occupations and in virtually all state benefits.

In manufacturing occupations women generally earned only about half the average weekly earnings of men. Table 11 shows female earnings as a proportion of men's for five of the major industrial occupations for women; only in textiles did women earn significantly above 50 per cent of male earnings. The gap closed slightly during the war, but reopened between 1945 and 1948. Women's lower earnings may be explained largely by the lower rates of pay they received for women's jobs. But even in the few areas where

Table 11: Average earnings: females as a percentage of those for males, selected industrial groups, 1906–1935

Groups	1906	1924	1931	1935
Textiles	58.5	56.1	56.0	55.9
Clothing	46.3	49.1	50.2	51.2
Food, Drink, Tobacco	41.5	48.1	48.7	47.0
Paper, Printing	36.4	39.6	39.4	37.3
Metal Industries	38.1	44.7	47.6	45.7
Total (all industries)	43.7	47.7	48.3	48.0

Source: Derived from A.L. Bowley, *Wages and Income in the U.K. since 1860* (Cambridge University Press, 1937).

the task *and* the rate was the same for men and women—textile weaving was the outstanding example—women rarely earned the same. In 1938 male weavers earned 36% more per hour than women. They managed this first, by working a larger number of looms: in 1937 30 per cent of men but only 16 per cent of women operated more than four looms, and, while the difference in pay between a weaver working two and four looms was less than 2/- per week, the difference between working four and six looms was 6/-. In the second place, men retained their work of tuning and adjusting the looms, for which as much as 10 per cent was deducted from the women's scale. Thirdly, some factories tended to give male workers the better paying work, and finally men tended to work longer hours; in 1938 women weavers worked 93.3 per cent of men's hours.[9] The number of hours worked also became significant in rather a different way in respect to shift systems. During the 1930s automatic weaving looms had to be worked in a double shift, and although women were permitted to do this from 1920 onwards, a special Home Office order was required. Employers were therefore able to drive a harder wage bargain with their female employees.[10] Nevertheless, in the many trades which escaped, or avoided, protective legislation regarding women's hours, women's pay was still low. Seasonal trades such as dressmaking and millinery were legally permitted to work overtime for 48 days in the year. But illegal overtime was also common, whereby women worked through their meal breaks, took work home, or, in the manner of the workroom portrayed in Edith Lyttleton's play *Warp and Woof*, were herded into a back room at the appearance of the factory inspector.[11]

New methods of wage payment introduced in the late nineteenth and early twentieth centuries were also used to reinforce the idea of a woman's rate. Women were more often paid on piece (as opposed to time) rates than were men, and found their rates lowered if they earned 'too much'. As one employer remarked to a factory inspector during World War I: 'What can one do when a girl is earning as much as 15/- a week but lower the piece rate?'[12] Piece rates for the same job were also liable to vary widely. In tailoring, for example, it was common for outworkers to be paid less than indoor hands for the same task. Premium bonus schemes, introduced during the 1900s, were another form of payment by results whereby a rate fixer set a time for the completion of a task and if the job was completed more quickly, the savings were divided between the worker and employer rather than the proceeds of the extra product going to the worker, as with the straight piecework system. Such schemes were implemented for male and female workers and were often extremely complicated. Barbara Drake described them as being a 'hybrid between a piece and time rate'.[13] For example, women munition workers during World War I were allowed a certain number of hours for the job and the worker finishing it just in time received the basic rate. The worker finishing the job in less time received in addition a bonus on output, or premium bonus, equivalent to one half (or some other fixed proportion) of the basic rate for each hour saved. Thus the employer extracted from the worker a piecework effort at a timework rate without having to go through the difficult process of reducing the piece rate. Many women employed under these systems could only guess at what they might receive by way of payment at the end of the week. Moreover, not only might premiums be added but, especially prior to World War I, fines might be deducted.

Employers found it relatively easy to impose a system of fines and deductions on their docile female employees. However, it was the issue of fines that proved the catalyst for the famous Bryant and May's match girl strike in 1883. The girls were fined 3d if the ground around their benches was left untidy, 1/- if 'burnts' (matches that caught fire during work) were set on the bench, and latecomers were shut out all morning and had 5d deducted from their wages.[14] In the 1890s, the Royal Commission on Labour reported cases of fines ranging from 1d to 6d for lateness, fines for damages, and, in the case of shop assistants, fines on materials that remained unsold. Margaret Bondfield, at that time the Assistant General Secretary of the National Union of Shop Assistants, gave evidence to a 1907 government committee that shop assistants were fined amounts varying from 3d to 5/- for addressing the customer as Miss rather than Madam, for not using string or paper economically, for wrongly adding up bills, wrongly addressing parcels, answering the shopwalker impolitely or losing an invoice. Barbara Hutchins claimed that as late as 1915 it was not unknown for a girl to be fined her entire earnings.[15]

Non-manual women workers generally earned a higher percentage of the average male earnings. Women shop assistants earned about 65 per cent as much as men in 1900, but here the differential was purely the result of discrimination, as women and men did the same work and women often worked rather longer hours. In the case of teachers, the 1919 Standing Joint Committee on Teachers' Salaries formally set the differential between female and male teachers' pay at a ratio of 4:5, somewhat lower than the 25 per cent differential that prevailed before the war. However, women clerks earned on average less than one-third of the average male clerk's earnings in 1914. This was because women clerks tended to occupy positions at the bottom of the occupations' hierarchy; because of their youth; and because many were temporary workers. Within particular grades of the early twentieth-century civil service, women clerks were usually paid about 75 per cent as much as men, although in 1914 women typists started work at £1 a week and men typists at £3.[16]

In all-female occupations, women often did worst of all. Nineteenth-century nurses were often paid little more than domestic servants. Indeed, their pay was actually lowered in order to attract middle class applicants who did not need the money. Clara Collet roundly condemned the way in which late nineteenth-century middle class parents often permitted their daughters to work for pocket money, because they considered that a tiny wage rendered the work respectable and genteel by making it more akin to voluntary work.[17] Likewise, the respectability that accrued from 'living-in' made the job of shop assistant more popular than it might otherwise have been. However, the system did little to improve the workers' standard of living. Clementina Black commented that shop assistants were usually boarded in extremely overcrowded and insanitary conditions so that they were 'carefully dressed as to the head but very inadequately washed'.[18] In one instance a firm handed over the catering for its 1000 live-in employees to a company which allowed 3½d a day per person and made their profit from the extra food the assistants were forced to buy. Derry and Toms openly admitted that despite abolishing living-in for men they were not prepared to do so for women because it would mean a financial loss.[19] The only area where men's and women's rates of pay (although, again, not necessarily earnings) were usually the same was in the higher professions. But, in the 1920s, only 3,600 of the higher professional bodies' total membership of 107,705 was female, 2,580 of these being women doctors. If the rate for the job was one of the hallmarks of a fully-fledged profession and the demand for a 'family wage' more characteristic of trade unionism, the semi-professions, such as teaching, found themselves in a difficult position.[20] Many male teachers were swayed more by material than professional considerations and the National Association of Schoolmasters strongly resisted equal pay.

The substantial differential between men's and women's earnings ensured that women were for the most part low paid, although Dorothea Barton complained in 1919 that the sweated rates of homeworkers attracted more attention than the 'adequate earnings' of factory and workshop workers who outnumbered homeworkers by ten to one; a view more recently reiterated by E. H. Hunt, who points out that the average wage of 18/8d paid to women in the cotton trade in 1906 was more than the pay of the average male farm labourer in most southern counties. A housemaid, earning £18 to £20 a year plus board and lodging in 1900 probably did almost as well as cotton workers. (A lady's maid or housekeeper would have earned considerably more and a 'between' maid considerably less.[21]) The movement of semi-skilled women's wages for the first half of the twentieth century has been charted by Guy Routh. Cotton workers experienced a relative decline in wages throughout the period, shop assistants between 1906 and 1924, and domestic servants between 1935 and 1955. What is particularly interesting is the tendency to fix women's pay without particular regard to the skill or intelligence required, but rather either in relation to a notional women's rate (of about 10/- to 12/- a week in 1906), or as a fixed percentage of the male rate.[22]

It is in fact striking how many women workers failed to achieve either the 14/- to 16/- that Cadbury and Shann believed necessary for a single woman to subsist in 1906, or the £1 a week Rowntree thought requisite in 1914.[23] In 1906 the average wage for all adult women textile workers was 15/5d; even in cotton, 27 per cent earned less than 14/-. For clothing workers the average was 13/6d, in the metal trades 12/8d, for those in printing 12/2d, and in the food and tobacco trades, 11/3d. The average wage for women over eighteen in non-textile industries was 12/11d.[24] The minimum wage set by the trade boards, which by the 1920s covered one-sixth of women workers (who were by definition among the most poorly paid), dropped below the Cadbury and Shann subsistence minimum prior to World War I and continued to fall well below Rowntree's 'human needs' standard of 30/9d set in 1937. Nevertheless, when the rates were set for the first group of workers in 1909, they represented a considerable advance for many women workers; hollow-ware makers, for example, received a 33 per cent increase. In any event, substantial evasion of trade board rates was documented. The early boards, such as that for the tailoring trade, allowed 20 per cent of the workforce to earn below the minimum wage, but in his pre-war sample of Colchester and London homeworkers, Tawney found that as many as 50 per cent were falling below the minimum. Boards set up after the war permitted between 25 and 35 per cent of workers to earn less than the minimum rate and evasion increased dramatically during the 1930s Depression.[25]

Low pay made it very difficult for women to support themselves or to take responsibility for maintaining other kin. In 1915 the Fabian Women's Group found that of 2,830 middle class women, 85 per cent were self-supporting and nearly 50 per cent were entirely or partially maintaining others. Seebohm Rowntree found that of 13,637 women over eighteen in eleven industrial towns, 88 per cent supported themselves, but only 12 per cent supported others.[26] Many working girls lived with relatives as a means of mutual support. A 1911 Board of Trade report on the expenditure of wage-earning women and girls pointed out that a machinist earning only 4/10½d due to short-time working paid 3¾d to her mother for board and lodging; if she had lived by herself her costs would have risen to 8/-. A clerk earning the relatively good wage of 23/1d managed to save more than fifty per cent of it for spending on non-essentials by living in one room and paying a total of 8/6d for rent, food and laundry.[27] A World War I welfare supervisor reported that girl applicants were frequently asked whether they lived with their parents. It was said that the inquiry was intended as a check on the applicant's morals, but the welfare supervisor believed that it served 'as a kind of rough-hewn shield for the employer who wishes to pay his girl workers less than must be spent on their maintenance'. The Oxford graduate who worked as a domestic servant during the 1930s in order to become acquainted with their conditions of work, made a similar observation about the attitudes of employers towards the wages of daily servants.[28] Rent was the largest expense the single working woman faced, and in 1909, five hundred women signed a petition demanding that the London County Council build housing for single women workers. Manchester City Council opened a lodging house for 200 women in 1910, but this was a rare experiment. During the inter-war years, hostels for women workers provided small cubicles with minimal privacy, breakfast on weekdays, all meals at weekends and laundry for 30/- a week, which was substantially more than half the wages of a civil service clerk and nearer three quarters of those of a clerk employed in the industrial and commercial sector.[29]

Girls under eighteen, who accounted for one-sixth of all women workers in 1919, faced still more severe problems. In the clothing trade girls were often taken on as 'learners' during the busy season, paid a few shillings a week and then discharged. Because of the competition for jobs that were considered respectable, employers could 'train' girls for up to three years on processes that took only six months to learn, paying them small wages.[30] Before the 1920s and the growth of the ready-made trade, it was common for girls entering dressmaking to be paid 2/6d or nothing at all for two to three years, sometimes also paying a premium to learn the trade. In 1890, at the age of thirteen, Louise Jermy was apprenticed for two years at no wages to a dressmaker who demanded a three guinea premium. Her parents were disgusted when at the end of her apprenticeship she earned only 7/6d a week.[31] Such wages made it virtually impossible for young girls to live away from home.

Thus women workers have tended to find themselves in the more monotonous, low status, low-paid jobs where their turnover rate was high. Even the idea of the faithful family retainer was something of a myth. A survey of 1,864 households in late nineteenth-century London revealed that a minority of servants were long-serving and that the vast majority were peripatetic, staying a maximum of one or two years. Servants' pay varied little between jobs, but conditions varied enormously and the high turnover rate probably represented the search for 'a better place'.[32] During the inter-war years there seems to be rather more evidence of women moving swiftly from one unskilled job to another. Thus Edith Hall, a working class Londoner, listed a series of jobs she held between the ages of fourteen and seventeen which included three production line jobs in electrical engineering, metal working and in a sweet factory; two posts as a domestic servant; one as a shop assistant and one as a factory tea trolley girl.[33]

Women's attachment to the labour force was additionally weakened by their customary decision to renounce full-time employment on marriage (reinforced by the marriage bar in many non-manual jobs). Both Mostyn Bird and Barbara Hutchins felt that women's expectation of a 'Visionary Deliverer' in the form of a husband explained their low level of job commitment. It is as likely that the characteristics of the jobs rather than the workers were to blame, but either way women's lowly position in the workforce found its reflection in their low levels of trade union organisation, which in turn served to reinforce their low pay and low status.[34]

Table 12 shows that women's trade union membership underwent a steady, absolute and relative increase during the period, but the proportion of working women as against men who joined trade unions was always less than one-half. The level of organisation varied immensely between occupations. In 1900 textile workers accounted for three-fifths of all organised women.[35] Late nineteenth- and early twentieth-century female textile workers earned good wages compared to other women workers, and the percentage of women who stayed in the factory after marriage was also high. These factors, together with the ease of organising the closely knit textile communities, produced a high density of union organisation. But in other industries where both men and women worked, for example in engineering, women were

Table 12: Trade Union membership and density[a]: males and females, Great Britain [b], 1896–1951.

Year	*Males Membership (000s)*	*Density*	*Females Membership (000s)*	*Density*	*Females as % Total Membership*
1896	1356	14.0	116	2.7	7.9
1901	1781	17.2	124	2.9	6.5
1911	2799	24.5	331	6.6	10.6
1921	5526	46.3	986	18.8	15.1
1931	3820	29.5	749	12.8	16.4
1941	5664	42.4	1384	22.2	19.6
1951	7515	55.2	1751	24.7	18.9

a. Percentage of total labour force union members
b. Trade unions with their headquarters in Great Britain

Source: G.S. Bain and R. Price, *Profiles of Union Growth*, (Oxford: Blackwell, 1980).

often excluded from the male trade unions; the Amalgamated Society of Engineers did not accept women members until 1943. Male unionists feared that women would undercut their wages and they therefore implemented a policy of exclusion in order to keep them confined to 'women's processes'. In the growing areas of female employment in offices and shops, male and female levels of unionisation were typically low, and in the large and predominantly female sector of domestic service, no effective union was ever formed, largely because of the isolated nature of the work. As Mary MacArthur noted prior to World War I, women's 'low standard of living may be stated to be at once the cause and consequence of women's lack of organisation'.[36]

What is so difficult to explain is the persistence of low paid, sexually segregated and poorly organised work as the norm for women, despite profound shifts in occupational distribution and in the nature of jobs. Early commentators on the problem, such as Sidney Webb (who confined himself to the issue of unequal pay), concluded that women's inferior earnings were mainly due to 'natural' causes: women's productive power was usually inferior to men's both in quantity and quality.[37] The idea that sexual divisions in the labour market are in some way natural has been long-lived. Modern neo-classicist economists assume that women's reproductive function makes the sexual division of labour in the home—whereby women perform the childcare and household tasks—natural. From this they argue that women's low-paid and low-status jobs are largely a matter of individual choice: because of their prior commitment to marriage, childbearing and childcare (or to the 'Visionary Deliverer' in Bird's phrase) women will not be prepared to invest in long training programmes or apprenticeships, will seek work near home, have interrupted work careers, and be prone to absenteeism. Such a model thus treats the possibility of sex discrimination as a residual factor and ignores the systemic processes which trap women as a group, rather than as individuals, within certain grades and kinds of work.[38]

As Deborah Thom has observed, 'natural' and 'historical' explanations of women's work have often been conflated by investigators. The 1919 War Cabinet Committee on Women in Industry, for example, accepted the idea that the historic divisions between male and female jobs were rooted in innate differences,[39] but the historical process itself was not further explored. In fact women's position in the labour market can only be explained by the complex changes in the relationship between women and men workers, trade unions, employers and the state, and in relation to the changing nature and structure of jobs, which is in turn dependent on the scale and technique of production and methods of work organisation.[40]

Modern economic and social theorists who have rejected the idea that the sexual division of labour is natural and a matter of choice on the part of women, have pointed to the existence of primary and secondary (i.e. dual) labour markets, in which 'primary' workers are assured a stable career with rising wages, and 'secondary' workers, who are often unskilled or who possess highly transferable skills, come to be seen as unstable workers. A large proportion of the latter will be women. More radical versions of this 'dual labour market' theory have suggested that it is not so much job specific skills that explain the development of career hierarchies and grading structures, but rather the process of 'deskilling', which, according to its leading exponent, Braverman, leads to a breakdown of gradings and skill differentials functional to capitalism.[41]

These ideas provide further insight into the position women workers find themselves in, but they are essentially descriptive and do not explain why the overwhelming majority of *women* workers occupy positions in the secondary labour market. The dual labour market theorists who rely on the argument that job specific skills and knowledge are the important differentiating factors, tend to fall back, like the neo-classicist economists, on the argument that women do not develop such skills because of their home commitments. And, in its original formulation, the argument that deskilling provided the mechanism by which a segregated labour market was created, portrays both male and female workers as the victims of capitalist 'divide and rule' strategies, recognising only that sexual and racial divisions in the workforce provided employers with ways of fracturing the workforce.

However, consideration of the changes in the level and balance of skill, whereby new jobs have been created, both at the managerial and technical level and on the shop floor (at the semi- and unskilled rather than skilled level), does provide a way into considering the complex historical changes in work relations and the labour process which are the key to explaining women's position in the workforce. It appears that skilled work has become, by definition, work that is not performed by women; thus while oxyacetylene-welding was classed as skilled work prior to 1914, as soon as women entered the trade during the war employers reduced the pay by 50 per cent. In this case the women formed a union and won a partial victory. Women in the felt hat trade were not so fortunate. From 1920 onwards the skilled work traditionally done by men in this trade was increasingly performed by semi- and unskilled machine operators, so that by 1945 the only genuinely skilled workers left were women.[42] But when it came to wages, the men were still classed as skilled and the women as semi-skilled. In both these examples skill may be seen to have been 'socially constructed'. The women workers were possessed of genuine skills but lacked the power to pursue successful wage bargaining negotiations.[43]

Women workers were also denied access to the means of acquiring real skills by their exclusion from training and apprenticeship programmes by both employers and male trade unionists. Even when male workers in a particular trade 'lost' skill or were not strongly organised, they demonstrated the capacity to exclude women from skilled processes. For example, after the big lockout of 1895, employers in the boot and shoe trade were able to convert to mass production methods in integrated factories using largely semi-skilled labour. Male and female processes remained distinct and the National Union of Boot and Shoe Operatives, while it admitted women from the 1880s, failed to press for piecework statements for women fitters and machinists until 1907. During World War I the union fought strongly against the introduction of women into the traditionally male processes of clicking (cutting out) and 'making' shoes. A Leicestershire clicker declared himself a married man with 'a certain amount of respect for the ladies', but urged the Union to 'stand first for the men' and be careful to see that their positions were not undermined. Finally, the Union agreed to let women work on male processes for the duration of the war as long as no male worker could be found.[44]

This pattern of male dominance and control at the workplace must be related to power relationships within the family, for it has been hypothesised that male domination of the pre-industrial family work unit and the practice of sexually segregating work processes was carried over into the factory when the workplace separated from the home.[45] Men and women did not always perform the same kind of tasks in the factory as they had in the home,[46] but the boundary between men's and women's work was defended in the face of technological change (which threatened to blur sexual boundaries), by means of union exclusiveness and the control skilled men managed to exert both over apprenticeship and via their power to subcontract work. This line of argument is in tune with the revisions to Braverman's original deskilling thesis, which stressed the need to consider worker resistance to changes in grading resulting from technological change, rather than regarding the workforce solely as victims.[47]

This is not to make the male worker the only instrument determining women's position in the workforce, as once the workplace and home were separated there existed a perceived need to decide what was suitable work for women and what women were suited for. As Beatrice Webb observed in 1919 in her criticism of the Majority Report of the War Cabinet Committee on Women in Industry, paid employment was assumed to be the prerogative of the male:

> To concentrate the whole attention of the readers of the Report upon the employment of women past, present and future and upon their physiological and social needs, without any corresponding survey of the employment of men and of their physiological and social needs, is to assume, perhaps inadvertently, that industry is normally a function of the male, and that women, like non-adults, are only to be permitted to work for wages at special hours, for special rates of wages, under special supervision and subject to special restrictions of the Legislature. I cannot accept this assumption.[48]

The conclusions reached as to what was suitable work for women differed from place to place and between social classes, but were largely *shared* by male workers, employers, government and women workers themselves. Employers did not proceed to engage women wholesale when male union control was weak despite their cheapness. State policies not only reinforced the assumption that women's wage-earning was secondary to their reproductive function, but also attempted to impose limits on work that was considered unsuitable for women by means of protective legislation, and to channel women into suitable occupations by the manipulation of national insurance regulations during the inter-war years. Nor is there evidence that a majority of women were by any means opposed to the sexual division of labour, as the attitude of the women printing workers quoted at the beginning of this chapter shows. The fact that the sexual division of labour was commonly believed to be natural made it difficult for both male and female workers to transcend it without stigma. In addition, working class women in particular may have supported men's claim to higher-status, better-paid work because it improved family welfare, accepting the fact that this was achieved at their expense as workers and that it involved a strengthening of the traditional sexual division of labour at home.[49] Given that their work experience and work expectations were likely to be confined to unskilled and fairly monotonous jobs, it is understandable that women should have thought of their paid employment as secondary and in relation to their family's needs and concerns. It is therefore doubtful how far the majority of unskilled women workers have *ever* moved away from the idea of working at the dictates of the family economy and towards a more individualistic notion of working for their own satisfaction.[50]

Women who had obtained secondary and possibly higher education or training were likely to feel more positive about their work, but they were also likely to have encountered more directly discriminatory practices, such as the marriage bar. It is perhaps not surprising that within the Civil Service women in the lower grades favoured the marriage bar because it entitled them to claim one month's pay for each complete year of service to a maximum of twelve months salary (which served as a partial compensation for total loss of pension rights), whereas women in the upper grades fought hard for its abolition.[51] The following sections explore the work relations and work processes determining women's position in the workplace in more detail, before returning to the issue of equal pay which, unlike the sexual segregation of labour, was a matter of contemporary debate.

WOMEN'S AND MEN'S WORK IN MANUAL OCCUPATIONS

Women and Men Workers and the Labour Process

Within the category of manual occupations there are trades such as textiles, where women have always worked, and where sexual divisions established in the domestic system prior to industrialisation were taken into the factory and survived technological change, albeit often changing their form in the process. There are also industries in which very few women worked in the mid-nineteenth century, but where technological change created a space for the introduction of female workers at the bottom of the labour hierarchy. Engineering is one such example. And there are occupations, like domestic service, which remained predominantly female preserves. Domestic service was also atypical in remaining relatively untouched by technological change; housework by its very nature defies rationalisation.[52]

Women's early waged labour was often an extension of the home-based skills they were traditionally assumed to exercise and sometimes represented an extension of the early domestic division of labour in a particular trade. Domestic service and laundry work had obvious connections with women's household labour, but nursing was also linked closely to women's domestic work. Not until 1891 did the census introduce the term 'sick nurse' to differentiate hospital nurses from household servants, and even then the Census Report considered that the two categories could be treated together. As women's work, nursing was not far removed from domestic labour.[53]

Where families worked at particular trades there was usually a sexual division of labour. In the tailoring trade, male tailors used their wives to make button holes, turn cuffs and fell seams, tasks that continued to be considered women's work throughout the century.[54] In early nineteenth-century Leicester hosiery families, the father worked the knitting frame, while children wound bobbins and the mother seamed stockings. Alternatively, older daughters helped with seaming, while the wife or older son worked a second frame. The departure of men to workshops to work the wide knitting frames served to sharpen the sexual division of labour. Women remained at home working only on seaming stockings; the wide frame knitting machines increasing the volume of their work.[55] Sometimes, as with cotton textiles, the family work group survived the transition to the factory. The male cotton mule spinner of the 1830s and 1840s hired his own children as piecers and scavengers. In other trades which remained substantially outside the factory system at the end of the century the family work unit also remained important. In nail and chainmaking a junior factory inspector estimated there to be 10,000 domestic workshops with an average of three or four workers in each in 1876. One witness reported disapprovingly to the Select Committee on Sweating on the arrangement of such domestic workshops:

> Suppose this person's house is this table, the shop is here (*pointing to a chair close to the table*), and in many instances there is a door communicating between the kitchen and the shop so that you step out of the shop into the house. . . and perform the duties of one or the duties of the other as best you may.[56]

Here men and women were largely employed on the same work, women making the small and men the larger chains. In some areas the boot and shoe trade was also carried on in family homes. A man writing of Wellingborough in the 1890s recalled that his father's brother 'was an outworker... his wife and daughter were closers [fitting together and sewing the uppers], all the work was done in the kitchen, and the meals were cooked during work time'.[57] Here the division of labour between closing, making and clicking paralleled that in the factory.

Within the factory system male workers were able to defend their craft skills by excluding women and male unskilled workers from their organisations. The danger of undercutting by cheap female labour was real enough. The Women's Protective and Provident League, formed in 1874 (it became the Women's Trade Union League in 1889), was cautious about advising male trade unionists to withdraw restrictions on women workers in the absence of an assurance that the women would be strong enough to observe trade union conditions. Thus, when three women mule spinners were introduced at Lostock Mill on women's rates of pay and the male spinners stopped taking women piecers as a result, the League did not take action.[58] It was the fear of women's cheap labour that prompted the famous letter to Mary MacArthur (a leading women trade unionist), from a group of male unionists in the Midlands, asking her to 'send the organiser immediately for our Amalgamated Society has decided that if the women of this town cannot be organised, they must be exterminated'.[59]

Efficient organisation of women workers was an alternative solution to the problem posed by women's cheap labour, but in the nineteenth and often in the early twentieth centuries, exclusion was the dominant practice. Male unionists tended to see adult women as mothers first and workers second. Tom Mann, a socialist organiser of semi- and unskilled workers, declared to the Royal Commission of Labour in 1894 that he was 'very loth to see mothers of families working in factories at all', adding that he considered 'their employment has nearly always a prejudicial effect on the wages of the male worker'. Will Thorn, a fellow socialist and unionist, similarly believed that women's household tasks prevented them from becoming good trade unionists and that the energies of union organisers were better employed working with male workers.[60]

By the late nineteenth century male unionists were committed to the fight for a family wage, which as Henry Broadhurst made clear from the platform of the TUC Annual Conference in 1877, carried with it a duty on the part of male unionists 'as men and husbands to use their utmost efforts to bring about a condition of things, where their wives should be in their proper sphere at home, instead of being dragged into competition for livelihood against the great and strong men of the world'.[61] It was against this background that middle class feminists construed all protective legislation as yet another attempt to exclude women from the labour market. In fact it is likely that many rank and file male unionists in occupations such as textile weaving and hosiery, where a family wage was not paid, had ambivalent feelings about women's work. In all probability these resolved themselves into the belief that women's contribution to the family economy was necessary and right provided it came from work on traditional women's tasks. This is certainly the conclusion reached by Nancy Osterud from her analysis of the Leicestershire hosiery industry.[62] In 1877 the TUC Annual Conference also passed a resolution favouring the prohibition of women from work in the nail and chain trades where women's work at the forge was often considered immodest. Similarly in 1908 the National Society of Amalgamated Brassworkers, who had refused to organise women, passed a resolution calling for legislation to prevent the employment of women in metal polishing, turning and screwing. In 1921, 87 of 209 mixed unions affiliated to the TUC accepted women, 41 per cent of all trade unions.[63]

Because women were excluded from so many trade unions, the Women's Trade Union League (WTUL) founded the National Federation of Women Workers (NFWW) in 1906 as a general labour union for women, open to all women belonging to unorganised trades. Between 1914 and 1918, the NFWW increased its membership from 20,000 to 80,000. Its wartime success was largely due to its alliance with the Amalgamated Society of Engineers (ASE), which made it a doubtful model for women's trade unionism in the years after the war. In fact the NFWW never aimed to do more than organise unorganised women, and as soon as an established union was ready to take a particular group the NFWW willingly passed them over.[64] Thus the amalgamation of the NFWW with the National Union of General Workers (NUGW) in 1919 was not out of line with its general philosophy, but the number of women organisers immediately dropped and by 1930 no women representatives were sent by the NUGW to the TUC conference. Similarly, the WTUL merged into the Women's Department of the General Council of the TUC after the war where it was dominated by the male secretaries of unions with large female memberships. It was replaced by the Women's Advisory Committee in 1931 which remained something of a marginal body: thus the problems of women workers never found a proper forum within the TUC.[65] Where women were accepted in male unions they tended to be confined throughout the period to special sections paying lower contributions and getting lower benefits. In the Bolton Amalgamation, Bleachers' Dyers' and Finishers' Association before World War I, men qualified as full members, boys as half members and women as one-third members. Women's low scale of contributions tended further to hinder them from holding trade union office.[66]

Men's defence of their craft status varied considerably between industries and regions according to the nature of technological change and the work relations existing in the particular industry. In Lancashire cotton textiles, the male mule spinners successfully resisted attempts to introduce women (who were quite able to handle the smaller spinning mules), largely because the men provided the employer with an efficient system of labour control; spinners subcontracted their own piecers, paying them out of their wages.[67] Women were expelled from the Spinners' Union when it was reformed in 1870, but continued to work as piecers in areas such as Wigan and Manchester, where male labour was scarce. Indeed, because not all piecers could become spinners in their turn, women were sometimes welcomed as a means of avoiding employing young men in dead-end jobs, a problem which received considerable attention from social investigators in the 1900s. It was felt that the notoriously low pay the piecer received would prove less of a grievance to women. However, in Oldham, Stockport and Preston, it was considered unsuitable for women to be employed in any capacity in the spinning rooms, the official reason given being the heat and the objection to women being scantily clad.[68] When the new method of ring spinning (using female labour) was introduced in the late nineteenth century the male mule spinners took no action against the women. Male spinners viewed any spinning disdainfully as unskilled work. If the new method threatened them with displacement their response was to cooperate with management to cut unit costs, for example by accepting inferior cotton, to overcome the net advantage of the new method. The cotton manufacturers were too divided by competition with one another to develop a coherent strategy of their own and ring spinning advanced very slowly in England. Seemingly as long as sexual segregation was maintained the male craft workers were satisfied, and women ring spinners remained poorly paid and organised.[69] In the Leicester hosiery industry the introduction of automatic knitting machinery after 1870 did involve massive shifts in the sexual segregation of labour and the rapid substitution of female for male labour, but again, there was little male resistance, because in this instance displaced male labour found a ready outlet in the growing Leicester boot and shoe industry.

It is interesting to compare these developments in cotton spinning with those in weaving where a much greater equality between men and women apparently prevailed. In the weaving sheds and cardrooms women and men shared a common piece list and trade unions were open to both sexes. However women's union activity tended to be limited. Women needed courage to stand for election. The Oldham Weavers' Association had a woman President in the 1890s, but union meeting places were often a men's club or pub, which were not considered respectable for women.[70] In addition, within the weaving and cardroom amalgamations there were groups of male workers able to restrict entry to their occupations. In weaving the male tapesizers worked by themselves, setting the size of the warp and controlling the winding of the yarn on the weaver's beam. Traditionally they were given complete control over their work and, as late as the 1920s, some tapesizers kept the size and proportions of their threads a secret.[71] The overlookers in the weaving sheds were also able to exclude women by their position as supervisors and by reserving the work of tuning the looms for themselves. The relationship between these male supervisors and the female weavers often involved the exercise of both economic and sexual power. During the 1880s and early 1890s the practice of paying the overlookers by results spread and they were thus tempted to 'drive' the weavers. Evidence of sexual exploitation in such situations is common. (The position of women in the tailoring trade, where they were subordinate to the male cutter sometimes resulted in similar incidents.) One notorious case of sexual harrassment by an overlooker in Nelson provoked a strike by the women workers during the early 1890s, in which the clergy acted as arbiter. One woman reported that during the inter-war period some women learned to maintain their own looms in order to avoid the attentions of the loom mechanic.[72]

In the cardroom the male 'strippers and grinders' managed to gain skilled status during the late nineteenth and early twentieth centuries by exploiting technical change to extend their control over machinery and simultaneously monopolising the trade union offices in the Cardroom Association, 90 per cent of whose membership was female. By 1914, they had created apprenticeship barriers, and eventually reached earnings parity with the spinners.[73]

The cotton manufacturing industry thus provides an example of a sexual division of labour maintained in face of technological change. The male spinners were able to defend their position by use of the subcontract system to block female recruitment and because of the lack of a coherent strategy by employers. The control exerted by the tapesizers resulted from their isolated position, and that of the overlookers from their status as loom mechanics (in virtually all industries women were considered unable to tune and adjust machinery). Both the overlookers and the strippers and grinders in the cardroom managed to achieve disproportionate control of their unions despite the fact that these admitted women.

In the tailoring trade the picture was rather different. Male tailors excluded women from their union as early as 1834,[74] but themselves became an increasingly endangered species as the market for ready-made clothing expanded. As the process of making a garment became increasingly subdivided, the demand for women's labour to stitch seams and finish the ready-made goods increased, but men continued to preserve their control over the bespoke trade. Thus technological change in the tailoring trade merely served to strengthen and deepen the existing sexual segregation of labour, rather than to threaten it. Ada Nield Chew complained bitterly to a local newspaper that when the government inspector came round a Crewe clothing factory the job of sewing in the sleeves of tunics, usually done by women, was passed to the men because the contractor's estimate had been based on male pay rates.[75] Such a direct observation was rarely possible in the tailoring trades, which were organised by an elaborate and virtually impenetrable system of internal and external subcontracts. For example, women machinists in a workroom might subcontract some work to other women working on sewing machines at home, and firms might subcontract parts of orders to outworkers working either in small workrooms or at home. With the rapid diffusion of the sewing machine during the late nineteenth century, it is likely that the number of outworkers substantially increased. Paradoxically, factory legislation of the period probably also served to increase their number, because MPs were reluctant to interfere with the running of small premises where no young children were employed or with domestic workshops (usually homes), where only family members worked. It is also possible that the Factory and Workshop Acts of 1891 and 1895, with their more effective regulation of workshops, had the unintended effect of increasing the number of homeworkers, although the evidence here is less clear.[76] In her investigation of the tailoring trade for Charles Booth's survey of London, published in 1889, Clara Collet found that in some cases the subcontractor did not know where a set of shirts went to and the finisher did not know where they had come from.[77] As in the case of spinners and piecers in the cotton textile industry, the system of subcontract tended to be mutually exploitative. Moreover, modes of thought associated with the system persisted long after its effective demise. In tailoring it was the women finishers in particular, who, at the bottom of the labour heap, tended to suffer most from the system. These women were consistently described by contemporaries as 'nervous and timid' and were prepared to take work at whatever price it was offered.[78]

If in tailoring and clothing the sexual division of labour was reinforced during the late nineteenth and early twentieth centuries, in bookbinding it was broken down. Sexual divisions in the bookbinding trade were well-established during the early nineteenth century and respected by both sexes. Women did the work of folding, gathering the folded sheets, collating and sewing, and men handled most of the subsequent processes: pressing and rounding the back of the book, covering it with board and cloth and lettering the cover.[79] Trade union organisation was separate, but there was cooperation between male and female workers. The introduction of machines to fold, sew, gather, cut round, and back books cut across the sexual division of labour. The cases were now made separately and glued to the book, and the machines were operated by unskilled workers, mainly women. The breakdown of traditional sexual divisions in the trade led to considerable bitterness and women were not permitted to join the men's bookbinding union until after 1918.[80]

In the allied industry of printing women initially had no place, and male printers fiercely resisted women's entry to the trade. Resistance was all the stronger because printing appeared eminently 'suitable' for women: middle class feminists set up their own Victoria Press in 1860 with the intention of teaching women composing and reading, while the Women's Protective and Provident League started the Women's Printing Society in 1876 to teach girls all aspects of the trade. Male printers correctly feared that women workers might undercut the male rate, and in a strike of compositors in Edinburgh in

1872, the employer broke the hold of Scottish print unions for many years by bringing in female strike breakers. The male unionists' response was to press for the exclusion of women from the trade altogether, rather than to organise them and to press for equal pay. In 1886 the Typographical Association decided to admit women on the same terms as men:

> ... while strongly of the opinion that women are not physically capable of performing the duties of a compositor, the Conference recommends their admission to membership of the various Typographical unions, upon the same conditions as journeymen, provided always the females are paid strictly in accordance with the scale.

Women were of course not paid on the same scale as men and so they were effectively shut out. Only one woman succeeded in fulfilling the conditions and was admitted to membership in 1892. As in the spinning sheds, women were confined to the dead-end job of layers-on, and the male print unions succeeded in retaining control over the new linotype and monotype processes which were introduced in the 1890s to replace hand compositing.[81]

It is against the background of a shifting but nevertheless persistent sexual segregation of labour that the well-known conflict over the introduction of female workers during World War I must be seen. Rather than the war accelerating the entry of women into the labour market and the process being cut short by the post-war depression, it would be more accurate to see the wartime experience as a brief period when male unionists, employers and government (the male workers often under duress) agreed to abandon traditional designations of men's and women's work for the duration of the emergency.[82] Women unionists were conspicuously absent from the negotiations which resulted in large numbers of them being drawn into the workforce; 22 per cent of all women working in insured trades in 1917 were previously unemployed.[83] It is only during World Wars I and II when government took control of the labour force and initiated proposals to introduce women into hitherto male areas of unemployment, that *all* women became 'a reserve army' of labour,[84] and women's roles as wives and mothers became temporarily subsidiary to their relationship to the labour market, although they were never entirely ignored. The complex set of interactions between capital, labour and the state, and the nature and volume of the production process, which normally determined women's entry and exit from the labour market, were closely controlled for the duration of the conflict.

The major area of controversy in respect to the introduction of women's labour during World War I was the engineering industry. The technical change of the late nineteenth century, particularly in the machine shops where semi-automatic lathes, drilling machines and fully automatic presses and stampers were introduced, put the skilled turners and fitters, who dominated the Amalgamated Society of Engineers, on the defensive against both the encroachment of the semi- and unskilled worker and the increasing control employers attempted to exercise over the new machinery. In the decade and a half before the war, lower grades of work employed an increasingly disproportionate number of women. Women had been largely absent from the nineteenth-century engineering trade, other than in very low-paid work such as the nail and chainmaking trades. When in 1901 the ASE decided to admit a new class of semi-skilled male member, comprising those who had worked for not less than two years on one type of machine and earning not less than 70 per cent of the standard rate, the union remained closed to women.[85]

The wartime Treasury Agreement between the government and the engineering unions (given legislative form in the Munitions Act of 1915), sanctioned the entry of women into the munitions industry, but the Agreement was bitterly resisted by male workers, particularly on Clydeside. The introduction of women 'dilutees' was accompanied by more rapid 'deskilling'.[86] The substitution of women for men on a one to one basis was achieved in only about 17 per cent of cases. The setting up of an automatic machine, such as a capstan lathe, was separated from its operation, and women performing only the latter took a crash training course of five to six weeks instead of the usual five to seven years' apprenticeship served by men.[87] The Treasury Agreement made it clear that women were to be employed on men's processes only for the duration of the national emergency, but the ending of the established pattern of sexual segregation, accompanied as it was by a further subdivision of work processes, evoked fears that women would undercut the male wage rate. Under a government circular issued in 1916, skilled women workers in government-controlled munitions factories secured equal piece rates, but not equal time rates; while no such agreement was achieved by those women working in semi- and unskilled processes. Women also failed to secure equal pay increases during the war. The wages of women engaged in what was traditionally regarded as women's work were raised substantially by government order, but often remained lower than £1 per week. The War Cabinet Committee on Women in Industry admitted that 'the popular notion of munitions work as a gold mine for the operatives was not borne out by the facts'. In 1916, the Woolwich Board of Guardians ordered a woman munitions worker to pay £1/7/1d for her child in care on the assumption that she earned over £2. She in fact earned 17/6d.[88] Munitions work was often exhausting and the hours were long. Elizabeth Flint's mother went to work in a London munitions factory but only lasted a week, and Rosina Whyatt recalled the dangers posed by sharp-edged brass parts which lacerated the fingers, and of TNT poisoning as well as the endurance needed to work a 72-hour week, for which she received 30/-.[89]

As Deborah Thom has pointed out, women trade unionists accepted that women's work was temporary and that motherhood was their most important work. The National Federation of Women Workers fought with the help of the ASE for pay agreements that would ensure women workers did not threaten the male rate, but did not take up the issue of the division between male and female jobs.[90] While the ASE undertook to campaign for the organisation of women in the NFWW, the NFWW agreed to withdraw its members from occupations claimed by the ASE on behalf of its male members at the end of the war.[91] This arrangement reflected the NFWW's paramount concern with recruitment and that of the ASE with retaining control over the skilled sector of the engineering labour market. Three Fabians, G. D. H. Cole, Monica Ewer and W. Mellor summed up the prevalent labour movement view at the end of the war when they wrote that the fulfilment of the wartime pledges to dismiss women doing men's work at the end of the conflict was 'from the social point of view, far less disastrous than the overwhelming of the Trade Unions by the breaking down of their standard rates, rules and customs, i.e. their economic strength. The hope for women both as wives and as workers, no less than for men, lies in the strengthening of trade unionism'.[92] Government committees investigating women's labour at the end of the war also envisaged that while women's employment would expand, they would be confined to light, repetitive unskilled processes requiring manual dexterity. Most employers would have agreed with the remark of one manager of a munitions factory that 'On mass production she will come first every time... we were never able in this particular class of work to get the men to cope with it, they would not stand it. Men will not stand the monotony of a fast repetition job like women, they will not stand by a machine pressing all their lives, but a woman will'.[93] Women's greater output on repetitive work was regarded as proof of their unique suitability for the boredom of the assembly line.

Thus, after the war, the trend towards employing women in light, repetitive jobs on the production line continued. During the 1930s, the number of insured women workers increased faster than that of men, and female unemployment, while very hard to measure, appears to have averaged about two-thirds of the male rate during the 1920s and 1930s.[94] Irene Bruegel has argued that the sexual segregation of the labour market and women's low pay may well serve to cushion women in aggregate from economic downturn.[95] During the inter-war years it appears that an expansion of 'women's work', particularly in the new light industries and in office work, served to offset the high rate of unemployment in traditional occupations like textiles. However, the concomitant decline in skilled work for women was dramatic. Between 1911 and 1951 the number of skilled male workers increased by 11 per cent, while the number of skilled women workers decreased by 34 per cent, reflecting primarily the deteriorating position of the textile industry. No skilled occupational categories emerged to replace that of weaver.[96] In engineering, the increase in the number of women workers was matched by an increase in the proportion of unskilled and semi-skilled workers. In the London engineering trades, one worker in fifty was female in 1891 and one in five by 1929, and whereas 60 per cent of workers in the industry as a whole were skilled in 1914, by 1933 the percentage had dropped to 32 per cent.[97] Increasing numbers of women in the scientific instrument and electrical engineering sectors of the industry, for example, worked on light press machines and automatic lathes. The 1929 government committee investigating the distribution of women in industry noted the increasing numbers of women working automatic machines and commented: 'Though this work is, if judged by ordinary standards, dull and monotonous, the women seem to be perfectly contented with it'.[98]

In fact women's passivity has probably been greatly exaggerated. Even unorganised women's industries provided some impressive exhibitions of female solidarity in the early period, including the Bryant and May's matchgirls' strike; the action taken by the Cradley Heath chainmakers against the employers' attempt to delay implementing the new trade board rates in 1910; the spontaneous strike action of jam and pickle workers, rag pickers, biscuit makers, bottle washers, tinbox and cocoa makers and distilling workers in the hot summer of 1911; and the strike of 600 unorganised clothing workers at Rego clothiers in North London in 1928. Nor is there any evidence that an increase in the proportion of women in a particular industry (for example, textiles) brought a decrease in the propensity to strike.[99] During the inter-war period, women and men workers in industries where skilled processes had already been substantially subdivided, stood together against the introduction of Bedaux schemes which were designed to determine the exact proportion of work and rest needed for the completion of any task, and which permitted comparisons of the relative efficiency of workers doing different tasks. In 1931 and 1932, 4000 women workers at Wolsey's Leicestershire works and 10,000 at the Birmingham Lucas factory struck against the speed-up which resulted from the implementation of such schemes. Similarly between 1929 and 1935 disputes in the Lancashire weaving industry were almost continuous over the introduction of the "more-looms" system, by which workers were given financial incentives to work six or more looms. Both women and men struck, though the women probably had rather more cause, for as one observer recorded: 'Although there has never been any specific recommendation regarding the composition of the weavers to be engaged for 'more-looms' working it may reasonably be inferred that the intention was that men weavers with family responsibilities should be retained wherever possible'.[100]

World War II did not see a repeat of the bitter struggle against women dilutees that characterised World War I. Wage rates were more precisely agreed than in World War I and gave women the rate for the job on tasks they performed without help or supervision. In order to avoid paying equal rates, however, many employers insisted that women either needed male help to tune and adjust their machines, or that they were actually employed on 'women's work'. Training was extremely limited and over 90 per cent of women employed in the engineering and metal industries were engaged on unskilled assembly line work.[101] The Amalgamated Engineering Union (the successor to the ASE) accepted the trend to deskilling as inevitable during the war and with it, women members. But by this time women's sphere of work in the engineering trades was clearly defined as essentially unskilled.

Women's Work, Employers and the State

Even in trades and occupations where there was no impediment in the form of an established sexual division of labour and male craft-control to hiring large numbers of women workers, employers rarely did so. This can be largely explained by the prevalence of certain shared beliefs regarding women's capacities and what jobs were suitable for them. The assumptions underlying the views of Mr Assheton, the Minister of Labour, speaking during the course of the 1941 debate on registering women for war service, were in most respects typical:

> I have discovered that women are not only not inferior to men but are superior to them in many respects. They are much more law-abiding than men, as our criminal statistics show... They are more patient, more faithful and no less courageous than men... It is, however, clear that women are more individualistic and perhaps less easily used to discipline than men... in addition women are certainly very much attached to their homes... we have clearly, therefore, to move very carefully.[102]

Mr Assheton assumed that he could generalise about all women and that they should be regarded as inferior workers until proved otherwise.

Furthermore, female economic independence was judged potentially morally corrupting. A government committee investigating the increased cost of living at the end of World War I reported a 93 per cent increase in working class girls' clothing expenditure, and one writer believed that the increased economic independence of women had resulted in more women applying for separations.[103] Certain types of work were regarded as posing a much greater threat to female virtue than others. Angela John has shown how the late nineteenth-century move to stop women from sizing and sorting coal at the pit brow was related to the popular image of pit-brow women as essentially masculine figures. Many of the women wore trousers—'fustian unmentionables'—and these, together with their shovels and black faces, gave rise to the use of animal imagery by those campaigning to exclude them from the work.[104]

Factory girls, however, were more likely to be condemned as flirts. Ada Nield Chew felt it necessary to apologise for the 'faults' of factory girls of the 1890s, whom she admitted to be 'essentially a noisy class', before she went on to ask the readers of the *Crewe Chronicle* to consider the 'injustices of their economic position'.[105] Clementina Black, by no means an unfriendly observer, commented at length on the roughness of the factory girl. She referred to the 'hideous vernacular' of the factory girls in the East End of London and, like many social investigators and social workers, she favoured the organisation of clubs by middle class women in order to tame their 'exuberence and energy': 'To watch the rapid development of refinement and gentleness consequent upon joining a good club is to feel how sound is the national character and how lamentable the yearly waste of admirable human material'.[106] In his investigation of women's work in Birmingham, Edward Cadbury recorded his view that factory girls were very like 'big children' and susceptible to good influence, although he feared that clubs were in danger of keeping the girls away from home too much. The Girls' Friendly Society was one of the most active clubs for working class girls with 197,493 members in 1913, all of whom were expected to be devout, kindly, serious-minded, uncomplaining and relatively uninterested in the opposite sex.[107] Trade unionism was also often encouraged among women during the late nineteenth and early twentieth centuries in the belief that its 'social and moral advantages' were 'equal if not superior to the economic'.[108]

Most observers regarded factory girls as 'low types'. Clara Collet believed that the morals of East End pickle and jam factory girls were additionally jeopardised by their contact with sexually experienced and 'rough' married women workers.[109] During World War I the behaviour of munitions workers was felt to pose a severe threat to moral order. The National Union of Women Workers (NUWW), an organisation of middle class women founded in 1910 'to face the problems of sin and suffering in a covenant of sympathy and purpose and to promote the social and moral and religious welfare of women' joined forced with the YWCA, the Mothers' Union, the Church Army, the Girls' Friendly Society and the National Union of Women's Suffrage Societies in the Voluntary Women's Patrols, which, together with the Women Police Volunteers, patrolled public parks and garrison and munitions towns primarily in order to supervise the behaviour of young women.[110] Within factories, the increasing numbers of welfare supervisors, some paid, some voluntary, and all middle class, often made themselves unpopular by making it their business to restrict the liberty and independence of the female workforce. One observer commented approvingly on an interview between a welfare superintendent and a young munitions worker: 'I don't think you would a bad looking girl if you hadn't such a dirty face... all that red stuff and then that hat... Awful. Go and take it off and have a wash and then perhaps we can do something'.[111] Even during World War II women workers (but not men) at the Hillingdon Rolls Royce factory were forbidden to smoke at their machines, presumably for reasons of propriety.[112] Officials administering unemployment benefits during the inter-war years also made judgements on the moral character of young women applicants. Case files usually recorded whether the applicant was a 'high' or 'low' type (terms also commonly used by working class women). Cathie

Wothergroon, a nineteen-year-old unemployed Glaswegian paperworker, was dismissed as having 'peroxide hair, plucked eyebrows and make up. Large paste earrings. Very poor and unsatisfactory type', for whom it was impossible to recommend a domestic service.[113]

Despite being acknowleged as sweated work, homework was sometimes viewed as a more suitable form of employment for women than factory work and domestic service was invariably seen as the most acceptable type of female occupation. Late-nineteenth and early twentieth-century girl children in the care of either the Poor Law authorities or voluntary organisations like Dr Barnardo's were given no option but to work as domestic servants. The great advantage of domestic work for women was held to be the training that it provided for marriage and motherhood. Women who had been domestic servants were considered unlikely to become the neglectful housewives and mothers described by the infant welfare movement. A 1924 report on the nutrition of miners and their families concluded that 'the most encouraging result' of the investigation was the high standard of nutrition observed in households where the wife had been a domestic servant.[114]

Nineteenth-century employers, such as Courtauld, the silk manufacturers, who had no reservations about employing a predominantly female labour force, nevertheless also organised mothers' meetings and an evening school for its young female workers to teach the principles of mothercraft and a respect for domestic ideals. Huntley and Palmer sought to maintain a sense of propriety among their female biscuit workers by having separate workrooms for men and women who entered and left the workplace at different times. Between 1898 and 1911 Huntley and Palmer quadrupled its female workforce who were all subject to automatic dismissal on marriage.[115] The implementation of a marriage bar in industrial employment was not only in line with accepted ideas about women's place but also provided employers with the means to secure a younger and cheaper workforce.

Employers accepted the stereotypical ideas of women's capacities, often without any direct experience of employing women. Sidney Webb noted in 1891 that because women were rarely fully trained and rarely performed tasks like tuning their own machines, employers tended to accept the popular idea that they were indeed of inferior value as a workforce.[116] The argument came full circle when employers declared that women were not worth training because of their tendency to leave on marriage. Most employers were quite prepared to employ women on low-grade repetitive jobs, but nothing more. During World War II, despite Ministry of Labour and National Service pamphlets showing the various ways of using women's labour, employers in traditionally male industries, such as shipbuilding, were notably reluctant to try women. There were employers who said that it was impossible for women to work on capstan lathes even though they were doing so elsewhere.[117]

Some employers were converted to the idea of employing women during World War I chiefly because they were cheap, but were unable to retain them because of the dilution agreements made at the beginning of the war. A Women's Industrial Council questionnaire administered to 764 firms, found that almost half would have liked to continue to employ women and specifically mentioned trade union opposition as a reason for not doing so.[118] However, not all employers were convinced that women provided a cheap labour force. One large-scale employer of women told an academic investigator during the early 1930s that he would not consider taking a man off a particular class of work and putting a woman on it. His firm did not favour 'the indiscriminate working of men and women together', and in the comparatively few cases where they did work on the same process the women were put under the separate control of a forewoman. As the investigator commented, this policy meant that any change in the sexual division of labour required the complete transferral of a whole section of work from men to women which was necessarily expensive.[119]

Many employers also considered the employment of married women particularly problematic because of their high rates of absenteeism. The Engineering and National Employers' Federations reported that women's timekeeping was consistently worse than that of men during World War II, although managers of National Projectile Factories declared women to be more reliable.[120] The long hours worked by women in wartime (often on twelve-hour shifts) probably contributed more to their absenteeism than any other single factor, and made the constant comparisons between men and women war workers invidious. During World War II, women lost 65 per cent more time through sickness than did single women, which the Royal Commission on Equal Pay attributed to the fatigue of doing two jobs. Of 1,000 women on nightshift, 40 per cent reported that they had less than six hours sleep.[121] Some employers nevertheless reported that they preferred married women despite their absenteeism because they were more stable and patriotic, but in the years following the war the firms surveyed by Viola Klein showed that they regarded the employment of married women as a necessary expedient to tide them over the post-war labour shortage.[122] Employers also complained about the costs of the supervision women required, the separate welfare provisions that had to be made for them (particularly from 1914 onwards), and the limitations put on their work by protective legislation, although one bookbinding firm found that it was still cheaper in the 1890s to use the new bookfolding machinery only at night (when women were not allowed to work) and to continue to use women in the traditional way by day.[123] Certainly a government committee appointed in 1929 to study the impact of protective legislation on the distribution of women in industry concluded that it did not have a decisive effect.[124]

Direct government intervention in respect to female employment, by way of protective legislation and, after 1911, the manipulation of state benefit regulations, undoubtedly helped to sustain ideas as to what was suitable and unsuitable work for women. The predominant concern of proponents of protective legislation, particularly in the nineteenth century, was morality. The statements of commissioners and witnesses investigating the work of women in the mines and of women chainmakers operating the 'oliver'—the heavy sledgehammer used to cut cold iron—show that their main concern was with the indecency and immorality of a woman performing hard physical labour in male company.[125] During the early twentieth century, pressure was exerted in Parliament to restrict the employment of barmaids, who were, as Mostyn Bird commented, 'more discussed and quarrelled over than any other women who stand behind the counter'. A committee of representatives from women's groups, the labour movement and the clergy deplored the presence of women in a place where 'vile language' was frequently heard and argued that 'a woman cannot be a "moralising influence" unless she is free to show her disapproval of whatever offends her sense of propriety; and she cannot be such in the drinking bar as long as her employer refuses to allow her to do this'.[126]

Proponents of protective legislation were also concerned about the effect of certain kinds of work on women as potential mothers. J. A. Hobson, the economist, asked how the women chainmakers of Cradley Heath 'engaged in wielding large sledge hammers, or carrying on their neck a hundred weight of chain for twelve or fourteen hours a day, in order to earn two or seven shillings a week, bear or rear healthy children?' In 1894 the Royal Commission on Labour took evidence from Medical Officers of Health on the danger married women's work posed to infant life and particular attention was drawn to the white lead industry because of the increased risk of miscarriage as a result of lead poisoning.[127] The Open Door Council continued to resist attempts to exclude women from all lead industries throughout the inter-war period arguing that women needed proper trade union organisation not protection, and that much of women's domestic work was as heavy and dangerous as the factory jobs covered by legislation. Certainly little attention was paid to occupational welfare when the conditions did not relate directly to issues of female morality or motherhood. There seems, for example, to have been no discussion of the Woolwich Medical Officer of Health's revelation in 1903 that one-third of barmaids died of pulmonary tuberculosis. Similarly, the issue of TNT poisoning amongst female munitions workers (popularly referred to as 'canary girls' because of the way the disease turned the skin yellow) did not attract as much attention as lead poisoning which related more directly to maternity.[128] Women trade unionists supported protective legislation and few women would have welcomed the complete relaxation of legislation respecting hours of work such as took place during World War I, but there is some evidence to suggest that women in particular occupations may have found certain aspects of the protective laws irksome. The 1894 Royal Commission on Labour reported that laundresses would have preferred to work four long days and then take the rest of the week off. Similarly, women in early twentieth-century Birmingham did not like the hours of labour set by the Factory Acts, preferring to start and finish later. As it was, they stopped at 7 pm as decreed by the Act, but refused to start earlier than 9 am, thus succeeding in substantially cutting their hours of work.[129] It is thus reasonable to suggest that women in manual trades objected to the rigidity of the Factory Acts rather than the principle of protective legislation *per se*.

Just as protective legislation sought to impose limitations on work considered unsuitable for women, so governments used state benefit regulations to push women into occupations considered particularly appropriate for them. At the end of World War I 'out-of-work donation'—the dole—was offered to all who could prove that they had paid national health insurance contributions for at least three months during 1918. In 1919 the Ministry of Labour became convinced that the dole was being widely abused by married women who had been munitions workers and were therefore entitled to donation, even if they did not intend to go on working. In particular, it was believed that women were refusing readily available work as domestic servants, preferring to draw the dole. A Committee of Inquiry into Out-of-Work Donation warned in 1919 that:

> There are many cases, particularly among women, where the rate of remuneration paid for work of a temporary character during the War has been much higher than that which they can reasonably expect to receive at the present time, many women who during the War were engaged in factories must now enter domestic service if they are to be employed at all...[130]

There was widespread support in the editorial and letter columns of the press for forcing women back into domestic service. A typical writer to *The Times* in 1922 expressed her anger that the dole was being paid to a quarter of a million women when an estimated million homes were without servants. The *Daily Mail*'s 'Scandals of the Dole' series which ran during the April of 1923, finally prompted a government inquiry which found no substance in the charges of abuse. This was not surprising, since no woman applicant for relief was allowed to turn down a 'suitable' vacancy, and no woman who had once been a domestic servant was considered eligible for benefit.[131]

Welfare workers at munitions factories assisted in this drive for women to return to domestic work. Lilian Barker at Woolwich pointed out to women workers 'that if they took 25/- a week and gave nothing in return they were impoverishing the country... we persuaded nearly 3,000 women to go back to domestic service...'[132]. Women claimants also found that the Courts of Referees, which included no women assessors, applied the regulations with vigour and in a manner that was often insensitive. Officials of the NFWW described the case of a 25-year-old member, who refused the offer of daily domestic work in Newcastle at 6/- a week and had her dole money cut off as a result; the decision was upheld by the Referees. The President and Secretary of the Society of Women Welders gave a more vivid description of the experience of one of their members:

> In one case the member and the Society's representative arrived at the Exchange [to appear before the Referees] at 10.20, having been summoned for 10.30. They waited in a small room, with 20 or 30 other women, and as there were only 7 chairs most of them had to stand. It was February and intensely cold, but there was no fire though there was an attempt to light one, abandoned because it did not immediately succeed. Our case was not heard until nearly 12.00, by which time, between cold and apprehension, our member, like the other applicants, was very miserable.[133]

The Society of Women Welders complained bitterly of skilled women being forced to accept unskilled jobs as servants.

During the inter-war years, the administration of state unemployment benefits for women was premised on the dual idea that if the woman applicant had to work, every effort should be made to encourage her to enter domestic service, and if she were married, she should be supported by her husband. The Report of the Royal Commission on Unemployment Insurance stated in 1931:

> It is clear that it is the exception rather than the rule for women after marriage to earn their living by insured employment. It *follows* that in the case of married women as a *class*, industrial employment cannot be regarded as the *normal* condition. (My italics).[134]

The authorities were convinced that married women had a 'different attitude towards wage earning'. This was true in so far as married women often assessed their need to earn in terms of the state of the family economy, but this did not justify the conclusion that their contributions were unnecessary. The Anomalies Act of 1931 assumed that a married woman who left the labour force for any reason had effectively retired. Married women had to satisfy a Court of Referees that they had not withdrawn from employment as a result of marriage and could reasonably expect to obtain insured employment locally in line with their previous work experience, (the assumption being that married women were constrained by their husbands' location in their search for employment). The Act hit married women textile workers particularly hard. Between 1931 and 1933 almost one-third of applications for benefit from married women came from north west England. Of the women's claims considered between 13 October and 3 December 1931, 48 per cent were disallowed and benefit stopped, compared with 4 per cent of those of men.[135]

Domestic service was the only job for which a retraining scheme was offered to unemployed women during the inter-war period. The Central Committee for Women's Employment, set up during World War I, was provided with half a million pounds in 1920 to organise centres to train women in horticulture, hairdressing, journalism and domestic work, but by 1921 its grant was tied exclusively to domestic service training.[136] Formal training for domestic service was also welcomed by government committees set up to examine the servant problem as the best way of raising the status of the work. The 1919 Committee of Inquiry recommended full-time training for 14–16-year-old girls in special schools. The two members of the committee who were active in the labour movement were unable to accept that training was the way to improve the status and conditions of servants, but it was nevertheless given a central place in the Labour Party's Domestic Workers' Charter, published in 1931.[137] The 1932 Royal Commission on Unemployment Insurance reported that 55,000 women and girls had received domestic service training between 1920 and 1931.[138] Nor was domestic service perceived solely in terms of a solution to female unemployment. Another government committee was appointed to investigate the issue during World War II, led by Violet Markham, who like many politicians and policy makers, including Beveridge, was convinced that 'grave questions' arose 'out of the domestic help shortage—the problem of population, the problem of home life, the problem of the professional woman who is carrying an intolerable dual burden'.[139] In the years following the war, Markham succeeded in setting up a National Institute of Houseworkers to promote domestic service as a skilled craft.

Women themselves largely accepted the idea that some work was more suitable for women than others, but by the inter-war years there was a substantial current of opinion flowing against the idea of domestic service as the 'natural' occupation for women, more because of the poor conditions of work than the nature of the job itself. In 1906 working girls were invited by a social investigator to write essays on why they preferred either domestic service or factory work. A domestic servant wrote that servants were 'quieter (*sic*) and more ladylike', but the factory girls' criticisms were focussed firmly on lack of personal liberty. This point came through still more strongly in the survey results published by the Women's Industrial Council in 1916.[140] Loneliness, due in large part to the 'no followers' rule, made domestic service dull, while the deferential relations between servant and mistress often made it additionally humiliating. In the years of full employment following World War II, women workers were able to vote with their feet and leave domestic service for good.

Nevertheless women workers felt a strong sense of the divide between 'rough' and respectable occupations. Domestic service, for all its drawbacks, was respectable. Laundry work, on the other hand, tended to be 'rough', although the sorters, despite the need to handle dirty linen, seem to have enjoyed a higher status and were addressed as 'Miss', while other laundry workers were called by their first names.[141] Barbara Hutchins classified non-textile occupations for women into three broad groups: very rough work, such as rag sorting; machine work; and finishing or warehouse work, considered the most 'superior'. The wages in the last were very low, but it enjoyed high status because it was light and clean. As Sidney Webb commented: 'For women's work the "gentility" of the occupation is still accepted as part payment'.[142] The status ranking of occupations became quite complicated within trades; in textiles the cardroom workers were considered to occupy the lowest place in the hierarchy, while in metal working, lacquering girls were considered the 'ladies' and would not eat with the 'dippers', whom they regarded as their social inferiors. Mostyn Bird wrote that 'the workers of one factory will refuse to recognise those of another in the same street, and one workroom will ignore the other where the work is dirtier or heavier'. The reaction of social investigators to the rigid sense of status distinctions prevailing amongst women workers was ambivalent. The Webbs recognised that the competition for respectable jobs drove down wage rates in those occupations. However, other investigators approved and sought to encourage the apparent desire by so many women workers to achieve respectability: 'As they climb laboriously up into a more and more rarefied air of respectability the codes of etiquette become more rigid and exacting, and many harmless diversions and pleasures have to be sacrificed to their totem. But it is a thing to advance in them and its influence for good is incalculable'.[143] The assumption here that a desire to 'better oneself' was a step towards accepting middle class values may well have been wishful thinking. Many working class women doubtless had good reasons of their own for wanting more 'respectable' jobs. For example, Alice Foley's sister, Cissie, hated her work in the cotton mill and persuaded Alice to become a shop assistant. But dislike of factory work was not accompanied by a wholesale adoption of middle class notions of gentility. Cissie was, on the contrary, active in the suffrage and labour movements.[144]

Women in manual occupations nevertheless tended to share the assumption that their work was temporary and secondary, and to accept that they would be paid less than men. Working class girls often gained little independence from wage earning, because of the amount they contributed to the family exchequer. Girls usually gave up a much greater proportion of their wage than boys. Indeed, the relationship of young women to the workplace and to trade unionism tended to be mediated by the family. After 1907, working class girls were sometimes offered the chance of a secondary school education through the bursary system, which stated that secondary schools receiving government grants had to award one-quarter of their places to 'scholarship children'. Prior to the 1944 Education Act (which secured free secondary education for all) only 20 per cent of children obtained a secondary education, and competition for the free places was strong, especially in rural areas where places were fewest. Some working class women's autobiographies highlight the disappointment experienced when family circumstances and/or the belief that a secondary education was wasted on a girl, prevented a scholarship winner from staying on at school, although others seem to have accepted the decision as inevitable and normal. A Birmingham elementary school log for 1928 shows that fourteen girls passed the scholarship examination but that only four accepted places.[145] For those who did go, poverty often caused additional problems. Molly Weir agonised over the fact that her tunic was made of gaberdine rather than the regulation serge, and Doris Frances was acutely embarrassed when the headmistress required her hair to be washed with soft green soap and combed with a fine (nit) comb. For the small number of working class girls leaving secondary school during the inter-war years there were even fewer job opportunities. In Jean Rennie's case, this meant the additional bitterness of having to work first in the mill and then as a domestic servant.[146]

The majority of girls who left school at a relatively young age were often found jobs by relatives. Very few apprenticeship trades were open to women and the few technical education institutions for girls concentrated on traditional women's occupations such as domestic service.[147] Women's membership of trade unions also tended to be mediated by the family. The rules of the Northern Counties Textiles Trade Federation stated that 'it should be the duty of all members of Amalgamations comprising this Federation to see that all members of their families, over whom they have control, are members of the Associations connected with the trades in which they are working'. Similarly, the Blackburn Association of cotton weavers provided that no 'person' should be eligible for office in the society if 'his wife and children' were not trade union members. In fact girls' trade union subscriptions were usually paid by their mothers.[148]

As adult workers, women accepted that their primary responsibility would be to home and family. A 1947 survey of 2,807 women found that a majority felt they could work only if it did not interfere with their domestic duties. The author of the survey report stressed that no appeal to unoccupied women to ease the post-war labour shortage by returning to work would be successful unless 'practical steps were taken to deal with the problems that face them [married women]'.[149] The strain of combining two jobs, together with the monotonous and uncongenial nature of most work open to women manual workers, were potent reasons for putting family first.

WOMEN'S WORK AND MEN'S WORK IN NON-MANUAL OCCUPATIONS

In line with Olive Schreiner's perception of industrialisation as the cause of middle class women's retreat from productive labour, the Women's Employment Committee of the Ministry of Reconstruction commented in 1918 that with the introduction of the factory system, middle class women had lost their 'natural role' as supervisors of female labour. The Committee saw the appointment of the first woman factory inspector in 1893 as beginning the restoration of middle class women to their rightful place.[150] In fact much of the higher-status work in the service sector that was considered suitable for women during the late nineteenth and early twentieth centuries was done on a voluntary basis. The Prison Commissioners for example commented:

We are strongly in favour of the superintendence and visitation of female prisoners by philanthropic ladies, and we are of the opinion that this recommendation may be adequately met by the extension of voluntary effort. Moreover... the object aimed at by the Committee would be so attained without cost to the state.[151]

The official reason for not appointing more women Poor Law officials was similarly that the increasing number of ladies serving as Guardians made this unnecessary; but these women, like the vast majority of middle class women volunteers, were untrained. When particular aspects of the work traditionally performed by women volunteers were 'professionalised' they were usually strictly segregated from similar work performed by men. Women health officials, for example, were called health visitors, a title which was more closely connected with the visiting work women traditionally did for charitable organisations than with that of the sanitary inspector and which was therefore considered more feminine.[152] In London health visitors were paid half the salary paid to male sanitary inspectors. In keeping with the primary allegiance to family customarily expected of them, early twentieth-century women professionals also tended to take family obligations rather more seriously than might be the case today. Clara Collet cited the case of a teacher who did not take a holiday (and eventually suffered a mental breakdown in consequence) because her father was much averse to his only daughter spending any of her free time away from home.[153] Many women also gave up their careers to care for elderly parents.

Middle class Victorian feminists, highly conscious of the surplus woman problem, sought to open up new forms of paid employment to women. The Association for the Promotion of the Employment of Women, established during the late 1850s, lobbied for a wider variety of work for women as well as sponsoring Emily Faithful's experimental Victoria Press, which taught women printing through the 1860s and 1870s.[154] But many of the new middle class girls' schools and women's colleges encouraged their pupils to pursue a life of philanthropic service rather than paid employment. Miss Beale at Cheltenham and Mrs Toynbee at Oxford, for example, promoted settlement work as a suitable activity for girls after graduation.[155]

The number of women in jobs that required a good education remained very small throughout the period, women comprised only 6 per cent of the higher professions in 1911 and only 8 per cent in 1951.[156] The large increase in the number of female non-manual workers came in the lower-status jobs of shop assistant, teacher, nurse and clerk and owed more to changes in the demand for white-blouse workers than to feminist efforts to expand employment or educational opportunities. Moreover, the wages in some of the occupations, particularly the lowest grades of clerks and shop assistants, showed little improvement over the notoriously poor pay of the Victorian governess, whose plight had so angered middle class feminists.[157] Nevertheless feminists greeted any expansion of women's white-blouse work uncritically; Clara Collet's dry observation that she was not acquainted with any work one could love and honour all day long was atypical.[158]

In professional and white-blouse work employers tended to play a more direct and central role in maintaining patterns of sexual segregation than they did in manual work. In the higher professions employers were also the men who controlled entry to the profession. For example, until World War I very few teaching hospitals admitted women wishing to train as doctors despite the opening of the Medical Register to women in the early 1870s, and similarly, only a group of 183 rather small hospitals, originally organised and staffed by women and specialising in obstetrics, would accept women residents before 1917.[159] During World War I most of the major London teaching hospitals began to take women as students and residents due to the shortage of doctors and because, feminists suggested, the women students proved 'financially useful' to the hospitals in an otherwise difficult period. In 1919 the London hospitals began to close their doors again. The reasons given included the old one that women's 'innate modesty' made co-education an impossibility and that women had adequate training facilities in their own hospital, the Royal Free.[160] Only the Royal Free and University College Hospital continued to accept women students.

Women were also directly excluded from top posts in the Civil Service. Senior male civil servants refused to admit that women were capable of equal work of equal value. The few women appointed to senior posts, such as Mrs Nassau Senior, who was hired to inspect girls' education in workhouse schools in 1874, or Adelaide Anderson, who became the Chief Woman Inspector of Factories, were the social equals of the men they worked with; in the telling words of Warren Fisher, Permanent Secretary at the Treasury from 1919 to 1938, they were 'biggish women'.[161] In view of the role prescription for middle class women this made for particularly acute tensions between the women and their male colleagues. Mrs Nassau Senior had no doubt as to the strength of covert feeling against her appointment; she wrote in 1874 that she had no hope of gaining an assistant and might well lose her own position. In fact she resigned through ill health and was not replaced.[162]

The Civil Service continued to stress women's unsuitability for high office throughout the first half of the twentieth century. The report of the 1912 Royal Commission on the Civil Service concluded firmly that 'in power of sustained work, in the continuity of service, and in adaptability to varying service conditions, the advantage lies with men'. As Meta Zimmeck has shown, the effort of the Treasury to exclude women became more devious and intense after World War I, as increasing numbers of women gained an education that equipped them for administrative posts.[163] The report of the Treasury Committee on Civil Service Recruitment after the war concluded in 1919 that women lacked flexibility and could not be considered interchangeable with men:

> Even when the supply of ex-Service men has been exhausted and recruitment for Class I under normal conditions can be resumed, it will not be practicable to admit women generally to junior administrative posts throughout the service as interchangeable with men until experience has demonstrated not only that they can fill these posts satisfactorily, but that in the same proportion as men they will be competent to carry out the higher administrative duties for which junior administrative work constitutes the regular and necessary training.[164]

It was not clear how women were to acquire the requisite experience when the Committee also favoured preserving segregation of the sexes with a separate promotion line for women. In the 1920 reorganisation of the Civil Service, all classes of work were opened to men and women, but the pyramid structure of writing assistants and clerks at the bottom, and male executive and administrative grades above, was effectively preserved by manipulation of the examination system. As Virginia Woolf remarked on the fate of female examination candidates: '"Miss" transmits sex: and sex may carry with it an aroma'.[165] Only three competitive examinations open to men and women for executive posts were held between 1918 and 1932. Women candidates were required to be older than men, which meant that they faced financial problems during the period between graduation and sitting the exams. Women also tended to fail in disproportionate numbers at the interview stage, despite doing well in the written exams.[166]

In contrast to the administrative grades, very little opposition was encountered with respect to the introduction of women into the clerical and typing grade of the Civil Service. As with so many manual occupations, it was advances in technology, particularly in the form of the typewriter and the telegraph, that created space for women workers. Mid-nineteenth-century clerical work, based on male apprenticeship and personal service, was a high-status occupation. The Prudential Assurance head office of the 1850s employed half a dozen male clerks all of whom became socially mobile in the company. The introduction of the typewriter during the later part of the nineteenth century speeded up the process by which routine clerical work was hived off into a separate, watertight compartment with no possibility of promotion, and this became the preserve of women. Men took on other new jobs that were also created by the changing scale and organisation of office work: for example, accountant, office manager and commercial traveller.[167]

Henry Fawcett, the Postmaster General and husband of Millicant Fawcett, was the first civil servant to promote the employment of female clerks and telegraphists. A post office official commented at length on the advantages of employing women as telegraphists in 1871, maintaining that women were naturally endowed with a good 'eye and ear, and delicacy of touch', as well as patience and docility. Moreover a 'superior class' of female labour could be obtained for less wages than male workers would accept, and female employees, required very few salary increments because they left to get married.[168] The Post Office made resignation on marriage obligatory when women became established in 1875, which saved substantial sums on pension rights. On resignation women were granted a marriage gratuity, an arrangement that was supported not only by women in the lower grades of the service doing dull routine work, but also by older single women. The Federation of Women Civil Servants, however, spoke against the marriage bar because they believed it lowered wage rates.[169] The bar was not lifted in the Civil Service or in industry more generally until after World War II.

The segregation of women into separate grades and types of work made it easy for government departments, who would otherwise have been nervous about the propriety of employing women, to do so. Arrangements for the physical segregation of the sexes were often elaborate in the nineteenth century; women typists occupied separate rooms, took their work only from 'responsible' male officials, who were supplied with a special permit for the purpose, and left the building at different hours from the male workers. Male clerks feared the increasing competition from female labour. One wrote to the *Liverpool Echo* in 1911 to suggest that

> these intrepid 'typewriter pounders', instead of being allowed to gloat over love novels or do fancy crocheting during the time they are not 'pounding' should fill in their spare time washing out the offices and dusting same, which you will no doubt agree is more suited to their sex and maybe would give them a little practice and insight into the work they will be called upon to do should they so far demean themselves as to marry one of the poor male clerks whose living they are doing their utmost to take out of his hands at the present time.

The National Union of Clerks was too weak to defend the position of the male clerk by adopting a policy of exclusion and argued instead for equal pay, making it clear that this position was based on pragmatic considerations rather than principle:

> The low status of the male clerk is due to the fact of the female clerk working for less wages than her competitor; therefore, whether the product of female labour be equal to male labour or not, to raise the salary of the male we must also raise the salary of the female and value her work as equal to that of the male. If the male clerk be so unwise as to be antagonistic to or ignore the female he will make her his rival, and in time she would prove herself so powerful as to oust the male out of his position.[170]

Male teachers were similarly incensed at the growth in the numbers of women teachers. Between 1875 and 1914 the number of women elementary school teachers increased 862 per cent and that of men 292 per cent, with the result that the proportion of female elementary school teachers rose from 54 per cent in 1875 to 75 per cent in 1914.[171] By 1919, 62,000 of the National Union of Teachers' (NUT) 102,000 members were women and the Union had adopted the principle of equal pay. But the policy was pursued halfheartedly, in part because only one-third of the delegates at the 1919 conference were women, and also because of the controversy surrounding the policy. Both the National Association of Schoolmasters (NAS) and the National Union of Women Teachers (NUWT) seceded from the NUT over the issue, leaving the union to try not very successfully to pursue a middle path in the emotional debate.[172]

Unlike doctors and top civil servants, male teachers were not in a position to control recruitment, which was in the hands of the local authorities. The nineteenth-century pupil-teacher system had encouraged the entry of working class school girls into teaching. Like nurses, they learned on the job, attending classes and occasional demonstration lessons at a local day training college. Ellen Wilkinson, who became an MP, began her career as a pupil teacher, but managed to pass her matriculation examinations while at training college, enabling her to escape elementary school teaching altogether.[173] Pupil teaching did not enjoy a high status and it was not unusual for girls to consider it in the same bracket as clerical or shop work. Margaret Bondfield, for example, moved from pupil teaching to work as a shop assistant. Many women teachers remained uncertificated: in 1913 one woman teacher in three was uncertificated, whereas the ratio for men was one in nine. Moreover, the lowest grade of all in the elementary schools, that of supplementary teacher, was entirely female. Supplementary teachers were required only to be vaccinated and approved by an Inspector. Many were in fact the wives of male head teachers.[174]

After 1907, the bursary system of teacher training replaced the pupil-teacher system. Boys or girls intending to become teachers had to stay on longer at school and become student teachers at seventeen. As a result, more middle class women entered the profession and its status rose.[175] A similar development took place in midwifery, where the introduction of formal training in 1902 and its extension in 1916, 1924 and 1937 attracted a new type of recruit. Whereas in 1911, 83 per cent of all midwives were either married or widowed and 70 per cent were aged over 45, by 1931 the comparable percentages were 52 per cent and 48 per cent. The midwife was ceasing to be an older local resident and was becoming a younger, probably middle class, professional. Certainly traditional practitioners with little formal education were squeezed out.[176]

The increasing status of the female teacher posed a threat to male teachers, and as in the Civil Service, tension over the place of women in the profession heightened during the inter-war years. The National Association of Schoolmasters clearly stated the refusal of its members to serve under women. In 1939 its President declared: 'Only a nation heading for a madhouse would force upon men—many men with families—such a position as service under a spinster headmistress'. In fact, of 800 mixed schools in 1934, only fourteen had women head teachers. The NAS adopted as one of its main slogans 'Men teachers for boys', claiming that 'no woman could train a boy in the habits of manliness'. The London Schoolmasters' Association quoted Geddes and Thompson's views on the biological differences between men and women to make their point against equal pay. Not surprisingly, one female teacher in a boys' public school found a majority of boys convinced of women's inferiority.[177]

As employers, local authorities were prepared to employ increasing numbers of women teachers, although they were neither ready to grant equal pay, nor to treat women teachers equally in the promotion stakes. The experience of the fabled Miss Clare, an early twentieth-century elementary school teacher whose career was chronicled in a series of books, was perhaps typical. Miss Clare 'carried the school' during World War I, but after the war ended was passed over for the headship which went instead to a man.[178] From 1922 onwards most local education authorities adopted marriage bars as a publicly acceptable way of acting quickly to create jobs for unemployed college leavers and as a means of reducing expenses in the wake of the public expenditure cuts of 1921. As Alison Oram has pointed out, while the policy may have achieved its goals in the short term, it did nothing to solve the fundamental difficulties regarding either teacher supply and demand or educational financing.[179] Local authorities argued in support of the marriage bar that married women were less efficient. In an unsuccessful court case brought by 57 married women teachers against the Rhondda Urban District Council in 1923, the Council testified that married women's 'periodical temporary absences' were not beneficial from the educational point of view and were inconvenient for employers. The counsel for the women teachers attempted to invoke the Sex Disqualification (Removal) Act of 1919 which stated that 'a person should not be disqualified by sex or marriage from the exercise of any public function or from being appointed or holding any civil or judicial office or post or from entering or assuming or carrying on any civil profession or vocation'. But the court chose to interpret the clause negatively in the spirit of nineteenth-century equal rights legislation, ruling that while a woman was not *dis*qualified by virtue of marriage, this did not mean she was necessarily *entitled* to employment.[180] During the 1920s and 1930s, married women teachers who were permitted to continue in post because their husbands were sick or disabled were often subjected to humiliating inquiries as to the size of their household income. Oral evidence has suggested that some women took off their wedding rings and continued to work as single women, but it is impossible to establish the numbers who acted in this way.[181]

Women in non-manual occupations, particularly those in the professions, experienced rather more direct discrimination by employers in respect to recruitment and promotion than did manual workers. As the number of qualified women increased, and it became usual for middle class girls to work on leaving school, the lines of sexual segregation were increasingly closely defended, a pattern exacerbated rather than explained by the economic depression. Ideas regarding the proper role of married women in particular lay behind the introduction of the marriage bar, which assumed that all married women could be treated as a reserve army of labour because of the primary responsibility to home and family and because they could be expected to rely on their husbands for financial support. This view was more rigidly enforced in the case of professional women, who were the daughters and potential wives of the men implementing the marriage bar, and whose roles were the more rigidly prescribed.

WOMEN'S WAGES AND THE EQUAL PAY DEBATE

Women's low pay began to be defined as a problem towards the end of the nineteenth century, chiefly in relation to the problem of homework and the sweated trades. Sweated workers could not be dismissed as part of the idle, demoralised residuum; on the contrary they worked very hard for very little and it was this that aroused outcry from crusading journalists and social investigators. Moreover, there was always the fear that low wages would be supplemented via prostitution. William Acton's 1857 study of prostitution suggested that the prostitute moved into her trade by choice and left it after a few years without ill effect: 'they live an idle life, pass much of their time in the open air, are generally well-clothed and well fed, and then proceed in their career with a capacity of withstanding the attacks of disease and of bearing its results, which is denied to their respectable but poorer and harder worked sisters'. Frances Finnegan's study of York prostitutes between 1837 and 1857 suggests that the more traditional picture of a life-time's poverty, disease and degradation was in fact the more accurate one.[182] Certainly contemporaries hinted darkly at the connections between low wages and prostitution and one observer referred to the relationship as the 'one ghastly investigation still awaiting the economist'. Mrs Lyttleton's play *Warp and Woof* included a scene where a poor dressmaker prostituted herself in order to get money to help her dying sister.[183]

The Trade Boards Act of 1909, which laid down minimum male and female rates in particularly low paid trades, was perceived as necessary 'protective' legislation for women workers who were too weak to improve their lot. One of the major preoccupations of the promoters of the Act (as in the case of protective legislation governing hours and conditions of work) was the moral issue: the link between low wages and prostitution on the one hand and impoverished mothers and high infant mortality on the other.[184] It was not suggested that women's work was being undervalued. Sidney Webb and Professor F. Y. Edgeworth believed that women's inferior earnings were mainly due to inferior productive power, in terms of both quantity and quality.[185] Women's lack of resourcefulness, their propensity to marry and high absenteeism were regularly catalogued as causes of their low pay. A representative of the Yorkshire and Lancashire manufacturers complained that women stayed away from work for trivial reasons: 'A day's washing may be a very serious thing for a woman, but to stay away and leave her machine idle for a day's wash does not appear to be anything but trivial to her employer'.[186] A similar view was stated more forcefully by the Civil Service Commissioner, who agreed that women's family responsibilities were incompatible with devotion to the public service. Because of their role as potential and actual wives and mothers, women workers were considered a class apart. In 1897, the Webbs concluded that the sexual segregation of labour was desirable for moral and economic reasons and that both men and women should be secured separate minimum rates. Women, they argued, had dissimilar faculties, needs and expectations, which therefore required that they be employed on different tasks at different rates, although, noting women's much lower 'standard of comfort', Sidney Webb wondered whether they might not 'do more work, and better, if they learned to eat more'.[187]

Those lobbying for minimum wage legislation consciously eschewed sentimental arguments. Not only was a national minimum necessary for the future welfare of the race, but also for the efficiency of industry. R. H. Tawney argued that businesses should not be allowed to exist on artificially cheap labour, but should be forced to modernise. Like other proponents of a minimum wage, he realised that this would mean unemployment for some workers: 'Their disappearance may be regarded with sympathy for the individual, but without solicitude for the industry, for it is not upon them that its fate depends'. Two late nineteenth-century women trade unionists, Gertrude Tuckwell and Lady Dilke, argued that minimum wage legislation should be welcomed because it would both stop women dragging down wages and raise male incomes, thus making the work of married women unnecessary. Homeworkers in particular were regarded as largely inefficient workers who would be eliminated by the introduction of a minimum wage.[188]

Not all observers agreed that the additional protection afforded by a minimum wage was the answer to the problem of women's low pay. Millicent Fawcett and F. Y. Edgeworth argued that the major cause of women's low wages was that they were 'crowded' into particular occupations primarily because of trade union restrictive practices.[189] They maintained that if these and all other legal restrictions in the form of protective legislation were removed, women workers would become more evenly spread throughout the workforce and higher pay would follow.

Fawcett and Edgeworth were stating the classical case for the removal of barriers to equal opportunity at the individual level and assumed that once this was done any inequalities (in terms of job segregation and unequal pay) that remained would be natural and irremovable. Fawcett, in common with other commentators,[190] also believed that education of the woman worker and her employer was necessary to overcome the burden of traditional attitudes towards women's work. Female domestic servants, for example, should be taught to be more resourceful and the mistress should be dissuaded from paying a butler more than a parlourmaid. Unlike supporters of the minimum wage, Fawcett and Edgeworth recognised a connection between occupational segregation and low pay, but their solutions focused on removing inequalities at the individual level, with little consideration of the structures giving rise to those inequalities. In particular, they ignored the relationship between women's position in the family and their position in the labour market. Millicent Fawcett belonged to the feminist tradition which argued that women had to choose between wife and motherhood and a career. Eleanor Rathbone also believed this, but recognised nonetheless that the idea of a family wage, payable to a male breadwinner, affected the wage rates commanded by single women. Thus she promoted family allowances as a means of circumventing the arguments that men needed a family wage, put forward by male trade unionists and groups such as the National Association of Schoolmasters. If the state supported children, wages could be paid on a bachelor/spinster basis.[191] But to Fawcett and Edgeworth family allowances represented an unwelcome measure of state intervention which might undermine male work incentives.

Fawcett, Edgeworth and Rathbone developed their ideas in response to the debate over equal pay which came to the fore during World War I as a result of the rapid breakdown of sexual divisions in the workforce. Male and female unionists were concerned above all to ensure that women employed on men's work obtained the male rate. In general it was correctly assumed that the employment of women on men's work in manufacturing industry would cease at the end of the war, but the issue of equal pay for those who did stay and for women in white-blouse occupations, particularly in the civil service and in teaching, remained an important issue for debate by economists and government committees considering women's employment position after the war. The majority of participants in the debate shared the assumptions underlying the earlier discussions of women's low pay and the need for minimum wage legislation. Just as it had been considered that minimum wage legislation would mean the expulsion of women from the labour market because of their 'natural' inferiority, so it was argued that a policy of equal pay would result in large scale unemployment of women. Clementina Black testified to a government committee that 'although in equity one ought to pay both [men and women] alike,. . . in the present state of things it would be injurious to the women to pay them quite as much'. Eleanor Rathbone also argued that 'the attempt to establish strict arithmetical equality between them goes further than is necessary to protect the man against unfair competition and really weights the scales against the woman'.[192] Neither Fawcett nor Edgeworth favoured withholding equal pay for equal work for fear of rendering women unemployed, but both fully anticipated (like J.S. Mill before them) that women might well prove less productive and therefore less valuable to employers, which would be reflected in higher unemployment rates. There was never any discussion of making provision to pay women a higher rate if they proved to be *more* efficient workers.[193]

The Majority Report of the 1919 War Cabinet Committee on Women in Industry accepted the idea that the 'rate for the job' would weaken women's bargaining power and thus their employment prospects. It recommended that women doing similar, or the same work as men, should receive equal pay in proportion to output. In other words, it favoured equal piece rates but not equal time rates, believing that the former would be sufficient to protect men from unfair competition, with the additional advantage of enabling women to be hired at times of expanding trade and increased production. The Majority Report thus contemplated a limited equal pay strategy as a means to increasing the female reserve army of labour. The idea of comparing the value of women engaged in women's work (such as nursing) with work performed exclusively by men (such as mining) was rejected as impossible. In making provision for equal pay for women working on the same tasks as men the assumption was that only a minority of women workers would be affected, as the majority would continue to work on women's processes for which they would be paid a minimum women's rate. Barbara Drake agreed with the logic of this position, but observed that it was very important to fix the woman's rate as high as possible: 'The fight for equal pay may, indeed, be won or lost in *women*'s trades'[194] (her italics).

Beatrice Webb's Minority Report to the War Cabinet Committee advocated a single rate for the job, whether by piece or time rate. Webb perceived quite accurately (in the light of the experience of the 1970s equal pay legislation) that employers could avoid the injunction to pay equal wages for equal work by slightly altering a particular work process and paying a lower rate. Webb did not doubt that the rate for the job would lead to female unemployment because she also believed that most women were inferior workers. Like a minimum wage policy, equal pay would rid the labour market of its inefficient members. That a majority of these were likely to be women was no bad thing in her view, because women could always return to the home or train as domestic servants.[195] A similar point was made by Barbara Drake in evidence to the War Cabinet Committee: 'The residue of women could provide a margin of labour for periods of good trade. If either sex is to be short of employment it had better be the women'.[196] The decision on the part of some women active in the labour movement to accept exclusion from the labour market rather than unequal pay must be considered in the context of women trade unionists' preoccupation with the need to stop women undercutting the male rate. Little attention was paid to the problems posed by the occupational segregation. In this regard, Beatrice Webb maintained that any sexual segregation of the labour force remaining after the implementation of equal pay would be due to 'natural differences' between the sexes.[197] This attitude was similar to Millicent Fawcett's, except that Fawcett identified trade union discrimination against women as the root cause of the problem, while labour movement activists like Beatrice Webb blamed the practices of employers. Neither analysed, as Rathbone began to do, the implications of the division of resources and power within the family for women as workers, and no one questioned the assumption that women were inferior workers.

During World War I limited guarantees regarding equal pay were seen by government as the necessary price for dilution. The trade union movement had always pursued a policy of either excluding women from particular jobs or seeking equal pay, the emphasis being very much on the former, despite the TUC's resolution in favour of equal pay passed in 1888. During the war, male unionists continued to resist dilution. The removal of thousands of women from industry after the war solved the problem from all points of view, and even the moderate recommendations of the Majority Report of the War Cabinet Committee were ignored.[198] However, the position of women doing the same work as men in the Civil Service and in the teaching profession continued to attract attention. The House of Commons passed resolutions in favour of equal pay during 1920 and 1921, although there is evidence that the motives of some MPs were mixed. In 1935 Colonel Clifton Brown, 'greatly alarmed' by the increase in the employment of women in the Civil Service, advocated equal pay as a solution, the assumption being that all things being equal men would be preferred.[199]

It was not until the end of World War II that a strong campaign for equal pay as a matter of social justice was mounted, after the successful fight for equal compensation for civilian war injuries.[200] Equal pay for teachers passed the House of Commons as part of the 1944 Education Bill by one vote, a decision that was reversed only by Churchill making the issue a vote of confidence and promising to set up a Royal Commission on the subject. The equal pay campaign became an essentially middle class movement.[201] The Standing Joint Committee of Working Women's Organisations remained suspicious of middle class feminists and did not take part, although women workers showed themselves willing to strike for equal pay during the War. Male trade unionists no longer aimed to keep women out of industry. George Woodcock, speaking for the TUC said plainly: 'We are asking for equal pay not for prohibition'. With full employment, greater productivity and family allowances, the TUC was optimistic that equal pay could be achieved without damaging the position of the male worker.[202] Nevertheless, trade unions were suspicious of state intervention to set wage rates and were more favourably inclined towards equal pay in the public service than in industry.[203]

The Majority Report of the Royal Commission on Equal Pay firmly rejected the idea that 'individual justice' was the main principle to be considered: 'the ultimate question for decision is *what price*, in the shape of departure from exact distributive justice as between individuals, is worth paying for what degree of social advantage of other kinds'. The Commissioners continued to fear female unemployment if wages were levelled up to the male rate and male displacement if they were levelled down, and it therefore recommended, in similar fashion to the War Cabinet Committee of 1919, equal pay for occupations where men and women were engaged on the same tasks, and fixed male and female rates for jobs defined as predominantly men's or women's work. The Commissioners' desire to cause as little disruption as possible to the labour market thus led to a recommendation to maintain sexual segregation. As the Minority Report compiled by the three female commissioners (Anne Loughlin, the first woman President of the TUC; Dr. Janet Vaughan, a former civil servant and medical doctor; and Lucy Frances Nettlefold, a company director) pointed out, the Majority Report feared two results of equal pay that were not in fact compatible with each other. First it speculated on the 'embarrassing' number of women equal pay might attract to the administrative level of the Civil Service and gave serious consideration to Mr. R.F. Harrod's warnings that motherhood must not be made to unattractive, while second, it continued to assert that equal pay would in all probability mean an increase in female unemployment. The female commissioners were nevertheless still convinced as to female inferiority in the workplace, though not to the tune of existing wage differentials.[204]

Equal pay was not achieved in the immediate post-war period chiefly because of the Labour government's refusal to contemplate the cost of implementing it during a national austerity campaign and because of the TUC agreement to back down on the issue.[205] Trade unions, including the Engineers, now pursued a policy of female recruitment, but women workers remained largely confined to low-paid, low-status occupations and their union density remained static. By the 1930s, unions were condemning trade boards as inimical to trade union organisation amongst women (it appears that while trade boards initially stimulated increases in women's trade union membership, these soon tailed off),[206] but unions were never successful in organising low paid women workers. The failure of both unions and government to recognise the structural factors affecting women's relationship to the labour market (particularly their reproductive role and the domestic division of labour), other than to conceptualise them as handicaps rendering women in need of protection, has meant that there has been little change in the overall position of women workers.

NOTES

1. John Hodgson to May Tennant, 12 July 1901, Coll. Misc. 486, BLPES.
2. Judy Lown, 'Not so much a Factory, More a Form of Patriarchy: Gender and Class during Industrialisation', in *Gender Class and Work*, eds. Eva Gmarnikow *et.al.* (Heinemann, 1983), pp.28-45.
3. J. Ramsay McDonald, *Women in the Printing Trades* (P.S. King, 1904), pp. viii, 65-6.
4. Raphael Samuel ed., *Miners, Quarrymen and Saltworkers* (Routledge & Kegan Paul, 1977), p. xii.
4. Catherine Hakim, Occupational Segregation, Research Paper No. 9 (Dept. Of Employment, 1979), pp. 22-34.
6. Sidney Webb, 'The Alleged Differences in the Wages Paid to Men and to Women for Similar Work', *Economic Journal* **1** (December 1891), pp. 635-662.
7. PP., 'Report of the War Cabinet Committee on Women in Industry', Cmd. 135, 1919, XXXI, 241, p. 89.
8. PP., 'Report from the Select Committee on Equal Compensation' (53), 1942-3, III, 41, p. 7.
9. PP., 'Report of the Royal Commission on Equal Pay', Cmd 6937, 1945-6, XI, 651, p. 52; E.M. Gray, *The Weaver's Wage* (Manchester: Manchester University Press, 1937), pp. 12-3; Barbara Drake, *Women in Trade Unions* (Labour Research Dept., 1920), p. 27; Amy Bulley and Margaret Whitely, *Women's Work* (Methuen, 1894), p. 97.
10. Gray, *Weaver's Wage*, pp. 35-6.
11. PP., 'Final Report of the Royal Commission on Labour', C. 7421, 1894, XXXV, 9, p. 92; Edith Lyttleton, *Warp and Woof* (T. Fisher Unwin, 1908).
12. Barbara Drake, *Women in the Engineering Trades* (Fabian Research Dept., 1917), p. 19; see also Adelaide Anderson, *Women in the Factory. An Administrative Adventure, 1832-1921* (John Murray, 1922), p. 67.
13. Drake, *Women in the Engineering Trades*, p. 20. On premium bonus systems see, Craig Littler, 'Deskilling and Changing Structures of Control', in *The Degredation of Work?*, ed. Stephen Wood (Hutchinson, 1982), p. 136; Richard Price, 'The Labour Process and Labour History', *Social History* **8** (January 1983), p. 67; and Jonathan Zeitlin, 'Craft Control and the Division of Labour: Engineers and Compositors in Britain 1890-1930', *Cambridge Journal of Economics* **3** (September 1979), p. 268.
14. Sarah Boston, *Women Workers and the Trade Union Movement* (Davis Poynter, 1980), p. 48.
15. C. 7421, p. 484; Drake, *Women in Trade Unions*, pp. 58-9; and B.L. Hutchins, *Women in Modern Industry* (G. Bell, 1915), p.101.
16. Lee Holcombe, *Victorian Ladies at Work. Middle Class Working Women in England and Wales 1850-1914* (Hamden, Conn.: Archon Books, 1973), pp. 111 and 151; Joseph Hallsworth and Rhys J. Davies, *The Working Life of Shop*

Assistants (Manchester: by the authors, 1910), p. 66; Alison Oram, '"Sex Antagonism" in the Teaching Profession: Employment Issues and the Woman Teacher in Elementary Education, 1910-39', PhD. thesis in progress, University of Bristol, and Theresa Davy, 'Female Shorthand Typists and Typists, 1900-1939', unpublished M.A. Diss. University of Essex, 1980, pp. 37-8.

17. Charles Booth, *London Life and Labour*, Vol. IV, 1st edn. 1889 (Macmillan, 1902), pp. 320-321.
18. Clementina Black, *Sweated Industry and the Minimum Wage* (Duckworth, 1907), p. 49.
19. M. Mostyn Bird, *Women at Work* (Chapman Hall, 1911), p. 70; and Holcombe, *Victorian Ladies at Work*, p. 135.
20. Neal A Ferguson, 'Women's Work: Employment Opportunities and Economic Roles 1918-1939', *Albion* **7** (Spring 1975), p. 61; and Oram, '"Sex Antagonism"'.
21. Dorothea M. Barton, 'The Course of Women's Wages', *Journal of the Royal Statistical Society* LXXXII (July 1919), p. 508; and E.H. Hunt, *British Labour History 1815–1914* (Weidenfeld and Nicolson, 1982), p. 106. On servants wages see also J.A. Banks, *Prosperity and Parenthood* (Routledge & Kegan Paul, 1954), p. 79.
22. Guy Routh, *Occupation and Pay 1906–1960* (Cambridge: Cambridge University Press, 1965), pp. 95 and 99.
23. Edward Cadbury, Cecile M. Matheson and George Shann, *Women's Work and Wages* (T. Fisher Unwin, 1906), pp. 14–15; and B. Seebohm Rowntree, *The Human Needs of Labour* (Thomas Nelson, 1918), p. 117.
24. Drake, *Women in Trade Unions*, p.44.
25. R.H. Tawney, *The Establishment of Minimum Rates in the Tailoring Industry* (G. Bell, 1915), p. 48 and 205; B. Seebohm Rowntree, *The Human Needs of Labour* (Longman, 1937), p. 107; and Dorothy Sells, *The British Trade Boards System* (P.S. King, 1923), pp. 40-41, 83, and *British Wages Boards* (Washington D.C.: Brookings Institute, 1939), pp. 235, 282-5.
26. Ellen Smith, *Wage-Earning Women and their Dependants* (Fabian Women's Group, 1915); and B. Seebohm Rowntree and Frank D. Stuart, *The Responsibility of Women Workers for Dependants* (Oxford: Clarendon Press, 1921).
27. PP., 'Accounts of Expenditure of Wage Earning Women and Girls', Cd. 5963, 1911, LXXXIX, 531, pp. 73 and 81.
28. Dorothea E. Proud, *Welfare Work* (G. Bell, 1918), p. 85; and C. Fremlin, *The Seven Chars of Chelsea* (Methuen, 1940), p.15.
29. Jane Marcus ed., *The Young Rebecca: Writings of Rebecca West 1911-17* (Virago, 1983), p. 356; and Mary Higgs, *Where Shall She Live? The Homelessness of the Woman Worker* (P.S. King, 1910), p. 149.
30. PP., 'Fifth Report of the Select Committee of the House of Lords on the Sweating System' (165), 1890, XVII, 257, p. viii; and Joan Beauchamp,

Women Who Work (Lawrence and Wishart, 1937), p. 22.

31. Louise Jermy, *The Memories of a Working Woman* (Norwich: Goose and Son, 1934), p. 42.
32. Theresa McBride, *The Domestic Revolution* (New York: Holmes and Meier, 1976), p. 74; and PP., 'Report by Miss Collet on the Money Wages of Indoor Domestic Servants', C. 9346, 1899, XCII, 1, p. 15.
33. Penelope Summerfield, 'Women Workers in the Second World War. A Study of the Interplay in Official Policy between the Need to Mobilise Women for War and Conventional Expectations about their Roles at Work and at Home, in the period 1939–45', unpublished PhD. Diss., University of Sussex, 1982, p. 2.
34. Bird, *Women at Work*, p. 3; and Hutchins, *Women in Modern Industry*, p. xiii. For a recent theoretical analysis of the relationship between the characteristics of jobs and workers, see R.D. Barron and G.M. Norris, 'Sexual Divisions and the Dual Labour Market', in *Dependence and Exploitation in Work and Marriage*, eds. D.L. Barker and Sheila Allen (Longman, 1976), pp. 47-69.
35. Norbert C. Soldon, *Women in British Trade Unions, 1874-1976* (Totowa, NJ: Rowan and Littlefield, 1978), p. 40.
36. Drake, *Women in Trade Unions*, p.45.
37. Webb, 'Alleged Differences in Wages', p. 649.
38. See for example, Brian Chiplin and C. Sloane, *Sex Discrimination and the Labour Market* (Croom Helm, 1976). For a review of various theories of women's position in the labour market see Alice Amsden, *The Economics of Women's Work* (Harmondsworth: Penguin, 1980); and Irene Bruegel, 'Women's Employment, Legislation and the Labour Market' in *Women's Welfare/Women's Rights*, ed. Jane Lewis (Croom Helm, 1983), p. 130-169.
39. Deborah Thom, 'The Ideology of Women's Work 1914–24, with Special Reference to the National Federation of Women Workers and other Trade Unions', unpublished PhD. Diss., Thames Polytechnic, 1982, p. 127.
40. Jill Rubery, 'Structured Labour Markets, Worker Organisation and Low Pay', *Cambridge Journal of Economics* **2** (1978), pp. 17-36.
41. Harry Braverman, *Labour and Monopoly Capital* (New York: Monthly Review Press, 1974). On dual labour market theory see Barron and Norris, 'Sexual Divisions and the Dual Labour Market'.
42. Drake, *Women in the Engineering Trades*, p. 66; and Sheila T. Lewenhak, *Women and Trade Unions* (E Benn, 1977) p. 93. On sex and skill generally see, Anne Phillips and Barbara Taylor, 'Sex and Skill: Notes Towards a Feminist Economics', *Feminist Review* No. 6 (1980), pp. 79-88.
43. On the concepts of socially constructed and genuine skill see Charles More, *Skill and the English Working Class, 1870-1914* (Croom Helm, 1980); and Veronica Beechey, 'The Sexual Division of Labour and the Labour Process', in *The Degradation of Work?*, ed. Stephen Wood, pp. 54-73.
44. Alan Fox, *A History of the National Union of Boot and Shoe Operatives, 1874–1957*

(Oxford: Blackwell, 1958), pp. 261, 308, 369-70.

45. Sally Alexander, 'Women's Work in Nineteenth Century London. A Study of the Years 1820–40', in *The Rights and Wrongs of Women*, ed. Juliet Mitchell and Ann Oakley (Harmondsworth: Penguin, 1976), pp. 59-111; and Michele Barrett, *Women's Oppression Today* (Verso, 1980).
46. Catherine Hall, 'The Home Turned Upside Down? The Working Class Family in Cotton Textiles, 1780–1850', in *The Changing Experience of Women*, eds. Elizabeth Whitelegg *et.al.* (Oxford: Martin Robertson, 1982), pp. 17-29.
47. Price, 'Labour Process and Labour History'; Rubery, 'Structured Labour Markets'; and Wood, *The Degradation of Work*?.
48. Cmd. 135, p. 257.
49. Jane Humphries, 'Class Struggle and the Resistance of the Working Class Family', *Cambridge Journal of Economics* **1** (September 1977), pp. 241-58; see above, p. 50.
50. As it is argued by Louise Tilly and Joan Scott, *Women, Work and Family* (New York: Holt Rinehart, 1978).
51. PP., 'Report of the Civil Service National Whitley Council Committee on the Marriage Bar in the Civil Service', Cmd. 6886, 1945–6, X. 871, p. 4.
52. Leonore Davidoff, 'The Rationalisation of Housework', in *Dependence and Exploitation in Work and Marriage*, eds. Barker and Allen, pp. 121–51.
53. Celia Davies, 'Making Sense of the Census in Britain and the USA: the Changing Occupational Classification and the Position of Nurses', *Sociological Review* **28** (1980), pp. 581-609.
54. Jenny Morris, 'The Sweated Trades, Women Workers and the Trade Boards Act of 1909: An Exercise in Social Control', unpublished PhD. Diss., LSE, 1982, p. 38.
55. Nancy Grey Osterud, 'Women's Work in Nineteenth Century Leicester: A Case Study in the Sexual Division of Labour', paper given at the 4th Berkshire Conference, Mount Holyoke, Mass., 1978.
56. Duncan Bythell, *The Sweated Trades* (Batsford, 1978), p. 125; and PP., 'Third Report of the Select Committee of the House of Lords on the 'Sweating System' (165), 1889, XIII, 1, Q. 18507.
57. Fox, *History of the National Union of Boot and Shoe Operatives*, p. 17, footnote.
58. Drake, *Women in Trade Unions*, p. 23.
59. Gertrude Tuckwell, *Women in Industry from Seven Points of View* (Duckworth, 1908), p. 65.
60. PP., 'Minutes of Evidence taken before the Royal Commission on Labour', C. 7063, 1893–4, 39, Q. 4447; and Boston, *Women Workers and the Trade Union Movement*, p. 56.
61. Drake, *Women in Trade Unions*, p. 17.
62. Osterud, 'Women's Work in Nineteenth Century Leicester'.
63. Boston, *Women Workers and the Trade Union Movement*, p. 86; Drake, *Women in Trade Unions*, p. 66; Sheila Lewenhak, 'Trade Unionism among Women

and Girls in the U.K., 1920–65', unpub. PhD. Diss., LSE, 1971, p. 137.

64. Marion Kosak, 'Women Munition Workers during the First World War', unpublished PhD. Diss., University of Hull, 1976, pp. 298 and 304.
65. Boston, *Women Workers in the Trade Union Movement*, p. 150; and Soldon, *Women in British Trade Unions*, p. 161.
66. Drake, *Women in Trade Unions*, p. 137; and Lewenhak, 'Trade Unionism among Women and Girls', p. 153.
67. William Lazonick, 'Industrial Relations and Technical change: the Case of the Self Acting Mule', *Cambridge Journal of Economics* **3** (September 1979), pp. 231-262.
68. N. Adler and R.H. Tawney, *Boy and Girl Labour* (Women's Industrial Council, 1909); Hutchins, *Women in Modern Industry*, p. 192; and PP., 'A Study of the Factors which have Operated in the Past and those which are Operating now to Determine the Distribution of Women in Industry', Cmd 3508, 1929–30, XVII, 1019, p. 10.
69. H. A. Turner, *Trade Union Structure and Policy* (Allen and Unwin, 1962), p. 143; Beatrice Webb and Sidney Webb, *Industrial Democracy* (Longman, 1919), p. 424; William Lazonick, 'Industrial Relations and Technical Change', and 'Production Relations, Labour Productivity, and Choice of Technique: British and US Cotton Spinning' *Journal of Economic History* XLI (September 1981), pp. 491-516. I am also grateful to Roger Penn for a personal communication on these issues.
70. Drake, *Women in Trade Unions*, p. 61.
71. L.H.C. Tippett, *A Portrait of the Lancashire Textile Industry* (Oxford: Oxford University Press, 1969), pp. 69-71. I am grateful to Jill Liddington for this reference.
72. H.A. Clegg, A. Fox and A.F. Thompson, *A History of British Trade Unions Since 1889*, vol. I (Oxford: Clarendon, 1964), p. 119; C. 7421, p. 537; Bulley and Whitely, *Women's Work*, p. 98; Webb and Webb, *Industrial Democracy*, p. 497 note 1; Caroline Foley, 'Review of the Royal Commission on Labour', *Economic Journal* **4** (March 1894), p. 187; Margaret Hewitt, *Wives and Mothers in Victorian Industry* (Rockliff, 1958) pp. 50-5; and Susan Bruley, 'Socialism and Feminism in the Communist Party of Great Britain, 1920–39; unpublished PhD. Diss., 1980, p. 201.
73. Turner, *Trade Union Structure*, pp. 164, 260, 293; and Roger Penn, 'Trade Union Organisation and Skill in the Cotton and Engineering Industries in Britain 1850–1960', *Social History* **8** (January 1983), pp. 37-56.
74. Barbara Taylor, *Eve and the New Jerusalem* (Virago, 1983), pp. 83–117.
75. Doris Nield Chew, *Ada Nield Chew: The Life and Writings of a Working Woman* (Virago, 1982), p. 13.
76. B.L. Hutchins and A. Harrison, *A History of Factory Legislation* (P.S. King, 1907), pp. 176–183; and the debate between Jenny Morris, 'State Reform and the Local Economy' and James A. Smiechen, 'State Reform and the Local Economy: A Reply', *Economic History Review* XXXV (May 1982), pp. 292–305.

77. Charles Booth, *London Life and Labour*, Vol. IV (Macmillan, 1902), pp. 261-2.
78. Booth, *Life and Labour*, Vol. IV, p. 258; and V. de Vessilitsky, *The Homeworker and her Outlook* (G. Bell, 1916), p. 27.
79. MacDonald, *Women in the Printing Trades*, pp. 4–5.
80. Felicity Hunt, 'Women in the Nineteenth Century Bookbinding and Printing Trades, 1790-1914', unpublished M.A. Diss., University of Essex, 1979, p. 77. Hunt's article, 'The London Trade in the Printing and Binding of Books: An Experience in Exclusion, Dilution and De-skilling for Women Workers', Women's Studies International Forum 6 (1983), pp. 517-24, appeared after this chapter was written.
81. McDonald, *Women in the Printing Trades*, p.28; Hunt, 'Women in the Nineteenth Century Bookbinding and Printing Trades', pp. 65-70 and 78-9; Zeitlin, 'Craft Control and the Division of Labour', p.264.
82. Thom, 'The Ideology of Women's Work', is clearest on this and effectively refutes the argument of Arthur Marwick in *Women at War 1914-18* (Fontana, 1977).
83. Drake, *Women in the Engineering Trades*, p.18; Gail Braybon, *Women Workers in the First World War* (New York: Barnes and Noble, 1981), p.48.
84. Thom, 'The Ideology of Women's Work', p.48.
85. J.W.F. Rowe, *Wages in Practice and Theory* (Routledge & Kegan Paul, 1928), pp.93, 110; and Roger Penn, 'Skilled Manual Workers in the Labour Process 1856–1964', in *The Degradation of Work?*, ed. Wood, p.92; Zeitlin, 'Craft Control and the Division of Labour', p.271; and Drake, *Women in the Engineering Trades*, p.8.
86. James Hinton, *The First Shop Stewards' Movement* (Allen and Unwin, 1973), is the classic work on the dilution struggles of World War I, but he unfortunately does not discuss the position of women.
87. Braybon, *Women Workers in the First World War*, pp. 60–1; Kosak, 'Women Munition Workers', pp. 99 and 102; and PP., 'Report of the Women's Employment Committee of the Ministry of Reconstruction', Cd. 9239, 1918, XIV, 783, p. 82.
88. Cmd. 135, pp. 122, 197, 255; and Kosak, 'Women Munition Workers', p. 159.
89. Elizabeth Flint, *Hot Bread and Chips* (Museum Press, 1963), p. 32; and John Burnett, *Useful Toil* (Harmondsworth: Penguin, 1974), pp. 125-132.
90. Thom, 'The Ideology of Women's Work', pp. 73 and 140.
91. Kosak, 'Women Munition Workers', p. 317.
92. Drake, *Women in the Engineering Trades*, p. 109.
93. Cmd. 135, p. 83.
94. Ministry of Labour, *22nd. Abstract of Labour Statistics of the UK, 1922–36* (HMSO, 1927). Any measure of unemployment must be treated with extreme caution. As W.R. Garside has pointed out, official statistics represent 'not a complete census but merely a count of those individuals who, according to the law and administrative practice of the time, felt it

worthwhile to record themselves as out of work at an Employment Exchange' [*The Measurement of Unemployment, Methods and Sources in Great Britain, 1850–1979* (Oxford: Blackwell, 1980), p. 48].

95. Irene Bruegel, 'Women as a Reserve Army of Labour: A Note on the Recent British Experience', *Feminist Review* No. 3 (1979), pp. 12-23.
96. Guy Routh, *Occupation and Pay 1906–60* (Cambridge: Cambridge University Press, 1965), p. 31.
97. H. Llewellyn Smith, *New Survey of London Life and Labour* Vol. II (P.S. King, 1931), p. 19; and Penn, 'Skilled Manual Workers', p. 97.
98. Cmd. 3508, p. 14. Press work involved inserting a small sheet of metal between metal guides on a machine which it had been cut to fit and by which it was correctly centred over the die. Pressing a lever then brought down the press and simultaneously drew a metal guard across the mouth of the machine to protect the worker's hand. The press rose automatically and the part was removed and dropped into a receptacle. The whole process took about a quarter of a minute.
99. Boston, *Women Workers and the Trade Union Movement*, p. 65; Hutchins, *Women in Modern Industry*, pp. 128-31; Bruley, 'Socialism and Feminism in the Communist Party of Great Britain', p. 193; and James E Cronin, *Industrial Conflict in Modern Britain* (Croom Helm, 1979), p. 184.
100. Bruley, 'Socialism and Feminism in the Communist Party of Great Britain', p. 197; Gray, *The Weaver's Wage*, p. 18; and J.H. Riley, 'The More-Looms System and Industrial Relations in the Lancashire Cotton Manufacturing Industry, 1928-35', unpublished M.A. Diss., University of Manchester.
101. Summerfield, 'Women Workers in the Second World War', p. 296.
102. House of Commons Debates, 1941, 370, c. 317.
103. Kosak, 'Women Munition Workers', pp. 404 and 406.
104. Angela V. John, *By the Sweat of their Brow. Women Workers at Victorian Coal Mines* (Croom Helm, 1980), pp. 181 and 219.
105. Chew, *Ada Nield Chew*, p. 82.
106. Black, *Sweated Industry*, pp. 136-7. See also Bird, *Women at Work*, p. 30.
107. Cadbury *et.al.*, *Women's Work and Wages*, pp. 214–2; and Brian Harrison, 'For Church, Queen and Family: The Girls' Friendly Society', *Past and Present*, No. 61 (November 1973), pp. 109 and 116.
108. C. 7421, p. 546.
109. Booth, *London Life and Labour* Vol. IV, pp. 313.
110. Braybon, *Women Workers in the First World War*, pp. 132–40; and Joan Loch, *The British Policewoman. Her Story* (Robert Hall, 1979), pp. 20-90.
111. Kosak, 'Women Munition Workers', p. 270.
112. Interview with Agnes McLean, shopsteward at Hillingdon during World War II, 15 March 1983. I am grateful to Tom Stephens and Jim McClymont for the transcripts of this interview.
113. Markham Papers 8/26, Case file of Glasgow Interviews, BLPES.
114. PP., 'Report of Mrs. Nassau Senior as to the effect on girls of the System of

Education at Pauper Schools', C. 1071, 1874, XXVI, 1; and Committee upon Quantitative Problems in Human Nutrition, *Report on the Nutrition of Miners and their Families*, MRC Special Report Series No. 87 (HMSO, 1924), p. 29.

115. Lown, 'Not so much a Factory, More a Form of Patriarchy', pp. 39-41; Sallie Heller Hogg, 'The Employment of Women in Great Britain, 1891–1921', unpublished D. Phil. Diss., Oxford University, 1967, p. 259; and Ebury and Preston, *Domestic Service*, p. 44.
116. Webb, 'Alleged Differences in the Wages Paid to Men and to Women', p. 659. For a modern analysis of this problem see E.S. Phelps, 'The Statistical Theory of Racism and Sexism', *American Economic Review* **62** (September 1972), pp. 659-61.
117. Cmd. 3508, p. 31; Vera Douie, *The Lesser Half* (Women's Publicity Planning Association, 1943), p. 55; Hogg, 'The Employment of Women', p. 456.
118. Braybon, *Women Workers in the First World War*, p. 183.
119. P. Sargant Florence, 'The Theory of Women's Wages', *Economic Journal* **41** (March 1931), p. 36.
120. Kosak, *Women Munition Workers*, p. 233.
121. Cmd. 135, p. 105; Thom, 'The Ideology of Women's Work', p. 153; Summerfield, 'Women Workers in the Second World War', p. 243; S. Wyatt, *A Study of Certified Sickness Absence among Women in Industry*, MRC Industrial Research Board, Report No. 86 (HMSO, 1945), p. 31 and *A Study of Women on War Work in Four Factories* MRC Industrial Research Board, Report No. 88 (HMSO, 1945), p. 42; and Cmd. 6937, p. 113.
122. Viola Klein, *Employing Married Women* (Institute of Personnel Management Occasional Papers, No. 17, 1961), p. 39.
123. Cmd. 135, p. 104; Braybon, *Women Workers in the First World War*, p. 85; and Hunt, 'Women in the Nineteenth Century Bookbinding and Printing Trades', p. 77.
124. Cmd. 3508, p. 28.
125. 'Third Report of the House of Lords on Sweating' (165), Qs. 18477 and 18510; and PP., 'Fifth Report of the Select Committee of the House of Lords on the Sweating System' (169), 1890, XVII, 257, p. xxxi.
126. Bird, *Women at Work*, p. 84; and Joint Committee on the Employment of Barmaids, *Women as Barmaids* (P.S. King, 1905).
127. J.A. Hobson, *Problems of Poverty* (Methuen, 1895), p. 168; and C. 7421, pp. 517-19.
128. Joseph Hallsworth and Rhys J. Davies, *The Working Life of Shop Assistants* (Manchester: by the authors, 1910), p. 93; and Thom, 'The Ideology of Women's Work', p. 77.
129. Cmd. 135, p. 108; C. 7421, p. 529; Cadbury *et.al.*, *Women's Work and Wages*, p. 36.
130. Alan Deacon, *In Search of the Scrounger*, Occasional Papers in Social Administration No. 60 (G. Bell, 1976), p. 24; and PP., 'Final Report of the Committee of Inquiry into the Scheme of Out of Work Donation', Cmd. 305, 1919, XXX, 201, p. 10.
131. *The Times*, 16 December, 1922, p. 8; and Ministry of Labour, *Report of the Committee Appointed to Enquire into the Present Conditions as to the Supply of*

Female Domestic Servants (HMSO, 1923).
132. Kosak, 'Women Munition Workers', p. 394.
133. PP., 'Minutes of Evidence of Committee of Enquiry into the Scheme of Out of Work Donation', Cmd. 407, 1919, XXX, 219, pp. 127 and 158.
134. PP., 'First Report of the Royal Commission on Unemployment Insurance', Cmd. 3872, 1930-1, XVII, 885, p. 43.
135. PP., 'Final Report of the Royal Commission on Unemployment Insurance', Cmd. 4185, 1931-2, XIII, 393, pp. 241 and 472; Deacon, *In Search of the Scrounger*, pp. 65 and 109; and Lewenhak, 'Trade Unionism among Women and Girls', p. 222, and *Women and Trade Unions*, p. 201.
136. Ministry of Labour, *2nd Interim Report of the Central Committee on Women's Training and Employment for the period ending Dec. 31st 1922* (HMSO, 1923).
137. PP., 'Report of the Women's Advisory Committee of the Ministry of Reconstruction on the Domestic Service Problem', Cmd. 67, 1919, XXIX, 7, p. 12; and Labour Party, *The Domestic Workers' Charter* (LP, 1931).
138. Cmd. 4185, p. 325.
139. PP., 'Report on the Post War Organisation of Private Domestic Employment', Cmd. 6650, 1944–5, V, 1; Markham Papers 12/2, Markham to Miss Smieton (Min. of Labour), 30 October 1945.
140. Cadbury *et.al.*, *Women's Work Wages*, p. 115; and C.V. Butler, *Domestic Service. An Enquiry by the Women's Industrial Council* (G. Bell, 1916), pp. 13–40.
141. Hogg, 'The Employment of Women', p. 197.
142. Hutchins, *Women in Modern Industry* p. 65; and Webb, 'The Alleged Differences in the Wages paid to Men and to Women', p. 653.
143. Jill Liddington and Jill Norris, *One Hand Tied Behind Us. The Rise of the Suffrage Movement* (Virago, 1978), p. 86; Cadbury *et.al.*, *Women's Work and Wages*, p. 70; Bird, *Women at Work*, pp. 16–17.
144. Alice Foley, *A Bolton Childhood* (Manchester: University of Manchester Extra Mural Dept., 1973), pp. 45 and 49. On the way in which the working class received middle class values generally, see Peter Bailey, *Leisure and Class in Victorian England* (Routledge & Kegan Paul, 1978), pp. 169-182.
145. John Burnett, *Destiny Obscure: Autobiographies of Childhood, Education and Family, From the 1920s to the 1920s* (Allen Lane, 1982), p. 140; and Pam Taylor, 'Women Domestic Servants 1919-39. The Final Phase', unpublished M.A. Diss., University of Birmingham, 1978, p. 70.
146. M. Weir, *Shoes were for Sunday* (Pan Books, 1970); Burnett, *Destiny Obscure*, p. 164; and Jean Rennie, *Every Other Sunday: The Autobiography of a Kitchen Maid* (Arthur Baker, 1955).
147. Clementina Black, 'Trade Schools for Girls in London', *Economic Journal* **16** (September 1906), p. 32.
148. Turner, *Trade Union Structure and Policy*, p. 160; Drake, *Women in Trade Unions*, p. 118; Joanna Bornat, 'Home and Work. A New Context for Trade Union History', *Radical America* **12** (September–October, 1978), pp. 53-69.
149. Geoffrey Thomas, *Women and Industry. An Inquiry into the Problem of Recruiting Women for Industry* (HMSO, 1948), pp. 1 and 15.
150. Cd. 9239, p. 60.
151. Hilda Martindale, *Women Servants of the State, 1870–1938* (Allen and Unwin, 1938), pp. 61-2.

152. E.J. Morley, *Women Workers in Seven Professions* (Routledge & Kegan Paul, 1914), pp. 221-234.
153. Clara Collet, *Educated Working Women* (P.S. King, 1902), p. 77.
154. Ray Strachey, *The Cause*, 1st edn. 1928 (Virago, 1978), p. 94.
155. Pauline Marks, 'Feminity in the Classroom: an Account of Changing Attitudes', in *The Rights and Wrongs of Women*, eds. Mitchell and Oakley, p. 185; Carol Dyhouse, *Girls Growing Up in Late Victorian and Edwardian England* (Routledge & Kegan Paul, 1981), p. 76; and J. S. Pedersen, 'Some Victorian Headmistresses: a Conservative Tradition of Social Reform', *Victorian Studies* **24** (Summer 1981), pp. 463-88.
156. Routh, *Occupation and Pay*, p. 16. Catherine Hakim, *Occupational Segregation. A Comparative Study of the Degree and Pattern of the Differentiation between Men and Women's Work in Britain, the United States and other Countries*, Research Paper No. 9 (Dept. of Employment 1979), p. 34, T. 20, gives the higher figure of 13% for 1911, but states that her data for local and central government officials included officers below the senior grades.
157. M. Jeanne Peterson, 'The Victorian Governess: Status Incongruence in Family and Society', in *Suffer and be Still*, ed. Martha Vicinus (Bloomington: Indiana University Press, 1975), pp. 3-19.
158. Collet, *Educated Working Women*, p. 125.
159. Strachey, *The Cause*, pp. 252-6; and E. Moberley Bell, *Storming the Citadel. The Rise of the Woman Doctor* (Constable, 1953), p. 88.
160. Neal A Ferguson, 'Women's Work: Employment Opportunities and Economic role 1918-39', *Albion* **7** (Spring 1975), p. 61; *The Women's Leader*, 31 October 1924, p. 288; and the view of Lord Knutsford of St. Mary's (closed to women in 1924), reported in *The Times*, 10 March 1922, p. 8, and 14 March 1922, p. 8.
161. Meta Zimmeck 'Strategies and Stratagems for the Employment of Women in the Civil Service 1919–39', *Historical Journal* (forthcoming).
162. Martindale, *Women Servants of the State*, p. 31.
163. Martindale, *Women Servants of the State*, p. 72; and Zimmeck, 'Strategies and Stratagems for the Employment of Women'.
164. PP., 'Final Report of the Treasury Committee on Civil Service Recruitment after the War', Cmd. 164, 1919, XI, 1919, p. 10.
165. Virginia Woolf, *Three Guineas* (Hogarth Press, 1938), p. 92.
166. Martindale, *Women Servants of the State*, p. 107.
167. Theresa Davy, 'Female Shorthand Typists and Typists 1900–39', pp. 26 and 32; and Braverman, *Labor and Monopoly Capital*, p. 293.
168. Martindale, *Women Servants of the State*, p. 17.
169. PP., 'Report of the Civil Service National Whitley Council Committee on the Marriage Bar in the Civil Service', Cmd 6886, 1945–6, X, 871, p. 4; Summerfield, 'Women Workers in the Second World War', p. 13.
170. Gregory Anderson, *Victorian Clerks* (Manchester: Manchester University Press, 1976), pp. 59, 132; and Linda Grant, 'Women's Work and Trade Unionism in Liverpool, 1890–1914' *North West Labour History Society Bulletin* No. 7 (1980–1), pp. 76-7.
171. Holcombe, *Victorian Ladies at Work*, p. 34.
172. Doris McLoughlin, '"Birds of Passage": Women Teachers in England,

Unions and Equal Pay 1930–60', unpublished, M.A. Diss., University of Essex, 1979, p. 35; and Oram, '"Sex Antagonism"'.

173. Betty D. Vernon, *Ellen Wilkinson* (Croom Helm, 1982).

174. Davy, 'Female Shorthand Typists and Typists', p. 54; Soldon, *Women in British Trade Unions*, p. 51; and G. Partingdon, *Women Teachers in the Twentieth Century* (NFER Publishing Col, 1976), p. 1.

175. Frances Widdowson, 'Elementary Teacher Training and the Middle Class Girl 1846–1914', unpublished M.A. Diss., University of Essex, pp. 60 and 76; and Miriam David, *The State, the Family and Education* (Routledge & Kegan Paul, 1980), pp. 130-1.

176. Jane Lewis, *The Politics of Motherhood* (Croom Helm, 1980), pp. 144-5; Margaret Llewellyn Davies, *Life as We Have Known It*, 1st edn. 1931 (Virago, 1977), p. 40.

177. Partingdon, *Women Teachers*, p. 37; NAS, *The Why and Wherefore of the NAS* (NAS Pamphlet No. 1, nd); and London School Masters Association, *Equal Pay and the Teaching Profession* (Evans Bros, 1921), p. 58.

178. 'Miss Read', *Miss Clare Remembers* (Michael Joseph, 1962).

179. Oram, '"Sex Antagonism"'.

180. Price v. Rhondda, 1923, 2 Ch. 372.

181. Partingdon, *Women Teachers*, p. 32; I am grateful to Jenny Hurstfield for information on the avoidance of the marriage bar.

182. Frances Finnegan, *Poverty and Prostitution* (Cambridge: Cambridge University Press, 1979), pp. 41, and 164-5.

183. Cadbury *et.al.*, *Women's Work and Wages*, p. 190; Isabelle O. Ford, *Women's Wages and the Conditions under Which they are Earned* (Williams Reeves, 1893); and Lyttleton, *Warp and Woof*.

184. See above, p. 33–34.

185. Webb, 'Alleged Differences in the Wages Paid to Men and to Women', p. 649; and F.Y. Edgeworth, 'Equal Pay to Men and Women for Equal Work', *Economic Journal* **32** (December 1922), p. 444.

186. Cmd. 135, p. 89.

187. Webb and Webb, *Industrial Democracy* pp. 504-5; and Webb, 'Alleged Differences in the Wages Paid to Men and to Women', p. 661.

188. F.J. Bayliss, *British Wages Councils* (Oxford: Blackwell, 1962), p. 8; R.H. Tawney, *The Establishment of Minimum Rates in the Tailoring Industry* (G. Bell, 1915), pp. 103-4, 116; and Morris, 'Sweated Trades', p. 143.

189. Edgeworth, 'Equal Pay to Men and Women'; and M.G. Fawcett, 'Equal Pay for Equal Work', *Economic Journal* XXVIII (March 1918), pp. 1-6. See Bruegel, 'Women's Employment, Legislation and the Labour Market' for a discussion of the recent development of 'crowding theory'.

190. For example, Helen Bosanquet, 'A Study in Women's Wages', *Economic Journal* **12** (March 1902), pp. 42-9.

191. Eleanor Rathbone, 'The Remuneration of Women's Services', *Economic Journal* XXVII (March 1971), pp. 55-68.

192. PP., 'Report of the Fair Wages Committee', Cd. 4422, 1908, XXXIV, 551, Q. 6493; and Rathbone, 'The Remuneration of Women's Services', p. 59.

193. Kosak, 'Women Munition Workers', p. 215; and Thom, 'The Ideology of Women's Work', p.51.

194. Cmd. 135, pp. 4, 180, 184, 187; and Drake, *Women in Trade Unions*, p. 226.
195. Cmd. 135, pp. 270, 302.
196. PP., 'Report of the Committee on Women in Industry—Appendices', Cmd. 167, 1919, XXI, 593, p. 17.
197. Cmd. 135, p. 299.
198. Harold Smith, 'The Issue of 'Equal Pay for Equal Work' in Great Britain 1914–19', *Societas* VIII (Winter 1978), p. 49.
199. Debates, House of Commons, 1934–5, 302, cols. 2213-14.
200. 'Report from the Select Committee on Equal Compensation' (53), Qs. 1019, 1063, 1679.
201. Harold Smith, 'The Problem of Equal Pay for Equal Work in Great Britain during World War II', *Journal of Modern History* **53** (December 1981), p. 660; and Allen Potter, 'The Equal Pay Campaign Committee: A Case Study of a Pressure Group', *Political Studies* V (February 1957), pp. 49-64.
202. Summerfield, 'Women Workers in the Second World War', p. 327 and 345; and Cmd. 6937, p. 161.
203. Smith, 'The Problem of Equal Pay for Equal Work... during World War II', p. 669, note 94.
204. Cmd. 6937, pp. 119, 143, 167-8, 170, 189
205. Summerfield, 'Women Workers in the Second World War', p. 350; and Boston, *Women Workers and the Trade Union Movement*, p. 235.
206. Bayliss, *British Wages Councils*, p. 139.

Epilogue

> Behind us lies the patriarchal system; the private house, with its nullity, its immorality, its hypocrisy, its servility. Before us lies the public world, the professional system, with its possessiveness, its jealousy, its pugnacity, its greed.
>
> Virginia Woolf, *Three Guineas* (1938)

The most startling development in the post-war period has been the huge increase in the number of married women working. By 1978 some 62 per cent of married women were classified as economically active, and above the age of 34, married women are now as likely to be employed as single women; indeed, the typical female worker has become the older married woman with children.[1]

This development was puzzling in view of economists' predictions that during a period of full employment and rising real wages people would opt to increase their leisure time. The most influential explanation of the unexpected increase in the number of married women going out to work recognises that women use their time in a more complex way than men and argues that household members will behave rationally to allocate their time between paid work, unpaid (domestic) work and leisure (including voluntary work), in such a way as to maximise the household's welfare. The underlying assumption that such an allocation can be established—usually between husband and wife—to the satisfaction of both is misleading. A husband earning a large salary may either demand the services of a full-time housewife, or feel that the paid work she could get would not be of sufficiently high status, irrespective of the wife's wishes. In any case, it is difficult to subsume all the factors involved in a woman's decision to work under a single theory of household choice.[2] Consideration of the husband's income and the social aspirations of both spouses; of the woman's educational attainment and the type of work she might reasonably obtain; and of her attitude towards the relative importance of her role as wife and mother versus the importance of paid work, either as a means to greater consumer power or personal fulfilment, requires considerable analysis. It may well be that at some point during the post-war years the wages women could command crossed a certain threshold leading them to conclude that their domestic duties were an uneconomic use of their time. But it is doubtful whether this would have been the only factor in the calculation, or even the essence of the calculation, in a majority of cases.

The largest increase in the number of working women has been in the area of part-time employment. Since 1951 the size of the full-time female labour force has remained steady at 5.6 million. The expansion of the total female workforce from 7.4 million in 1951 to 9.1 million by 1977 was the result of an increase of almost two million part-time jobs. In 1956 only 12 per cent of the female labour force worked part-time, by 1977 this had risen to 40 per cent, with the vast majority of these women confined to monotonous, low paying jobs. Many more casual workers continued to be omitted from the census. In 1980, the government again felt it necessary to set up an inquiry into homework,[3] which reported that a high percentage of homeworkers are now immigrant women whose husbands are low paid or unemployed, and who make such goods as ballpoint pens and Christmas cards rather than the matchboxes and tennis balls of earlier years.

A majority of women probably worked to pay for the 'extras' that were fast becoming considered necessities, but many continued to want work because the family economy demanded it. The 1979 Family Expenditure Survey showed that women's earnings were the major source of income for 10 per cent of households and contributed between one-third and one-half of wage income for a further 40 per cent. Two-parent households are three times as likely to be in poverty when the wife is not employed. Some better-qualified women may have found part-time office work as clerks and secretaries congenial, no matter that it was still low paid. 'A little job' warded off the isolation of the suburban housewife and was acceptable because it minimised conflict with household responsibilities. Indeed, the idea that work and marriage might not after all be incompatible may also help to explain what has been called the post-war 'marriage revolution': since World War II the mean age at marriage has decreased and the proportion of the population married increased.[4] Nevertheless, the movement of a large number of women out of the home must also have involved a significant change in the attitude of husbands. Pre-war male respectability required husbands to 'keep' their wives; when and why this component of masculinity changed is not clear. Recently it has even been suggested that the few wives who occupy well-paying, high status jobs are considered by husbands to add to, rather than detract from, their own status.

Household-choice theory predicts that because women continue to put home and family first they will tend neither to invest as much in training, nor to take paid work as 'seriously', as men. This is said to explain why a majority of women continue to find themselves in low paid, menial jobs. But while the presence of children certainly appears to be an accurate predictor of women's labour force participation,[5] it is not clear that this reflects their wishes. Evidence suggests that more women would like to work if childcare were available. During the 1970s the largest increase in the number of women working took place among women with children under five. Moreover, one recent analysis predicts that 70 per cent of the new jobs likely to be created between 1983 and 1990 will go to women,[6] thus decreasing female unemployment despite the threat posed to female clerical employment by the micro-chip. This does not reflect any slackening in the ideology of domesticity, which, since the work of Bowlby, has centred on the importance of childcare and the danger of maternal deprivation, nor is it a result of the influence of the feminist movement. Rather it signals the strength of sexual stereotyping and segregation in the labour market. The trend towards part-time, service sector jobs is predicted to continue, and such work tends to be low paid, poorly unionised, lacking in security and other employment benefits, and is labelled women's work. Had this sort of work existed in the 1930s, it is quite likely that the percentage of married women working would have been higher, for it is impossible to know how many women during that period were behaving as 'discouraged' workers and not seeking jobs because of the difficulty in finding them.

It is also notable that increasing numbers of women have pursued further education and training irrespective of expectations regarding marriage and motherhood, and yet the percentage of women in 'top jobs' other than medicine is not much greater than in 1911.[7] The kinds of direct discriminatory practices that kept women out of the upper echelons of the Civil Service or the medical profession during the inter-war years are much rarer, although a greater proportion of women still fail at the job interview stage (when the Board is invariably predominantly or entirely male), as was the case in the 1930s. It has also become clear that patterns of socialisation which mitigate against women becoming engineers or managers, for example, are important in explaining their absence from certain jobs, as are the continuing doubts in employers' minds (often divorced from any practical experience) as to whether women will prove capable of doing the job. Even where more women have entered a particular area, such as medicine, vertical segregation persists and few reach the high status jobs within the profession.

The equality laws of the 1970s (the Equal Pay and the Sex Discrimination Acts) followed the earlier pattern of providing women with equal rights to men in the public sphere although they represented a substantial departure from legislation such as the 1919 Sex Disqualification (Removal) Act in terms of their attempt to outlaw discriminatory practices rather than to merely remove barriers to women's advancement. The effects of the legislation were disappointing. There was convergence between male and female average pay until 1977, but the improvement was not maintained and, in 1980, full-time women workers earned only 71 per cent as much as men. Similarly, the degree of sexual segregation diminished between 1975 and 1977 only to revert to the 1973 level by 1979. Equal opportunities legislation treated particular manifestations of inequality in the lives of individual women, but ignored the structures that gave rise to those inequalities, in particular the complex patterns of female socialisation and the sexual division of labour in the home. Thus, like earlier equal rights legislation, it succeeded in increasing formal rather than substantive equality,[8] leaving those concerned to further improve the position of women to advocate 'positive action' in the form of an increase in the social wage (in respect to day care, for example), special education initiatives for girls and possibly a quota system in certain jobs to correct the historical burden of discrimination.

The feminist movement of the late 1960s and 1970s recognised both that equality could not be achieved on men's terms because women started unequal, and that to treat women as equal but different would only reinforce sexual stereotyping and divisions. It therefore called for liberation rather than equality, emphasising a search for more autonomy and choice in all areas of women's lives: in education, work, family arrangements and personal relationships. Liberation in the sense of personal freedom certainly increased dramatically during the 1960s and 1970s. More young women left home, travelled alone or with friends and slept with whomever they pleased. But more freedom did not necessarily bring liberation in the sense of greater autonomy and choice. With the sexual freedom of the 1960s came 'the amazing rise of illegitimacy'.[9] For complex reasons, not all young women chose to exercise the control over their own fertility made possible by the Pill. In contrast to the pre-war period, unmarried mothers were primarily urban working class girls who had had little or no intention of marrying. The rise in illegitimacy together with a 400 per cent increase in the divorce rate between 1960 and 1980 (made possible by increasing liberalisation of the divorce laws), caused a substantial increase in the number of single-parent families, and by 1980 they accounted for one in eight of all families.[10] In addition, the number of one-parent households, together with the increase in the number of elderly single women and widows, has meant a rise in female poverty. Both groups of women still tend to depend on state benefits and, in the case of single parents, the state continues to forbid cohabitation on the assumption that the presence of a male also indicates the presence of a breadwinner. In other areas of pension and social security legislation the movement towards a formal equality between the sexes has entailed the gradual abolition of the male-breadwinner assumption,[11] although the state's desire to promote traditional sex roles within the two-parent family remains, as Cabinet documents on family policy, leaked early in 1983, have shown.[12] In the case of divorced women, acceptance of the desirability of a formal equality between the sexes has resulted in an increased reluctance to award women a 'meal-ticket for life' in the form of alimony, but this ignores the fact that many women are deskilled by marriage and would anyway command a much lower wage than men.

Thus, in the name of equality, the protection accorded women during the late nineteenth and early twentieth centuries has been withdrawn, without women gaining the means to achieve effective economic and sexual independence. This problem had of course been foreseen by feminists of earlier generations, such as Millicent Fawcett and Edith Summerskill. Both the legal protection afforded late nineteenth-century women in respect to employment conditions and family law, and the customary exercise of chivalry, was of dubious value. Nevertheless, in male-dominated society the withdrawal of protection is also problematic. Late twentieth-century wives might have less cause to fear prostitution which in their confined and dependent late nineteenth century world they could do little about, but sexual violence towards women has increased in tandem with the growth in both women's personal freedom and their ability to dispense with a male social and economic protector.

The gains of the post-war period have tended to favour those women with a good education, who wished to enter particular jobs and who had the means to buy childcare, domestic appliances and, often, domestic help. The most glaring gap now lies between the teenage single parent, usually poorly educated and drawing supplementary benefit, and the increasing numbers of middle class well-educated women in their 30s, well-established in their careers, and, as a result, beginning to think that they can afford the time to have children. It is still easier to do a demanding job if marriage and motherhood are renounced, but with careful planning and the financial advantages provided by two incomes it can be accomplished. Moreover, as long as it is accomplished without a hitch, it is more likely to be applauded than denigrated. The ideal role prescription of 'Superwoman'[13] could hardly be more different from that offered nineteenth-century middle class women, and yet very little has changed in respect to women's continued responsibility for home and family.

An understanding of the period prior to World War II shows that substantial class differentials in the gains made by women are not new. It is also clear that while few women (and possibly few men) would wish to return to the world of the 1950s, let alone the 1870s, there has been no steady line of uninterrupted, unequivocal progress for women. Nineteenth-century feminists undoubtedly thought that the road to equality would prove more straightforward than it has been. Women in the late twentieth century find themselves in the paradoxical position of having more freedom and opportunity than ever before and yet facing inequalities that seem as deeply entrenched as ever. Finally it is apparent that the gains women made were achieved in the face of male resistance. Particular conjunctures—of which the decline in family size and the increased demand for women's labour are the most important—promoted change in women's position regardless of any conscious attempt by women to secure it. But any shift in the balance of sexual divisions provoked resistance. Neither the classical liberal philosophy of laissez-faire, with its regard for individual achievement, nor the urge to rationalise and reform, for example with respect to the law and education, could entirely transcend the paternalism that, at best, characterised domestic relationships between men and women. During the period 1870 to 1950 the defence of the boundary between public and private was strongest in respect to middle class women, although within manufacturing industry any threat to the sexual division of labour evoked an equally fierce resistance. Since the war, women have increasingly been permitted to compete in the public sphere without hindrance, albeit on men's terms.

Where women have tried to force the pace of change in respect to particular issues, such as the vote, resistance has been stronger still. It is in fact profoundly difficult to assess the role women themselves played in securing any change in their position. To a large extent, belief systems were shared, for example in respect to the position of working wives as secondary wage earners; and major decisions between spouses, such as the use of birth control, were in all probability negotiated. Middle class women who pursued their domestic mission beyond their own homes in the form of voluntary work did not perceive the inherent contradications of so doing, nor for the most part did they act out of any consciously feminist belief. But as Julia Matthaei has recently commented, their response to the rigid separation of spheres makes it unlikely that any new attempt to confine women to the home would stand any hope of long-term success.[14]

Women's changing expectations have undoubtedly been important, although whether as cause or result of the changes in women's position in society more generally, is difficult to determine. After World War I, the desire of many working class women for better housing appears often to have become a family priority. Similarly, many working class women recorded their determination not to repeat their mothers' experience of frequent pregnancies, although further consideration of other aspects of their lives and of men's attitudes is required to explain why that particular generation succeeded. The two world wars probably increased the confidence and sense of independence (and thus the expectations and aspirations) of individual women of all classes, and, despite the frustrations women experienced in the years following both wars, may have been comparable to the feminist movement of the 1970s in terms of their consciousness-raising effect. However, women's aspirations have often been confined to seeking improvement within the areas of activity already allotted to them. Feminists seeking change have always faced the dilemma of whether to prioritise what have always been regarded as 'women's', rather than human, issues (the conditions of maternity, for example), or to seek equality for women in respect to activities dominated by men. During the early twentieth century, the Women's Cooperative Guild had no hesitation in taking up 'women's issues', a pattern continued by middle class feminists during the inter-war years. However, any argument that a world in which women held power in proportion to their numbers would be significantly different runs the risk of reinforcing ideas of sexual difference, which in male-dominated society have always been used to limit women's range of activities. The nature of the equality to be sought, as well as how to achieve it, remains problematic.

NOTES

1. Catherine Hakim, *Occupational Segregation. A Comparative Study of the Degree and Pattern of the Differentiation between Men and Women's Work in Britain, the United States and Other Countries,* Research Paper No. 9, (Dept. of Employment 1979), pp. 3–10.
2. George Joseph, *Women at Work* (Oxford: Philip Allan, 1983), p. 8. See also the discussion in Irene Bruegel, 'Women's Employment, Legislation and the Labour Market', in *Women's Welfare/Women's Rights*, ed. Jane Lewis (Croom Helm, 1983), pp. 130-169, the statistics regarding women's employment which follow are also taken from this article.
3. PP., 'Report of the Employment Committee of the House of Commons on Home Working' (H.C. 39), 1981-2.
4. Joan Busfield and Michael Paddon, *Thinking about Children* (Cambridge: Cambridge University Press, 1977), pp. 116–32.
5. Heather Joshi, *Demographic Predictors of Women's Work Participation in Post-War Britain*, Centre for Population Studies Working Paper No. 81-3 (1981).
6. Peter Moss, 'The Current Situation', in *Mothers in Employment*, eds. N. Fonda and P. Moss (Brunel University, 1976), pp. 6–38; *Review of the Economy and Employment* (University of Warwick, 1983).
7. Hakim, *Occupational Segregation*, p. 34.
8. Janet Radcliffe Richards, *The Sceptical Feminist* (Routledge & Kegan Paul, 1980), p. 90.
9. Shirley Foster Hartley, 'The Amazing Rise of Illegitimacy', *Social Forces* **44** (June 1966) pp. 533–45.
10. Lesley Rimmer, *Families in Focus* (Study Commission on the Family, 1980).
11. On these aspects see Hilary Land, 'Who Still Cares for the Family? Recent Developments in Income Maintenance, Taxation and Family Law', and Dulcie Groves, 'Members and Survivors: Women and Retirement Pensions', both in *Women's Welfare/Women's Rights*, ed. Lewis, pp. 38-85. See also Miriam David and Hilary Land, 'Sex and Social Policy' in *The Future of the Welfare State*, ed. Howard Glennerster (Heinemann, 1983), pp. 138–156.
12. *The Guardian*, 17 February 1983, p. 4.
13. Shirley Conran, *Superwoman* (Harmondsworth: Penguin, 1977).
14. Julia A. Matthaei, *An Economic History of Women in America: Women's Work, the Sexual Division of Labor and the Development of Capitalism* (Harvester Press, 1982).

Guide to Further Reading

There are already good bibliographies covering the major part of the period discussed in this book: Barbara Kanner, 'The Women of England in a Century of Social Change 1815–1914: A Select Bibliography, Part I', in *Suffer and Be Still*, edited by Martha Vicinus (Indiana University Press, 1975), and her 'The Women of England in a Century of Social Change, 1815–1914: A Select Bibliography, Part II', in *A Widening Sphere*, edited by Vicinus (Indiana University Press, 1977); Neal A Ferguson, 'Women in Twentieth Century England' and Jeffrey Weeks, 'A survey of Primary Sources and Archives for the History of Early Twentieth Century Women', both in Barbara Kanner's *The Women of England from Anglo-Saxon Times to the Present* (Mansell, 1980). Less useful is the volume by Margaret Barrow: *Women 1870–1928* (Mansell, 1981).

The brief guide that follows is intended only to provide beginners wishing to follow up the topics covered in this volume, with a few starting points in respect to published work specifically relating to the history of women. As the notes to the book show, there is an enormous amount to be gleaned from government documents, work not specifically relating to the female experience (such as trade union histories, and social surveys) as well as unpublished material. Readers should be aware that at present there is still a lack of cross-fertilisation between the findings of the new women's history and more traditional historical approaches.

WOMEN'S HISTORY: PROBLEMS AND ISSUES

My own comments on the writing of women's history are contained in 'Women Lost and Found: The Impact of Feminism on History', in *Men's Studies Modified: The Impact of Feminism on the Academic Disciplines*, edited by Dale Spender (Pergamon, 1981. The development of the concept of sexual divisions put forward by Diana Leonard Barker and Sheila Allan (eds.) in *Sexual Divisions and Society* (Tavistock 1976) has been particularly important for the perspective used in this book. More recently a piece such as Judy Lown's, 'Not so Much a Factory, More a Form of Patriarchy: Gender and Class during Industrialisation', in *Gender Class and Work*, edited by Eva Gmarnikow *et.al.* (Heinemann, 1983), has taken the concept further, relating it to both class and power.

The crucial interplay between family and employment was first explored in detail by Louise Tilly and Joan Scott, 'Women's Work and the Family in

Nineteenth Century Europe', *Comparative Studies in Society and History* 17 (January 1975). On the range of questions asked by the new women's history, see Natalie Zemon Davies, 'Women's History in Transition: The European Case', *Feminist Studies* 3 (Spring-Summer 1976); and Berenice Carroll (ed.), *Liberating Women's History* (University of Illinois Press, 1976).

Part I

On demographic trends: the publications of the Cambridge Group are many. Especially important background reading are: Peter Laslett, Paula Oosterveen and Richard M. Smith (eds.) *Bastardy and its Comparative History* (Arnold, 1980), and Richard Wall, Jean Robin, and Peter Laslett, *Family Forms in Historic Europe* (Cambridge University Press, 1982). R.B. Outhwaite (ed.), *Marriages and Society: Studies in the Social History of Marriage* (Europa, 1981) is also useful. Qualitative evidence regarding affective relations tends to take a backseat in these volumes; thus on a subject such as illegitimacy, for example, the work of John Gillis, 'Servants, Sexual Relations and the Risks of Illegitimacy in London, 1801–1890', *Feminist Studies* 5 (Spring 1979) provides an important corrective. Some of the authors who do focus on qualitative evidence (for example, Edward Shorter, *The Making of the Modern Family*, Basic Books, 1975) give accounts which incorporate women but which do not attempt to come to terms with the complexity of the female experience.

On birth control and family size the most important books are: J.A. Banks, *Victorian Values. Secularism and the Size of Families* (Routledge & Kegan Paul, 1981); Diana Gittens, *Fair Sex. Family Size and Structure 1900–1939* (Heinemann, 1982), chapters 5 and 6; and Angus McLaren, *Birth Control in Nineteenth Century England* (Croom Helm, 1978). Linda Gordon, *Woman's Body, Woman's Right* (Penguin, 1976) covers the ground for the USA and raises many questions of fundamental importance for the study of fertility control. On women and old age, the literature is much more scarce, but see Jill Quadagno, *Aging in Early Industrial Society: Work Family and Social Policy in Nineteenth Century England* (Academic Press, 1982); Janet Roebuck, 'Ladies and Pensioners: Stereotypes and Public Policy Affecting Old Women in England, 1880-1940', *Journal of Social History* 13 (Fall 1979); and, the most useful, Pat Thane, 'Women and the Poor Law in Victorian and Edwardian England', *History Workshop Journal* No. 6 (Autumn 1978).

There is now quite an extensive literature on working class motherhood and the impact of ideologies of domesticity and maternalism: Anna Davin, 'Imperialism and Motherhood', *History Workshop Journal* No. 5 (Spring 1978); Carol Dyhouse, *Girls Growing Up in Later Victorian and Edwardian England* (Croom Helm, 1980); Jane Lewis, *The Politics of Motherhood* (Croom Helm, 1980); and Denise Riley, 'The Free Mothers; Pronatalism and Working Women in Industry at the End of the War', *History Workshop Journal* No. 11 (Spring 1981). Margaret Hewitt's older interpretation: *Wives and Mothers in Victorian Industry* (Rockcliffe, 1958) is questioned by Dyhouse and Lewis. Laura

Oren, 'The Welfare of Women in Labouring Families: England, 1860–1950', in *Clio's Consciousness Raised*, edited by Lois Banner and Mary Hartman (Harper and Row, 1974); Elizabeth Roberts, 'Working Wives and their Families', in *Population and Society in Britain, 1850–1980*, edited by Theo Barker and Michael Drake (Batsford 1982); and Ellen Ross, 'Women's Neighbourhood Sharing in London before World War II', *History Workshop Journal*, No. 15 (Spring, 1983), provide excellent analyses of the family life of working class women. Michelle Barrett, *The Oppression of Women Today* (Verso, 1980); Leonore Davidoff, 'The Separation of Home and Work? Landladies and Lodgers in the Nineteenth and Twentieth Centuries', in *Fit Work for Women*, edited by Sandra Burman (Croom Helm, 1979); and Hilary Land, 'The Family Wage', *Feminist Review* No. 6 (1980) give a good introduction to the vexed issue of the family wage.

I have tried to provide illustrations throughout the book from women's autobiographies. John Burnett has brought together good collections of these in *Useful Toil* (Penguin, 1974) and *Destiny Obscure* (Allen Lane, 1982). David Vincent's *Bread, Knowledge and Freedom: A Study of Nineteenth Century Working Class Autobiography* (Europa Pubs., 1981) is a useful guide to the genre. The Virgao Press reprint collection is invaluable in this connection and the Press has also reprinted such classics as Margaret Llewellyn Davies (ed.), *Maternity: Letters from Working Women* (1978); Magdalen Stuart Pember Reeves, *Round about a Pound a Week* (1979); Margery Spring Rice, *Working Class Wives* (1981); and Lady F. Bell, *At the Works* (forthcoming).

On sex role prescriptions there is a vast amount of material. For a useful warning of the methodological pitfalls of using prescriptive literature (taking child-rearing manuals as an example) see Jay Mechling, 'Advice to Historians on Advice to Mothers', *Journal of Social History* 9 (Fall 1979). Sara Delamont and Lorna Duffin (eds), *The Nineteenth Century Woman: Her Physical and Cultural World* (Croom Helm, 1978); and Janet Sayers, *Biological Politics. Feminist and Anti-Feminist Perspectives* (Tavistock, 1982) are perhaps the best introductions. See also J.N. Burstyn, *Victorian Education and the Ideal of Womanhood* (Croom Helm, 1982); and Deborah Gorham, *The Victorian Girl and the Feminist Ideal* (Croom Helm, 1982). Patricia Branca, *Silent Sisterhood* (Croom Helm, 1975) has peformed a useful service in asking how far their prescribed role matched the reality of middle class women's lives, although her interpretation of the manual literature on which the book is based has been criticised in its turn. For the home life of upper class Victorian women see Leonore Davidoff's original analysis in *The Best Circles* (Croom Helm, 1973). A fascinating insight into all aspects of the domestic worlds of women during the inter-war years is to be found in Nicola Beauman's study of the novels of the period: *A Very Great Profession. The Woman's Novel 1914–39* (Virago, 1983).

On women's position in law, which is particularly difficult to unravel, the lucid, chronological account in Appendix 5 of the Finer Report on one-parent families is the best starting place (Cmnd. 5629-I, 1974). The contributions by

Lee Holcombe, *Wives and Property. Reform of the Married Women's Property Law in Nineteenth Century England* (Toronto University Press, 1983); and Albie Sachs and Joan Hoff Wilson, *Sexism and the Law* (Martin Robertson, 1978) are also valuable. Erna Reiss, *The Rights and Duties of Englishwomen* (Sherrat and Hughes, 1936) is still useful for reference.

Some of the most impressive contributions to the literature have come in the area of sexual relations: Jeffrey Weeks, *Sex, Politics and Society. The Regulation of Sexuality since 1800* (Longman, 1981) is particularly valuable for its lucidity and range. Two thought provoking and original essays are those by Leonore Davidoff, 'Class and Gender in Victorian England: The Diaries of Arthur J. Munby and Hannah Culwick', *Feminist Studies* 5 (Spring 1979); and Judith R. Walkowitz, 'Male Vice and Feminist Virtue: Feminism and the Politics of Prostitution in Nineteenth Century Britain', *History Workshop Journal* 13 (Spring 1982). Susan Edwards' rather 'victim-oriented' study, *Female Sexuality and the Law* (Oxford: Martin Robertson, 1981) is useful for the leads it provides in a hitherto neglected area.

On philanthropy, traditionally seen as the middle class woman's bridge to the public sphere, see Anne Summers, who feels it to have been rather 'A Home from Home: Women's Philanthropic Work in the Nineteenth Century', in *Fit Work for Women*, edited by Burman; and Frank K. Prochaska's extensive study, *Women and Philanthropy in Nineteenth Century England* (Clarendon Press, 1980).

As Brian Harrison has shown in *Separate Spheres* (Croom Helm, 1978), the suffrage movement overlapped significantly with the philanthropic world. Harrison's contribution also draws attention to some hitherto neglected feminist pamphlet literature of the period. Olive Banks' *Faces of Feminism* (Martin Robertson, 1981) provides a clear and comprehensive account of feminism in England and the USA, and her interpretation differs markedly from the one offered in this volume. On working class women's suffragism see Jill Liddington and Jill Norris, *One Hand Tied Behind Us* (Virago, 1978), which locates working class women's political activism in relation to their domestic responsibilities and paid work. On the relationship between groups such as the Women's Cooperative Guild and the Women's Labour League, and their parent bodies, see Caroline Rowan, 'Women in the Labour Party 1906–20', *Feminist Review* No 12 (1982). Two valuable contributions setting ideas about women's place and feminism in the context of western political thought are John Charvet's *Feminism* (J.M. Dent, 1982); and Susan Moller Okin's *Women in Western Political Thought* (Virago, 1980).

Part II

On employment trends, most accounts concentrate on the twentieth century because of the data problems for the nineteenth. George Joseph, *Women at Work* (Philip Allan, 1983); and Catherine Hakim, *Occupational Segregation* (Dept. of Employment, 1979) provide the most comprehensive analyses. Guy

Routh, *Occupation and Pay 1906–79* (MacMillan, 1980) is also a useful basic source.

Alice Amsden, *The Economics of Woman and Work* (Penguin, 1980) and Irene Bruegel, 'Women's Employment, Legislation and the Labour Market', in *Women's Welfare/Women's Rights*, edited by Jane Lewis (Croom Helm, 1983) provide good introductions to theories of women's work, but there has been, as yet, little attempt by historians to test these theories empirically. Sally Alexander's essay for an earlier period provides some important leads and draws attention to the importance of women's work not recorded by the Census: 'Women's Work in Nineteenth Century London—A Study of the Years 1820–1850', in *The Rights and Wrongs of Women*, edited by Juliet Mitchell and Ann Oakley (Penguin, 1976). On women's casual employment see Duncan Bythell, *The Sweated Trades* (Batsford, 1978), but it is worth going back to the much older volumes by R.H. Tawney and Dorothy Sells.

Most of the standard accounts of women's work were published prior to World War I and are descriptive. Particularly useful are: Clementina Black, *Married Women's Work* (G. Bell, 1915); Edward Cadbury, *et. al.*, *Women's Work and Wages* (T. Fisher Unwin, 1906); and B.L. Hutchins, *Women in Modern Industry* (G. Bell, 1915). Lee Holcombe's more recent *Victorian Ladies at Work. Middle Class Working Women in England and Wales 1850-1914* (Archon Books, 1973) is also descriptive. Gail Braybon, *Women Workers in the First World War* (Barnes and Noble, 1981) is useful for the War years, although not as valuable as the two unpublished PhD. theses by Marion Kosak and Deborah Thom that I have drawn upon for this volume. There is no general account for the period after 1918. Three government documents serve to frame the period as a whole: The Report of the Royal Commission on Labour (C. 7421, 1894); the Report of the War Cabinet Committee on Women in Industry (Cmd. 135, 1919); and the Report of the Royal Commission on Equal Pay (Cmd. 6937, 1945–6).

We have the beginnings of a reinterpretation of women's position in particular occupations; for example: Angela V. John, *By the Sweat of their Brow: Women Workers at Victorian Coal Mines* (Croom Helm, 1980), which also provides a valuable commentary on protective legislation; J.S. Pedersen's work on schoolmistresses, for example 'Some Victorian Headmistresses: a Conservative tradition of Social Reform', *Victorian Studies* 24 (Summer 1981); and Meta Zimmeck's work on women and the Civil Service, 'Strategies and Strategems for the Employment of Women in the Civil Service', *Historical Journal* (forthcoming). Joanna Bornat, 'Home and Work. A New Context for Trade Union History', *Radical America* 12 (September–October 1978) has provided a valuable new interpretation of women's trade unionism that is more suggestive than the detailed descriptive accounts by Sarah Boston, *Women Workers and the Trade Union Movement* (Davis Poynter, 1980) and Norbert C. Soldon, *Women in British Trade Unions, 1874–1976* (Rowan and Littlefield, 1978).

Acknowledgements

I should like to thank the following for permission to cite or quote their unpublished work: Margaret Allen, Lucy Bland, Barbara Brookes, Susan Bruley, Theresa Davy, Martin Durham, Felicity Hunt, Sallie Hogg, Patricia Hollis, Marion Kosak, Sheila Lewenak, Doris McLoughlin, Ellen Mappen, Jenny Morris, Tim Murphy, Alison Oran, Nancy Grey Osterud, Shelley Pennington, Elizabeth Roberts, Pat Ryan, Penny Summerfield, Gillian Sutherland, Pam Taylor, Deborah Thom, Linda Ward, Frances Widdowson. Thanks are also due to the Department of Employment for permission to reprint statistical material from Catherine Hakim's *Occupational Segregation*, Research Paper No. 9, (London: Dept. of Employment, 1979); the *Manchester School* for material from Edward James, 'Women and Work in Twentieth Century Britain', *Manchester School of Economics and Social Science* XXX (Sept. 1962); and from Basil Blackwell for material from G. S. Bain and R. Price, *Profiles of* Union Growth (Oxford: Basil Blackwell, 1980).

Index